T0208794

LEAPING OFF

"THE TORTURED PATH TO FLIGHT"

G, ALAN DUGARD, COLONEL USAF (RET)

authorHOUSE®

AuthorHouse™
1663 Liberty Drive
Bloomington, IN 47403
www.authorhouse.com
Phone: 1 (800) 839-8640

Published by AuthorHouse 06/26/2020

ISBN: 978-1-7283-6535-0 (sc)
ISBN: 978-1-7283-6534-3 (e)

Library of Congress Control Number: 2020911527

Print information available on the last page.

This book is dedicated to Clyde M. Pinkerton (Pinky) and Class 56-H.

CONTENTS

PROLOGUE

There is a factor used in military parlance called the "pipeline" and it concerns the path to many skills, one of those being the path to gaining United States Air Force Silver Wings, known as becoming an Air Force Pilot. It has been modified from early days of flight. Wilbur Wright had his own method! World War I pilots were literally thrown into the fray, but as bigger and more powerful aircraft evolved between and during the two world wars it became necessary to create a system that would prepare future pilots for those aircraft. Billy Mitchell had convinced the naysayers that aircraft had a place in warfare and therefore men would have to be trained to fly various types of aircraft. The preparation wasn't honed to the finest degree, but it did sustain the need for manning the newer reciprocal aircraft that were being placed on the line. With the onset of World War II pilot training became a series of programs that of necessity took physically qualified men and gave them the bare necessities to fly. They counted on the large numbers pushed through abbreviated training in a wide pipeline to adequately sustain the need in the various theaters, European and Pacific, to fly the many aircraft that were designed and built through the end of that conflict. Newly minted pilots were then rushed to locations to aid in combating the Axis forces that were encountered throughout the world. Aircraft losses during the second world war were enormous, many because the pilots had to be rushed though, a training program that was programmed to sustain that "pipeline" at a very high level, due to the losses being recorded on both fronts. There was an abrupt end to the training of pilots to enter the Army Air Corps when the war ended in 1945. There was no great need for pilots as the onslaught of the war left a vacuum when the fighting ended. The need for pilots was not a priority and the "pipeline" closed or at least dwindled to a dribble. However, a factor evolved that awakened those leaders who had created the Army Air Corps. They could now see the need to continue a program that would accommodate the need for pilots to fly the revolutionary Jet aircraft that were now being developed. It was determined this new era of flight would require a more demanding training program for this peace time, yet evolving period was going to be needed. It began with the Army Air Corps, being made into a separate service, the United States Air Force. Initial efforts were implemented to use surviving and experienced World War II pilots who had left the service to initiate this newly designed rigorous training program. Strict physical parameters were established to be used in the selection of the future trainees. The long program would begin with a pre-flight portion where physical and mental aptitude would be tested. An intense personal physical would be administered, with very restrictive limitations applied. Successful completion of this month-long screening process would be followed by the first segment of flight training. This "Primary" phase would use former military, experienced, now civilian pilots to introduce individuals to flying in reciprocal engine aircraft; once completed the trainee would qualify to step up to "Basic" training and jet aircraft. The Basic phase would be their first encounter with instructors who were Air Force pilots. This vanguard of instructors would consist of the most qualified individuals who had successfully completed training in the new jet aircraft. For the Primary graduates, gravitating to and successfully completing the Basic flight training phase would qualify them as pilots; they then would be awarded their "wings". As new pilots they would be sent to "Advanced" lead-in training, an additional two to three months, to qualify in a specific aircraft. The final total time would be eighteen months from the beginning of pre-flight to combat-ready status before the new pilot would qualify to fly an on-line aircraft.

Pipeline levels would vary based on the need to replenish the attrition of pilots in the inventory. These numbers would be programmed as aircraft are developed, combined with the current need due to hostilities and the estimated loss of pilots.

AIR FORCE PILOT TRAINING

T he incident haunted me! After years of anticipation and over six months of flight training in all propeller-driven training aircraft, I had reached a point that I was unsure if I really wanted to continue on the path to achieve my silver wings, one already full of moments to remember, to be a United States Air Force pilot. The step up to flying jet aircraft seemed like a mountain to climb, especially after witnessing the crash of a student and instructor on their return from a training mission. Another accident! It had happened only two days after a solo student fatality on a night training flight. Supposedly that student, one close to graduation, experienced vertigo and slammed into a closed outdoor theater close to the base. This day was a clear cloudless late September morning in Laredo Texas, no wind and a mild temperature, perfect flying weather. I was a brown bar lieutenant and was exiting the flight planning center, parachute over my shoulder with my mentor, Lieutenant Doug Anson, a tall, lanky, dark haired Air Force instructor pilot. We were discussing my about-to-be last solo mission in the T-28, a reciprocal engine aircraft I really hadn't enjoyed much on my continuation into the second phase of Air Force pilot training, a phase called

Basic. It happened suddenly, as the T-33 jet training aircraft, returning from a training mission, on board a student pilot and his instructor, entered the overhead traffic pattern to finish off their flight. As all pilots do, we glanced up to see where the sound was coming from. The aircraft, an afore mentioned T-33 was on "initial", an entry position preparing for landing and executed by a "pitch-out", a forty-five-degree bank turn to enter a downwind leg. It was a standard abrupt left turn that stopped everyone in their tracks as the unforgettable happened; the left wing tip tank, bolted free, only to strike the aircraft's vertical stabilizer, jamming it and placing the aircraft in a skid to the right, veering wildly away from the traffic pattern. The aircraft was rapidly losing altitude. All viewing this mishap knew that to eject safely via the ejection seat you needed 1000 feet above ground for a safe escape. (It was four years later when "zero-zero" capability ejection systems were developed). They easily passed that safe escape altitude in the initial moment as we watched. From the ground, student pilots and instructor's eyes were glued on the effort to now control this out of control missile. At first it appeared control of the aircraft was gained as it slipped sideways, the nose of the aircraft trying to go in a sane direction, fighting the obvious rudder displacement, but then it was apparent that a lack of airspeed and now altitude made it a losing battle. It appeared they were trying to put it down in the desert south of the base, but responses to attain control seemed futile. Slowly the two pilots and the wounded bird were thrust into a death spiral and crashed in the South Texas desert and were consumed in flames. A towering cloud of black smoke filled the distant sky. Stunned, the now assembled groups of pilots were frozen, mesmerized by the latent, but the now apparent sound of the exploding aircraft and now unable to take their eyes off the lazy fireball at it rose far across the runway that the aircraft so futilely attempted to reach. Suddenly they were aware of the new sound, one of crash, fire engines racing across the ramp, followed by a couple of official Air Force vehicles and the always present ambulance. The group of pilots slowly turned to reenter the flight ready room. Words spilled out! "No chance", "What happened", "I can't believe what I just saw". "Poor bastards"! Expletives punctuated the scene from the group as they were trying to tell those still in the planning area what they saw. It was apparent there would be no more flying today. The silent, stunned student turned to Doug and was told to put his chute away. They re-entered the flight operations room. Doug's other two students of "Shotgun Flight", George Fong and Dick Clark were still at the flight table, who were awaiting Doug's return after he had finished seeing the young, blond- haired student pilot off on his solo mission. They had heard the muted explosion, but their response to it was one of wonder, not curious enough to wander outside to see what happened.

Seeing the group, of pilots re-enter they were now very aware that there was something terrible that had occurred and were stunned to hear what tragically had taken place while they sat at the training table. Doug was not a very animated person and he became silent about the accident, but the young student was now effusive in trying to relate to the two of them what he saw. Finally, Doug tried to bring them back to reality and capped off the discussion by talking about tomorrow's routine schedule. Fact of the matter was that flying would commence tomorrow where it left off today. Flying training simply was not to be interrupted for an extended period for an aircraft accident! The now fearful student would be taking his delayed, last solo flight in the T-28 tomorrow along with Dick Clark, who would also complete his last T-28 solo flight in the second half of the morning period. It turned out that George Fong would be getting an evaluation ride with another instructor, as his last training flight with Doug was a failing effort and if this flight tomorrow is no better, he would face elimination from the program. "Pink slips" (a name given to the form given to a student for an unqualified ride) at this stage of training are rare, but not out of the question. A roommate to me, Bob Duggan has an instructor named Helmut Meinig, whose call-sign was "Dead Eye" (the students called him "Herr") a former Luftwaffe pilot at 19, who threatens his students constantly, but has not given Bob a pink slip despite many warnings. Bob is a ham-handed student, so intelligent that simple, logical flying procedures are lost in the maze of his thoughts. During primary Bob was led by fellow students into the flight pattern when he was taking his final check-ride before graduation. He could not decipher the 45-degree entry into the downwind leg, preparing for landing, therefore I, as his roommate, on a solo flight waited to hear Bob's request to enter the pattern. His call sign would give him away, but his gruff voice was very distinguishable and easy to identify. I had been tailing Bob's aircraft, sped up and pulled in front of his yellow flying machine, cutting him off and led him on a 45-degree entry to the pattern. Despite being heavy on the controls, Bob was a good pilot and an interesting roommate for this 5"6-inch tall Loyola University ROTC graduate. Bob was a big guy who had rowed on one of the University of Washington competitive crew, strong and true to his size, a mild-mannered man. He often talked about his girlfriend, Martie, but didn't seem to be very serious about her.

The next day dawned as a hot, muggy, August day. The "A" flight student pilots of the 3640th Pilot Training Squadron formed in military ranks outside of their barracks at 0700 hours and then marched to the flight line. Conversation was light, mostly concerning what their mission was today. There was some mention of yesterday's accident; however, the most salient item to be learned was that those who saw the crash seemed to not want to talk about it. However, it was disclosed that the student involved was a West Point graduate and a member of the class that was a week away from getting their "wings". It was the third fatality in that class. The present class, my class was 56-H, was finishing the T-28 phase and to date has been accident free, in fact there were zero reportable incidents, something not mentioned by anyone, as to do so was thought to have a cascading effect and would jinx the group. The 56-H newly commissioned lieutenants and Aviation Cadets, hoping to make it through pilot training and the Av-cads being commissioned as officers, had initially reported at the end of December at Lackland AFB, in San Antonio for their pre-flight processing and training. It was a first step in filling the shrinking "pipe-line" for the Air Force pilot force.

THE PROCESS

RESERVE OFFICERS TRAINING CORPS (ROTC)

Entering college during the Korean War kept me from being drafted as I was a 1A type of young male. I didn't enter to avoid the draft as I was given a scholarship to play baseball, otherwise I would have joined the military and had talked about doing so until the baseball offer was given to me. Upon registering for classes I was told that all freshmen and sophomores had to take "Air Science" and be a member of the Air Force ROTC. I didn't mind as I had always admired military men and their uniforms and wanted to fly, but never had so much as taken a ride in an aircraft of any kind. I had worked for a friend of mine's father, who rebuilt old Bi-wing type aircraft and converted them into crop dusters. On one occasion he bought an AT-6 trainer from a Marine who had updated the instrument panel and he was going clean it up and sell it to a foreign country as a trainer type aircraft. He was in the business of refurbishing aircraft and then selling them to eager buyers. He flew it into the local area, Hawthorne Airport, and I went over to the airport to pick him up. I was told I could sit in the cockpit and see what it looked like. He had leaned in the cockpit with his smelly cigar in his mouth and pointed out the newer instruments. I was very impressed, even though I knew it was an old model of a WW II trainer. That was as close as I ever got into the air. At any rate the AFROTC was a boondoggle as I took an easy course in "Air Science" and had to march in uniform one day a week. I did learn how to march and how to salute and was very pleased when the entire corps would march in review every Wednesday. It was very impressive, as almost the entire male student body were in their brown uniforms, marching to marshal music, snapping eyes right as they passed by active duty staff on the reviewing stand. At the end of your sophomore year you could opt out, but I chose to stay. Entering my junior year, I became a flight leader and as now members of the senior portion of the corps, we were actually given a small stipend for participation in the corps. It was not a burden to wear a uniform and march one day a week and the junior/senior classes were interesting and an easy good grade, just show up. At the end of your junior year you were told you had to go to a summer camp. It would be three weeks long and it was to and acclimate you to the military way, and hone your military skills, such as getting comfortable with weapons such as a 38 or a 45 pistol and even a M-1 carbine rifle. In addition, you could take part in intense military regimens, long marching hikes in military boots, close order drill, climbing steep walls and ropes, and take part in military functions, hosted by barbaric drill instructors. It was capped off with an all-male party as a graduation benefit. I had taken the trip to George AFB in the California desert. It was mid-July and as I left the June type gloom of Southern California,

I thought it would be nice to see the sun again and once clear of the mountain range I was immediately impressed at the rising heat in my un-air-conditioned car. Getting to the gate of this Air Force base, I flashed my orders (Yes, we were given military orders to report on a given day, before a certain time) at the gate guard and he directed me to the housing /barracks I was to report to. Reporting in I saw a group of my classmates, some of my baseball team-members, but there was also a huge group of others from schools such as University of Utah, Brigham Young University and UCLA. We were given a barracks to report to and assigned wire strung cots by alphabetical order. All sizes and shapes lined up to receive bedding for our multi-bed barracks housing units. We also were given shorts, tee shirts and a set of military fatigues, plus socks and boots. The time was interesting to say the least.

Once assembled we were briefed on the routines that would be followed and introduced to our DIs (drill instructors), young looking enlisted individuals, sharply attired and standing in a brace and nodding their head when their name was called. We would start at 0600 hours tomorrow and were to be dressed in our fatigues. We were awakened and fell out in the same order as our bed-given names. We were welcomed by our DIs and warm morning air and told we would march to the mess-hall for breakfast. After breakfast, our days began with drill every morning, followed by a wide variety of things to familiarize us with military life. We spent a few afternoons on the firing range, which was the most interesting and least demanding of our brief military exposure. We were introduced to the various firing arms, the 38 and 45 handguns and the M-1 rifle. All of us were warned to be careful on the firing range on the use of the weapons on the stand in front of us. Not the actual firing of the gun, but that it would be very hot, due to the 90 + temperatures of every sun-shining day we were there. We were cautioned to cover the gun with the cleaning rag on each stand. We were also taught how to safely handle our weapons and fire them. I really enjoyed that part of the training and qualified as an expert in the 38, my choice of a weapon. To say it was a torrid three weeks is an understatement as we lived in non-air-conditioned barracks, however the desert nights were surprisingly cool and sleeping was not a problem. The real difficulty were the days. They started out pleasant, but by 1000 hours the rising temperature was hard to ignore. By 1300 it was more than hot. It was like a fire standing on the firing-line or, taking part in some wild physical activity. There were no clouds and the humidity was very low, (they called it dry heat, but you couldn't prove it by my drenched fatigues). You looked for shade, but it was hard to find and you prayed for the setting of the sun. Food was good and I was introduced to SOS for breakfast, toast covered with creamed chipped beef, it actually grew on you and was a staple whether you liked it or not. Just days before we were set to leave, the entire corps was scheduled for an induction (yes, they intended to make us enter the military after graduation; we had signed an innocent piece of paper) physical. We were split into groups, each starting one phase then going to another. I don't believe I had ever had a complete (I mean complete) physical in my life, but I never had a serious problem with my health, so wasn't concerned. I progressed from the spread your cheeks line to a doctor checking my lungs, heart, getting my blood pressure taken by a technician and then sent to a dental line, being told by a dentist I would lose my wisdom teeth when I came on active duty and finally went to a line checking mobility and vision. You had to display a range of motion, reaching to the ceiling and extending your arms and legs to show you could manipulate them freely. The vision line checked your depth perception using strings to pull two raised sticks until they stood even in a box a distance of 10-15 feet and then looked at a set of cascading letters to check whether you had the vision necessary to enter the military and qualify for pilot training. I had no trouble with them as I ended up seeing at the 20-15 range and was the first to pull the sticks together on the depth perception test. I was then pushed to a line to check my color perception. I was shown a book that had pages with a number with different small circles arranged in a large circle, one large circle per page. I was supposed to pick out the number hidden in the mélange of different colored circles. The technician tried three pages before I saw a number, those behind me were seeing numbers on every page. The technician actually traced a complete number with his finger on one page. I thought I saw something, but I gave him the wrong answer. They then gave me what they called a "Yarn" test. A gagle of different pieces of yarn in a box. I was told to pull out a series of colored pieces of yarn. I was able to pull out all the designated colors they asked for. It was easy, but despite that on my physical papers I was termed "color deficient". It would disqualify me from flight training! I was incredulous as I had no trouble seeing items of different colors; I could tell a red from a green light, in my opinion there was absolutely nothing wrong with my discernment of color.

Leaving at the end of our camp time I made the decision I would not stay in the Air Force ROTC as there didn't seem to be a reason to do so. If I couldn't fly, what else could I do in the military? I had courses I needed to take for graduation and not taking Air Science would allow me an easier senior year in college. During registration for my senior year for some reason I took a writing course that was not required for graduation instead of the Air Science course designated for seniors and settled in as a non-ROTC student. Being 1A on my draft card, I knew, as long as I stayed in school, I would be able to graduate and not be drafted. After two days in the writing course I felt I had been ambushed as the work for that one course would dominate the first semester of my senior year. I was really looking for a way out, when one of the sergeants I had become friendly with in the ROTC unit over three years saw me walking across campus and called out to me. I stopped and we exchanged hellos. He asked me why I had dropped out of the program and I told him I flunked the color-blind test and no longer could go to pilot training. He said why don't you come over to the office and let's talk. When we walked into the ROTC building, he sat me down and pulled out the same book I had seen during my physical. He showed me a couple of the green and yellow number mixes and I could easily make out the required number involved. He showed me the reds and blues mixtures and I couldn't make out the number. He convinced me that with "practice" I would pass that test. I'm not sure it was his words or the opportunity to re-enroll and take Air Science and drop the now burdensome writing class that convinced me to make the change, but it was a way to save my senior year class load. Everything was predicated on me retaking a physical and passing all phases in order to be commissioned and go to pilot training, otherwise I would not get that chance. I was happy with the choice I made but was unsure how I would pick out the mystery numbers on those charts. By chance my family intervened as my sister, Colleen was a nurse, working in a medical building in Los Angeles and upon hearing of my plight in one of our family suppers, offered to go to an optometrist office in the building and talk to a friend there. The next weekend she produced out of her large purse one of the books with the puzzling hidden colors and told me to study the pages and see if constant surveying of the numbers would help my identification of the proper number. The answers to each circle puzzle were on the back of the page. I proceeded to go over the individual pages, especially the ones I could not discern and after close examination I discovered a key, using the location of a pattern in each circle that would give me the answer. A number 97 had two dark blue circles bunched together in the lower, right corner of the page. Other tough numbers to distinguish had similar identifying patterns, giving me clues to the number I could not see. I was convinced I could pass the test with this information. I told the sergeant who urged me to come back to the unit that I wanted to take another physical, as I was convinced I could pass the color blind test now. He pulled out his copy of the phantom book (called the Ishihara test) and flipped to the difficult red-blue numbers and I gave him all the right answers. He said he would schedule a physical for me at the earliest possible time. It would take some time to get scheduled as that was the way things were. Finally, in an early second semester day I was told by my favorite sergeant I was scheduled to go to March AFB and take an induction physical for pilot training. It was a nice day in February with instructions to report to the base and go to the base hospital for my physical. I was to fast, eating nothing from midnight till I reported. I was to be there by 1000 hours. I was given directions to the base, but I already knew the way as I had spent summer weeks with a friends family in Riverside at their orange orchard. I had trouble sleeping the night before and had no trouble being in my car by 0630 and started to Riverside. I arrived at the main gate at 0900, with an hour to go, but showed my orders to the guard at the gate and he directed me down the main road on the base and arrived at the hospital with a lot of time to spare. I went to the main desk and was told to go into a section of the hospital where the physical would be administered. It was still early, but an airman called my name and brought me into a room and started the paperwork with me, once finished with the many pages of questions I returned it to the same individual who led me to a scale and wrote down my weight on one of the pages he had and did the same for my height. I was ushered into a room by a three-stripe airman, who took me into yet another room and checked my depth perception, range of motion my vision and pulled out the dreaded puzzle book. It was larger than the one I had used and studied. Instead of one combination per page, this had four per page. I instantly panicked, but saw they were the same ones I had studied, just placed differently. The airman pointed at one of the four. I stared for a second, not seeing any number, but checked and found the right key and answered the proper number. He tried one more on that page and again I found my key and answered the appropriate right number. He turned to the next foursome page, pointing to one more, which I immediately identified as it was one of the book numbers I could actually see. He shut the book and told me to go into the next room, sat me down and took out items to check my blood pressure. My heart was pounding at this juncture. He placed the cuff on my left arm and pumped up the cuff. My recorded blood pressure was well above the norm for acceptance into pilot training. I felt I passed the color test and now am flunking the blood pressure test. He glanced at me and I told him I was anxious, and he told me to breathe deeply and relax. He left the room and let me sit alone for about ten minutes. When he returned, he took it a second time and my blood pressure had gone down enough to pass the test. He told me the next step would have been to have me lie down. He was determined to have me pass that test. He led me down a hall, opened a door and told me to strip to my shorts and almost before I was ready a very tall and somber doctor came in, told me to pull down my shorts and went through the "cough" routine, checking my prostrate and then listened to my lungs and heart and told me to put my pants back on and handed me over to another individual who finished my paper work and gave me the information needed for my ROTC unit. I had succeeded in passing my flight physical. I was very pleased and when returning to the Air Force ROTC office at the university I gave my results to the sergeant who had convinced me to remain in the ROTC. He congratulated me and

I thanked him for his caring. I graduated from the university that June and the same afternoon was sworn into the Air Force as a second lieutenant with a reporting date for pre-flight training, the last obstacle to my goal of entering pilot training.

LACKLAND AFB /PREFLIGHT

With the end of the Korean War the demand for pilots, as with many skilled positions in the military slowed down to a crawl. The "pipe line" as it was called had narrowed to a point that the Air Force could be highly selective of those who they would choose for pilot training. With the surge of college ROTC (Reserve Officers Training Corps) graduates, spurred by the Korean War, creating now newly minted second lieutenants at its height in the fifties. This along with the long standing programs such as OCS (Officers Candidate School) and the Aviation Cadet Program had created a glut of individuals vying to fill those few pilot "slots" available due to the diminished need for new pilots as the Korean conflict was now over. Preflight was now actually a weeding out of those who could not physically or mentally meet the new, more rigorous standards set up for the pilot curriculum. Reporting to Lackland two days after Christmas in 1954 a large group of ROTC second lieutenants, recently commissioned after graduating from various Universities around the country, were about to be entering an unknown future, one with barriers created to preclude their success. It was the start of the weeding out process and it was intended to ensure that only those who could endure certain physical and mental rigors would be found capable to go to the next step, a pilot training position. Lackland AFB was known as the basic training base for all enlisted personnel, going through initial training before going to various commands of the Air Force. Many were unaware that it was also used for the indoctrination of new officers into this service. This was well before the establishment of the Air Force Academy and was therefore, along with the Aviation Cadets and Officer Candidate School (OCS), the only source for officers going to the various skills needed in the young Air Force. Upon arrival and signing in you were given an assigned place to live for the next thirty some odd days. Housing was in massive two-story barracks, with a central latrine, with multiple showers, on each floor. Beds were hard cots with hard mattresses arranged much like any other training group barrack. There was an office at the end, housing a sort of barrack's "mother". He was a senior enlisted person, more tuned to supervision than discipline. There was a requirement to make your bed and shine your shoes, but no real hassling of those living there. Everyone was formed into marching flights by barrack, going to and from various locations. I was in the "B" group. Various uniform items were distributed the first day, mostly warm weather clothes and PE shirts and shorts. An allotment was given to each officer to purchase a uniform and other more formal gear downtown in San Antonio. There would be classes in a theater environment on military customs and discipline, plus other mundane topics. A morning wakeup was at 0600 hours, followed by breakfast in the chow hall. Then the fun would begin! This was to be a demanding four weeks of physical regimen to include a mid-morning timed run, (stragglers and those unable to complete this three mile run were summarily eliminated by the end of the second week). This was followed by a series of daily obstacle events. These included water troughs, mud crawls, climbing walls and rope and tower climbs culminating in getting to the top of a tower which had five platforms, each a bit farther apart, starting at about five feet. This tower arched out about a foot from each platform, making it a "V" shape. To get from one level to the next you had to grab a bar on the outside of the platform above and pull yourself to the next level, thus hanging over the ground below. The first three levels were fairly simple, however the last two required effort and strength and you were now above twenty-five to thirty feet above the ground. There was a safety net below in the event you didn't make it, but most who failed this obstacle just didn't try to go to the top two levels. For the taller individuals it was a bit easier than for the five foot-six people like me, it was a good stretch, but doable. Winging out to get to the highest level seemed easy for me as I spent half my youth climbing trees. Few were eliminated for not reaching the top as physically not qualified was a combination of factors. There were also other timed runs, for instance you had to complete a mile and a half in less than twelve minutes. They used other methods of weeding out this force on the physical side, to include too much body fat, (I remember a football player from Syracuse, named Doblbrovsky, who was solid, but his weight versus height disqualified him), poor eyesight (20-20 vision was a standard factor), a color blind test (I never got another color blind test) and depth perception tests were among other means used to disqualify applicants. Spine length (more than 42 inches was the limit) and of course attitude. Many took the easy way out and applied to exit the pipe-line using what was called an "SIE" or "Self-Initiated Elimination". There were many incredible athletic individuals among this group who had played major sports, one in my barracks, Zeke Bratkowski, had been an all-American football quarterback from Georgia Tech, Bob Blaine had been a tight end in college and others who did well, (The "B" barracks won the flag football crown), but others had a difficult time making it through this elimination process. Most of my fellow graduates from my ROTC unit at Loyola University in Los Angeles were eliminated for one reason or another. By the end of the four weeks what had started with possibly as many as four hundred aspiring pilots was now down to 120. Some of those were eliminated for physical problems that didn't preclude a "rated" slot and opted to go to Navigator training, most of them failed the needed 20/20 eyesight requirement. The survivors going to pilot training would begin the primary phase of their training at three civilian-contract-run bases, one in Arizona, one in Florida and one in Missouri. Each of those selected for pilot training could choose their base, however one could easily see that the two warm weather bases, Florida and Arizona would be overwhelmed with volunteers, so using the advice of a native of the state, Bob Duncan, I along with a barracks mate, Bob Dugan and others chose Malden, Missouri, knowing we would end up there anyway. The training facility was situated in the boot-heel of the state, not too far from Cape Girardeau on the Mississippi River and approximately 60 miles south of St. Louis and very close to the state of Kentucky. Malden was a small mid- western town, couldn't have had a population of over three thousand and was a close neighbor to another town called Dexter. Dexter was the location of an alternate grass landing site for Malden aircraft. Orders were cut for the pilot training qualifiers with a reporting date in early February. We would be given four travel days to report, traveling from San Antonio Texas to the lower and eastern part of Missouri. The adventure had barely begun!

PRIMARY PILOT TRAINING
- MALDEN MISSOURI

The arrival of thirty-five new ROTC lieutenants joined by fifteen aviation cadets, four foreign exchange students, one from Venezuela, two from Italy and one from Iran (they arrived after the PA-18 flights) and ten OCS (Officer's Candidate School) graduates made up this Malden Section of Pilot Training Class 56-H. It was a cold end of a February day when this assemblage arrived in this southeast Missouri town. Upon arrival at the base all the single students were assigned in alphabetical fashion to on-base quarters. The housing for single individuals was four to a tar-paper two-bedroom, single bathroom building, no air-conditioning, but heated. Married students were obviously allowed to live off the base and were given a meager housing allowance to subsidize their rent. The Aviation Cadets were housed in barracks, close to the officer's quarters. The first day, after going for a breakfast on a freezing morning, we were marched to an area where we were given our necessary flight equipment. All were given two flight suits, flight gloves, boots, two jackets, one light, summer type and one for the artic blasts we would experience for the next month or so, sun glasses, heavy socks and a set of winter undergarments, top and bottom. There were separate formations for the officers and the aviation cadets, but we would all come together for the first time in the flight operations center, where a welcoming of sorts was given by the head of the civilian instructors. He outlined the flying process and explained the routine of flying and academics to us. He also introduced us to the flight instructor group, lounging next to one wall. Using some mysterious system, the entire group was summarily divided into two flights, "Eagle" (of which I would be a member) and "Hawk". One would be flying in the morning and the other in the afternoon, alternating week to week. While one group was flying the other would be going to academic classes on navigation, engineering, weather and various other topics to complement the flying of the two Primary aircraft, the PA-18 and the T-6G. The initial briefing did not set the stage for personal confidence as the new students were told, there were too many in the class and initial washouts were going to be made, based on adaptability to fly, both physically and mentally. This was plus the fact that the pipeline of needed pilots was at an all-time low due to the end of the Korean War and a seemingly peaceful time looking forward. With this sobering news we were given our group and reporting time for our introduction to our flight.

The morning formation for our first day found our group, clad in flight suits and winter jackets, some even wearing sun glasses, despite the overcast sky, marching to the flight line. (Jim Sexton, a graduate of USC was our Hollywood hot dog and was never without his sun glasses). We were followed closely by a sharp contingent of aviation cadets calling cadence as they marched. Eagle flight met for the first time and our flight-leader, Mr. Hubenthal, briefed us on what the routine would be. We were also "awarded" our flying ball caps, each having an eagle image emblazoned on the front. He then assigned us to individual instructors, who were standing by designated places, known as instructor "tables". We were told that every instructor was a former military pilot with thousands of flying hours, most from the Navy and all had seen action in WWII and were now part of a civilian contract group hired to teach Air Force want-to be pilots how to fly. They came in all sizes and demeanors. There were the quiet, non-assuming ones and the "yeller-screamer" ones. We would find out how we fared after our first couple of rides. Even though Malden was a civilian operation, contracted by the government, there were also a group of military check pilots who would be the final authority of who passes and who does not pass, primary flight training. There were two other sections at Malden ahead of 56-H, one about to graduate and one two months further along in training. There were also USAF doctors, nurses and Dentists on the base, two chaplains and even a Judge Advocate, in the event you were faced with legal problems. The base proper was made up of a ramp, full of T-6 aircraft, a runway and a grass strip, close to where the PA-18, high wing preliminary aircraft were parked, which was used for landings and take-offs when needed, a couple of maintenance hangers and a flight line ready room for the military check-pilots, where each student had to eventually go for a "forty-hour check-ride" and a final check ride before advancing to the next phase of their training where we would begin our "Jet" flying. There were also a few buildings used for class rooms, a dispensary and a dental clinic, plus a mess hall and a small chapel. It was totally uncomplicated. There were no fences around the base. The town of Malden, about two miles from the airstrip, was mainly a one street downtown, with a theater, a couple of decent and cheap restaurants, a movie, a couple of side-streets on each end of the town, with typical small town bars and a set of stores where you could buy mercantile and clothing items. It was not what you would call an exciting area to live, but it was clean and inhabited by very nice people.

Bob Dugan, who I shared a barracks, next bed with and I became roommates in one half of the housing unit with the other half given to First Lieutenant Joe Kelly, senior in rank to all of the class and he also outranked a couple of the military check-pilots. He was the lone occupant of the room due to his advanced rank, however he had to share the bathroom with Bob and me.

Due to the large number of students four students were at each instructors table with even the Flight Commander having two students (within a week of flying they had been farmed out due to the washout of two individuals) and the assistant flight commander having a table full of four aspiring pilots. The name of the assistant flight commander was Clyde M. Pinkerton, affectionately called Pinky, a red haired, former Navy pilot with a South Carolina drawl and the patience of a saint, but one who would not let a student proceed through training without the capability to be an Air Force pilot. As it turned out I was at this wise pilot's table. Pinky politely stated that first day" I can teach anyone how to fly, however time will not be wasted on an individual in this environment". Objectively, I was a good candidate to fly as I considered myself smart, and athletic, a former college baseball infielder, with good hands and dexterity. I was quick to grasp difficult situations and was a good listener. I tended to not ask questions, content to discover for myself what was needed, sometimes to my regret, as I was reluctant to feel I didn't know answers and truthfully, too shy to expose myself. The other three at my table were two other ROTC graduates and one aviation cadet, named Thurman Chamblee Jr. Roland Ford and Charlie Englehart were the two officers. We were all told at the outset that we would only be with Pinky until the washout rate would allow room at one of the other instructor's tables. They didn't anticipate a long wait! Pinky's other duties as the assistant flight commander dictated that he did not have students and so the students were on edge from the very beginning. Little did we know how fortunate we were to be placed with Pinky. He was a former Navy pilot, having flown many missions during the second world war and by his own admission "lost a couple of aircraft", and "dead-sticked" another damaged Corsair on an island beach in the Pacific theater.

After some preliminary instructions to the group at the table the instructors took their young and eager "Eagles" out to their first aircraft, the high wing PA-18, essentially a two seat, side-by-side aircraft. It basically was used to find those who have no adaptability to fly, or to discover a fear of flying. The T-6 was a gas guzzler, so using the economical PA-18 was a way to discover those who could not be trained to fly without using the T-6. In the initial briefing from Pinky he again explained that anyone could learn how to fly, however The Air Force does not have the time to train everyone the Air Force way. Everyone was to be given twelve to sixteen hours in the PA-18 before they would transition into the T-6. Pinky explained the basics of our PA-18 time and then told us that each student would get a twenty-minute introductory flight. A summary was made of the procedures that would be followed prior to flight, the walk around, looking for items that would impeded flight on the exterior of the aircraft, then told us that every aircraft had a check-list that outlined a series of items that must be adhered to. He handed out a thin checklist with a hard, yellow cover for us to study.

Later in the period all the student pilots were ushered over to a "Personal Equipment" building and were fitted for a parachute. A civilian employee explained to all of us how to check the chute "history" which was contained in a small book embedded on the left shoulder strap. We tried on a chute and were assisted in adjusting the straps, until the chute rode high on our backs and it was semi-comfortable to walk. The now fitted chute was yours for the duration of your student days at Malden. Each of us carried our chute back to our flight shack and placed it on an assigned rack in the adjoining room to our briefing area. Pinky then took the group to show them the interior of this tiny bird, showing them certain flight items and explaining what "needle, ball and airspeed" meant in this rudimentary small craft. The four peering into the tiny cockpit from both sides, with the slender southerner sitting in the instructor seat showing how to manipulate the controls and explaining how the reaction to each worked and how to trim the aircraft with the manual wheel, doing this in a factual and calm manner took time and it was cold outside. He then went over how to start the engine, following the "check-list" that he gave to us. You had to wonder how long has Pinky been doing this, but obviously he loved what he was doing this and you knew he had to be a very competent pilot? Actual flight could not be taken until the class had gone through their first engineering class on the makeup and flight capabilities of the PA-18, something we would be doing this afternoon. After leaving the flight line, we marched directly to the mess-hall, where we found really good food. There was a wide array of sandwiches, already made, hot soup and fresh milk from a local dairy. After lunch we had twenty minutes to change out of our flight suits into the winter, blue uniform and then hustled out to once again form as a military unit and march the short distance to our first classes. We would find the initial classes were very uplifting as it was very instructive, but the platform instructor encouraged each student to get into the stationary mock cockpits set up for students to familiarize themselves with the placement of and point out flight instruments. All of us were given rudimentary flight manuals of the PA-18, outlining flight limitations and procedures for everything from starting the engine and all the intricate aspects of the airplane, including what to do in an emergency. Next topic was how to wear a parachute and how to deploy it. It was one of the more interesting topics that were covered in this first four-hour block. At the end of the day and a reasonably good meal in the chow hall, this exhausted group was ready for a good night's sleep before the next morning baptism of flight. A 0600 wakeup to a dark sky outside and a chilly wind whistling over the housing shack was followed by breakfast and then immediately these mostly new lieutenants formed as a group outside the mess hall and marched with 1st Lieutenant Kelly, calling cadence, leading us to the flight line, again followed by the cadet group.

It was a cold morning, the temperature was hovering around 40 degrees, so after arriving at the flight building Kelly yelled "fall out" and we sprinted to get inside. We hurried into the warm room to find the instructors mostly at their tables awaiting the 56-H class on their first day of flight. Pinky was not at the table but appeared minutes later. He sort of half-sat down as the four students took their seats. He explained the order of flight and how each of them would be eased into the actual flying of the aircraft, as much would be demonstrated on this first flight. Each of the aspiring pilots were leafing through the thin flight manual and check list that had been given to them as they covered all phases of flight. The check list could be attached to the knee of your flight suit with a clip to ensure it didn't fall off. After this rather short briefing the group exited the building into the cold February air and walked to a parking area, short of the grass strip. The PA-18s were lined up awaiting someone to crank them up and fly them. Pinky opened the right-side door of our assigned aircraft and tightened his parachute straps and stepped into the cockpit. Roland was the first to go! He put his chute on and took the left side seat. The three of us stood fire guard with a fire extinguisher in hand in the event we were needed. He closed the door and within seconds the engine started and began to move slowly, taxing out to the grass field. This field ran almost perpendicular to the main runway. The remaining three students watched as the aircraft moved to the end and then heard the engine whine up and roll down the runway and shortly push into the sky. The aircraft took a turn away from the field into the clear, but cold sky. In mere minutes, the aircraft returned, bouncing onto the grass and returned to its parking spot. The engine shut down and Roland emerged from the left side of the small Piper product with a huge smile on his face. Pinky had indicated the order he would take each and I was next. I hopped into the already warm seat and nervously strapped the seat belt and shoulder harness on, then positioned the seat as Roland was a bit taller, with longer legs. Because the PA-18 was a propeller driven aircraft it would require rudder pressure to counter the rotation of the prop in order to keep the aircraft straight down the runway. I had my winter jacket on and suddenly I felt very warm. I grabbed the headset being handed to me by Pinky and placed it over my Eagle ball cap and adjusted the ear flaps for my head. Pinky went through the engine start procedure and introduced me to the before engine start checklist. Completing the checklist was then followed by another checklist, the before taxi checklist to prepare the aircraft for flight. Pinky was pointing and pushing as he read the checklist and motioning to me to put my hands-on various item to comply with the checklist. We then received clearance to taxi to the takeoff position and calmly led me in the turn onto the grass strip, pushed the throttle forward and stayed on the controls as he helped this nervous student into the air. Suddenly the ground passed from them and I was, for the first time in my life, was flying an aircraft. I had been around aircraft, but never had been in one. Pinky was talking about trimming the aircraft for a climb, and his instructions were totally confusing to this student. Nose up, nose down trim! It was a quick mystery that the instructor calmly explained and now it was my aircraft totally, with Pinky explaining turns and climbs and dives, trimming for all, then it was back in the pattern, going through another checklist. The use of flaps was explained as we entered what was called a base leg and flew toward the middle of the grass strip, with Pinky helping me through the final feet before landing and showing how a slight amount of back pressure would result in a smooth landing. After almost no roll on the runway we maneuvered the aircraft back to the remaining students, parked and following the checklist, shut down the engine. The total time of flight was less than twenty minutes! Emerging from the aircraft I felt a great sense of accomplishment as I made way for Charlie to enter for his initial flight. It followed the same routine as the previous two student-pilots and saw Charlie lift into the air and climb straight ahead, then making a gentle right hand turn away from the traffic on the T-6 runway. Roland exchanged his feeling about the first flight and both he and I admitted we were exhausted, but happy with how we felt; we had actually flown an aircraft. Thurman fidgeted as we shared our thoughts about our feat, but said nothing. The Aviation cadet was to be the last for his indoctrination flight and he was visibly nervous. Thurman was a typical, young southern boy. He had sandy hair, was raw-boned, fairly, tall and constantly talking, mostly to hide his apprehension. As a solo cadet at our table of three officers he felt a bit conscious of his position, but he was outgoing and had an answer for everything. Pinky and Charlie appeared from their short flight and taxied to the parking slot. Engine shut down and an excited Charlie stepped out of the left door with a customary huge smile on his face. Pinky, as before completed some notes on a knee pad he wore and motioned for Thurman to get in. Now taking the seat in the PA-18, Thurman was uncharacteristically quiet. As the engine roared into activity, the doors closed and the high-winged training aircraft rolled down to the takeoff area of the grass strip and as the three students watched the tiny bird launched into the air for the first indoctrination flight for Thurman Chamblee Jr. The three new PA-18 "veterans" began to share their flight time and all seemed to feel they were ready for more time in the air. Twenty minutes in control of a small aircraft had done this. All needed their newly acquired pilot log books so they could dutifully record their time and a single landing. Charlie was effusive talking about his turn at the controls of the PA-18, elaborating on his turns and use of the trim wheel. He was a person the others would soon realize had a propensity to exaggerate his experiences. As we talked, the now very familiar aircraft was taxiing back from its short flight. As it came to an abrupt stop we waited for the doors to open and from the left side Thurman exited with a smile on his face and slowly the right door opened and Pinky was involved in jotting something on his knee board. He casually exited, grabbed his chute and led us back to the "A" flight ready room. Charlie talking all the way back to the area. Arriving back at our table, chutes having been placed back on their racks, we were given an overall group summation of the flights we had all had. It seemed positive, but who knows after a mere twenty minutes in the air. Our instructor assigned all of us to go to the cockpit mockup in the simulator building and practice our checklist procedures until we knew them by rote. This would be a normal part of our day, while Pinky had a student in the air.

Ground School

The afternoon would begin with information being given to us about the theory and physics of the flight of an aircraft. We would learn about the universal functions of flight surfaces, what words like yaw and roll mean. How airflow impacts the surface of an aircraft and the function of the various flight instruments need for flight, rudimentary "needle, ball and airspeed", something I heard at least five times today in the first flight in the PT-18 from Pinky. Navigation class started and the first thing we learned was something called "dead reckoning". It seemed simple enough! Everyone received a local area map and they showed us the principal emergency landing areas in Cape Girardeau, Pine Bluff Arkansas and of course Dexter, locally. Pinky had already talked about the fact that everything locally is farm land and that using section lines and furrow direction, almost anywhere is a good place to put down an ailing aircraft. On the brief indoctrination flight the first thing Pinky pointed out was the flow of the land in this southeast Missouri "boot". Virtually acre after acre of farmland clearly cordoned off into large acre plots. Each plot of land is replete with fertile soil and clearly marked in furrows that can be seen easily from the air. Because this area had a long history of farmland there were very few hard obstacles, like rocks hidden in the soil. The glide distance of an aircraft without power is something a pilot must be familiar with, but in the local area any choice would more than likely be a good one. Weather would become a prime topic in our classes and we would learn how to discern what to avoid and what to accept as reasonable to fly in. This area of the country was prone to severe weather, blizzards in the winter and thunderstorms in the spring and summer. It was the goal of this group to make sure we respected the need for a pilot to be educated in all things leading to successfully and safely fly an aircraft. Our classes were all taught by qualified instructors, who had a background in the subject, some were military, but others were civilian part time flight instructors. The first need was to know the aircraft we were flying and that became our primary interest. A class in engineering describing facets of the PA-18 dominated the first days of academics. At the end of our first day everyone seemed overwhelmed with what we had to learn. To make it worse the mystery of how to trim was a hot topic and the first in a series of puzzling mysteries in this pursuit of learning how to fly.

The second day dawned as before with a murky sky and a cold, biting wind. As we assembled outside of the mess hall to march to the flight line we huddled to keep from facing the wind. The question was "will we fly today"? As we approached our flight center we noticed for the first time a flag pole outside flying a red flag. We found out as we entered the spacious briefing area that the red flag meant "no flying" as the instructors were casually sitting at their tables discussing the wind velocity and direction. The regular runway was situated in an east-west direction, but the grass field was more northerly, which was the direction the wind was coming from. As we approached Pinky at the table he appeared ready to spend time talking, but as we sat down

Mr. Hubenthall arrived and he and Pinky were discussing the possibility of using the grass runway for PA-18 flight activity. As the flight commander and assistant, it would be their decision. I heard Pinky say it would be a good instructional occasion and they could get a second flight in on all the students. Mr. H agreed and so the announcement was made that flight activity would commence after some preliminary safety factors would be presented. Pinky let us know at our table that we would change the order of flight to have Chamblee go first, followed by Charlie, then Roland and finally me. Due to the cold weather only the individual student and one posing as the fire guard would go with Pinky to the aircraft and each 30 minutes later, the following scheduled student would go to meet the aircraft and the finishing student would act as fire guard for the following flight. Mr. Hubenthall briefed the wind conditions and some flying items and then released the assembled instructors and students to start flying activity. He also told us to be prepared for turbulence and that each instructor would re-brief that topic before flights began. Pinky did so then left with Chamblee to get their chutes and told Charlie to meet him at the aircraft in 35 minutes. As they exited the building with others going to their assigned aircraft it was apparent that the wind seemed to be the only factor as the sun was shining through a few clouds. It was February and the flat terrain did little to slow the wind down. The temperature was announced as 47 degrees, but a new figure was thrown at us "wind chill"; this new item reduced the temperature to around 30 degrees. The blue winter jackets, heavy flight suits and thermal undergarments given to each student were not enough to keep one from feeling the cold temperatures, but they helped. We had been given the winter long-leg underwear, but most did not use them. They, like me, would tomorrow!

THE WINDY SECOND FLIGHT

C harlie had exited the ready flight room and Thurman very shortly afterwards sluggishly entered with a frown on his face and his chute over both shoulders. He threw his "Eagle" cap on the table and launched into a tirade on the conditions in the air. He said that Pinky talked about the turbulence they experienced and demonstrated various flight conditions, but they mostly stayed in the pattern. He then sat in his chair, picked up his flight manual and became silent. Roland and I had been in a conversation about personal background and it turns out that he is a member of a family that owns a pharmaceutical company, based in Chicago. It was a closed corporation with all its shareholders limited to his family. I asked if he was going to remain in the Air Force or leave to join that group. He indicated a love for flying, but as one of the few married officers, he was getting some pressure to not make a career out of his time in the service. That seemed to be the feeling of most of the student officers who came from the ROTC (Reserve Officers Training Corps) program. That feeling was not shared by the Aviation Cadets, nor was it by the OCS (Officers Candidate School) graduates. Those two groups had already spent a significant amount of time in the service, some for a few years, whereas the only service time the ROTC graduates had was spending three weeks in summer camp and close to five weeks in pre-flight conditioning. For Roland and I this was a great adventure, something we wanted to do, but we were living in the moment and had not extended our thoughts to the future. Roland had a great attitude about things and I would find he was a very giving person and eager to succeed. The subject was dropped as he said he better be going to meet Pinky and Charlie. He left to pick up his parachute from the adjacent room and waved as he left the building. I picked up the same manual that Thurman was reading and perused a couple of lines, but really wasn't too engrossed in what it said. I was more concerned about "trim". It was now an obsession with me! Why would you turn the wheel down, when the nose was coming up and vice versa? Shortly, Charlie entered with another huge smile on his face and launched into feats of experience and how the wind buffeted the aircraft and how he saved the day while being a fire-guard for the starting engine routine we have all been trained to do when starting the PA-18 engine. He was so glad he had worn his thermals as it was bitter cold outside. Charlie seemed to have experienced everything in his life and I had heard enough, so tried to engage Thurman into asking questions from our first day in ground school. He really didn't get what I was trying to do, but it did succeed in shutting down Charlie. I was still early but said I would go and wait at the parking slot for Pinky and Roland. I slowly picked up my chute I had been fitted with yesterday from the adjoining room and walked out the door to the flight line. It truly was cold! As I walked to the grass runway I noticed the red flag was still flying and remembered the T-6s could not fly due to the cross-wind I had heard about in our first taste of learning about flying hazards. The wind was hitting me on my left side, so I raised the fur flap on my jacked to save my face and pulled my hat down tight, but it didn't help my legs and now freezing, butt. I loved the pilot's sun glasses I was issued and felt they were secure on my face and truly added to the persona of being a pilot, even though I had only logged 20 minutes of flying time. I arrived at the parking area poised to wait for the aircraft and the two flyers, and was surprised to see them taxiing across the runway, turning off the end. I watched as they turned back on the runway and launched, if you can call it that, into the air. They appeared to be standing still as the wind was right in their face, holding them in a seemingly set position. Slowly they were gaining headway and climbed back to what I guessed was a cross-wind altitude at the far end of the airdrome. Still climbing they turned on a downwind (I learned all the terms yesterday). They were a blur on that heading as the wind at their back was propelling them rapidly to where they would make their turn to the base leg. They turned and continued around to heading straight down the runway. Again, they appeared to be standing still, but slowly let down to the end of the runway. There were a few other aircraft in the pattern, but most of the instructors were not at the point where they were shooting multiple landings. For Pinky and Roland after landing the aircraft came to a stop, it seemed almost instantly due to the wind. I would learn something about Pinky today. This time they turned and taxied toward me in the parking area, turned into the parking space and shut down the engine. I picked up the "chocks" for the set of tires and put them firmly in place as the two doors opened. Pinky shuffled a bit in his seat, but the one thing I remember was the smile on his face as he addressed Roland. It was obvious he liked what he saw with Lieutenant Ford.

I was poised to take the left seat as Roland left the aircraft, but he was sort of holding on as Pinky positioned his leg clip board on his right thigh and fastened it as he turned his page to cover the notes he had taken on Roland. I held the door as Roland left, nodding to me as he cleared the aircraft, grabbed the extinguisher and waited for me to start the engine. It was my turn now as I stepped into the cockpit, positioning my chute and snuggling in from the wind. Pinky repositioned his small bag, stuffed some papers in it, then shoved it to the side and smiled as he gave me the headset, saying "do you remember how to start the engine"? I nodded yes, having gone over it a trillion times in my mind since yesterday and proceeded to go through the checklist, while watching Roland outside with the fire extinguisher in hand in his role as the "fire guard". The engine roared into life and Roland scampered away with wheel chocks in hand, from the now alive PA-18, whose whole frame was shaking. The time practicing the checklist items in the mockup had really helped. I put on my newly issued flying gloves, having forgotten that I was supposed to have them on when entering the aircraft. Pinky didn't seem aware, but knew he was. I looked at him and he pointed to the runway. I released the brakes and started the roll on the grass parking area to the designated launch point. The chill of the outside was gone now, and I could feel the beginning of sweat coming out in my armpits as I nervously pulled into the takeoff position. There were two other PA-18s in the pattern, but they were not a factor. Pinky put his hand on mine as I touched the throttle and slowly pushed the throttle forward and the high winged little bird started to move. As the airspeed reached the lift-off point Pinky helped me take a lift-off attitude and we were airborne. All the time he was talking to me about flight attitude, trim and airspeed. He was explaining the use of the flight instruments, covering basically what we learned in ground school yesterday. As we were slowly climbing he demonstrated how to skid the aircraft, using the rudder and having me watch the needle and ball. I could see what effect his action had on this key instrument, the ball going one way and the vertical needle leaning the other. We leveled off at 4000 ft and spent the next twenty minutes going through gentle turns with varying bank angles after which we did a stall series, first power on and then power off. Each was meticulously demonstrated before telling me to do them. It seemed strange and very quiet when you pulled the throttle to idle and pulled the nose up waiting for the shutter of the aircraft to begin and the nose to fall on the power off stall but then even stranger when you set the throttle for a power-on stall and pulled the nose up waiting for the inevitable and once again the shutter followed by a recovery with stiff leg on the left rudder pedal and bringing the power back in to full power as the nose slips through the horizon. He seemed pleased with my efforts as I noticed we had really, never left the Malden Airfield environs. We let down to traffic pattern altitude and then went through how to enter on a forty-five degree entry angle to enter the downwind leg, managing airspeed for each phase of the pattern and now noticed that my headset was leaking water down my neck. For the first time since takeoff I became aware of the buffeting being experienced by the aircraft from the heavy wind. It was like being on a washboard as I tried valiantly to hold altitude, turning from the forty-five degree entry to the downwind leg. Pinky was talking calmly the entire time, making me cross check the instruments and making sure I had trimmed the aircraft for each phase. Yes, suddenly trim was making sense! In my mind I would try to think ahead, but I would find I was holding too much pressure on the stick as I wasn't keeping up with the trim. Finally, on final I felt I had total control. Pinky talked me through the landing and told me to add power to go around, which I did. Rudder pressure was needed to hold the aircraft straight down the grass strip. It was the first time I really felt the buffeting of the wind and the turbulent air. "Re-trim now" he called out. I realized the trim must change drastically as I added power to go-around. I was way behind but battled to get the trim where it belonged for takeoff as opposed to that needed for the landing attitude I had just left and now could feel I was strong arming the little aircraft through a tough wind, but was slowly winning the battle as I groped the stick with one hand and worked the trim with the other. I naturally overshot the pattern altitude. All the while Pinky had become very quiet and didn't utter a sound until I found the proper altitude on the cross-wind leg. I had stabilized the trim, but now discovered I had gone beyond the point that I had been given to turn downwind so tried to adjust and did an uncoordinated turn to get back to where I should be. I glanced at the "needle and ball" and found them in disarray also. Finally, I was on a downwind heading, a bit wide but on the proper altitude and trimmed, with an indicated airspeed close to what I was supposed to have. I squirmed in my now wet seat as the leak on my head had turned into a torrent of water down my back. I looked at the grass strip and estimated it was time to turn on a base leg. I made a surprisingly, smooth turn and started to descend when I noticed I was being blown away from the runway due to the wind. I set an angle of attack for the approach, which if seen from the ground would have approached a 45-degree angle of the runway heading. All the time Pinky was now calmly explaining what was happening to the aircraft and what I was doing to make it seem we were not trying to land. In a desperate angling move I was on a straight-in heading down the runway, trimming the whole time as my airspeed bled off and touched down on the end of the runway. As we taxied back to the parking spot Pinky had to remind me to "S" turn the aircraft as it was a tail-dragger, back to the parking spot. When we got to the spot, much to my surprise, the other three students were there. Pinky had told Roland to have them all meet the aircraft. I shut the engine down and Charlie reached under the aircraft to chock the wheels. I was so hot and when I opened the door after completing the engine shutdown checklist, the blast of cold air sent shivers down my wet body. I was waiting for Pinky to say anything, but he was vigorously writing on his knee pad. Finished he unfastened it, stuffed it into his bag, smiled and said, "let's go". We virtually ran to escape the wind back to our flight center. As we scurried back by sweating body turned to an ice cube. Those long-johns that I left in the room were now a needed item.

THE DEBRIEFING

As the five of us strode into the student pilot area there was no conversation, mostly because the wind was blowing directly into our faces and we were covering up to protect them. My Eagle hat came very close to blowing off my head, but I grabbed at it before it could fly away. My very wet underarms were now so sufficiently cold that I expected them to freeze over. Pinky and I were the only ones needing to rid ourselves of our chutes, so we worked our way to the equipment area and placed them on the appropriate stands. I noticed my flight suit was drenched, and Pinky's was dry. We then retreated to the student table for the group debrief. It was amazingly painless as Pinky did not really address us individually, but more as a group, occasionally referring to one of us for a deviation from the norm. Many of the items he cited needing work were things I had committed, but many were not. He said all of us showed that we had studied our checklist procedures and he was very pleased with that item. He felt we all would be better prepared for days like this in the future due to the limited experience we had in the aircraft and how we worked through the conditions. He promised we would start to love what we are doing and closed with the comment we all need to learn to stay ahead of the aircraft. It was not healthy to fall behind. I took that personally and hoped I wasn't the only one and was not being singled out.

The end of the morning period saw us released from our ready room and forming into our military formation with 1st Lieutenant Kelly counting cadence on our return to the barracks area. After falling out we walked to the mess hall for lunch and based on yesterday it would be sandwiches and milk. Joe Kelly and Bob Dugan saved me from sitting with Charlie and cut into the line ahead of me. It turned out that the go-to item was going to be hot soup with two choices and sandwiches. I filled a bowl with tomato soup and picked up a handful of saltines, filled up a glass with milk and found Joe, who was munching a sandwich and sat down at one of the four person tables. We were soon joined by Bob with two large sandwiches and a huge glass of milk. I noticed that Charlie had sat with Roland, who being the kind of guy he was, tolerated Charlie's boastful and never-ending chatting. All the Aviation Cadets sat in another section, cordoned off from the officers and Thurman was settled in the middle of a group and appeared to be exchanging the day's activity. Joe started talking about his flight and it was obvious we had similar problems "staying ahead of the aircraft". I felt a bit better about my flight now, especially when Dugan said he had a problem maintaining pattern altitudes and had no concept of what the pattern looked like. Joe laughed at Bob and hoped in his raspy, cigarette toned voice that he would have a better day tomorrow. The soup was great and the heat warmed my entire body. The march back had dried my flight suit and I was reasonably comfortable now. We had to be in class at 1300 hours.

The military time line was a constant and after the pre-flight at Lackland I was very accustomed to hearing it and no longer had to think about it. A change of clothes was in order as we were not to wear our flight suits to class. Fortunately, we were given permission to wear our flight jacket over our uniform, winter blues with tie. (with the clothing allowance I was given at Lackland I did not buy an official overcoat, didn't think I would need one). A bit late but I pulled on my thermals, even though I knew we would remain inside for the next three hours. After changing we all fell into the "route step" group and walked to the Academic building. Topics today would be Flight characteristics and dynamics (again) and weather. Two ninety-minute classes with a 20-minute break in between.

Various frontal systems were a topic of the first hour. How to identify a warm front from a cold front as opposed to a stationary front on a weather map and how they form was a very interesting item. This was followed by the types of clouds and their formation. What was meant by the three phases of a thunderstorm and the final result, an anvil appearing cloud that had lots of stuff in it and could actually throw it out, so don't fly too clos On top of that was the information on the building of an anvil and the currents of air up and down the interior of the cumulus cloud which were all discussed and how they affected flight was not only interesting, but essential to know. The class went by quickly and during the break we all agreed that what we heard in that class was only the beginning in our education on the meaning of what takes place in our weather systems. I was a bit surprised by the number of smokers among the Cadets as opposed to the officers.

Joe was the only officer I saw who went out in the cold to grab a smoke as he joined a flurry of "AvCads", as they were called. The individual comments on weather ended abruptly as we returned to the classroom to be greeted by yet another knowledgeable instructor, this time on the flight characteristics of the PA-18, to include previous flight experiences. Among them was icing, not just on a surface, but the icing of the Pitot Tube, a device that measured the wind through a tiny external tube and gives the pilot airspeed among other essential flight instruments. Pinky had made a comment on that item when he removed a small cover from an extended tube from the aircraft and briefly made a comment on what that tube was. One of the switches in the cockpit was for the heating of that tube. Frozen over meant no airspeed indication and other ram air instruments. The engine in the PA-18 was another item that brought questions from the students. There was one AvCad, named Hill who had been an aircraft engine mechanic and who had worked on a number of different aircraft engines, who added some salient comments on engines. He was one of the many smokers among his group, not that it had anything to do with his knowledge of engines. He was rather tall (most seem tall to me as I'm only 5'6) and rugged looking and had a very serious edge to him. I would almost call him unfriendly. However, having said that, he was very effusive and seemed knowledgeable in speaking of his extensive background and experience of working on engines.

Academics ended and we exited into a milder day. The sun was going down and the wind had subsided significantly, making it seem warmer that it had been. We did notice that there were a series of clouds forming to the northwest, masking the setting sun somewhat. Our new-found knowledge of clouds came into play and the recent picture of a front came to mind. Was it a cold front? Of course, said Charlie, "look where it's coming from?" We left it at that as we knew that question would come up tomorrow, if not at the student table, but surely during our weather class. Kelly, Dugan and I decided to go into town to eat after changing into civilian clothes. I volunteered to drive the short two miles into town. The route was a two-lane road off the main drag in a very rural area and finding a parking spot for his 54 Ford Victoria was not a problem. The eating place was on the corner at the near end of town as they entered the block-long downtown. It had been advertised at the field as an alternative to the food at the mess hall and seemed like a good idea to the three tired student pilots. It had also been recommended by some of the class ahead of them who Joe had become friendly with. It turned out to be an excellent place to eat. As we entered the place, the engaging young female greeter couldn't have been more exuberant about our coming. She immediately identified us as new students. She obviously was familiar with many of the other student pilots from the class in front of 56-H. She showed us to a table in the middle of the somewhat narrow, but deep confines of the restaurant. There were probably no more than twenty tables and four booths in the room, about half occupied. By the time we sat down everyone was aware we were from the field. Most were most assuredly from the town and no one was near to us in age, other than the waitress and the girl who greeted us at the door. We chatted with the pretty waitress, who was married and about our age. She told us that most of the things to do, outside of the movie were not local, but involved sort of weekend trips to Cape Girardeau. It was a decent menu and the food was very good and surprisingly cheap, which made it a good place for Dugan and I as we made $341 a month and that included $100 flight pay. Kelly as a first lieutenant made a smidgen more. As we left the restaurant Dugan saw a sign down the back side of the road away from town that indicated a possible place to visit. "Blondells" was the name on the sign. And underneath was an announcement that beer and spirits were sold there. We walked the half block from the restaurant, entered the darkened establishment and found a couple of our aviation cadets at a table and an attractive young woman behind the bar. We sat down at a table after acknowledging our classmates and the young woman came out from the bar and asked what she could get for us. Three beers were soon in front of us with frosted glasses and Dugan was launching into a conversation with the bar-maid. It turned out she was Blondell. Could she own a place like this at her age? Her father owned the bar, named it for his daughter, and she was old enough to be behind the bar on occasion, when he wasn't there. It was a Wednesday night in February, so the clientele was going to be sparse. She sat down with us and told us her story. There were not many jobs available and after finishing a junior college in Cape Girardeau, which was on the Mississippi River about forty miles away in the boot of Missouri, she said she wanted to just stay in Malden.

We left after one beer knowing that a 0600 hours wakeup was in front of us and we would all be in the air tomorrow. There was a flurry of snow in the air as we drove back on the narrow two lane road, now guided by the split beacon on the tower. Military field beacons are split, meaning that as they rotate they show the beacon with a pause, then light and then a break before the next split light shows. Civilian beacons are one constant light, before a break. We were learning slowly and were adjusting to the military way! It had been a good day and bed could not come soon enough.

The morning drill came and after breakfast the sun came up and we marched to the flight line in a fairly, calm, but cold morning. I would venture that all were well equipped with winter undergarments today. We commented on the few cirrus clouds which were in the sky, trying to exhibit our new knowledge of types of clouds and of course Charlie was still stuck on what kind of front we were involved in. Nobody seemed to care as it was good flying weather and the green flag flew above the ready room. As we entered there were no instructors in the room, but we heard voices from their private break room and wondered what the topic of their discussion was. The group slowly exited the room and took their seats at the appropriate table. There had been some direction to the group on detailing flight activities on anyone who had difficulty on their first two flights as the instructors all seemed to be aware of the crowded conditions. There were 36 students for nine flight instructors, including the flight commander and his assistant. A couple of them had five students, a situation they wanted to remedy quickly. It was reiterated to the students that there was a path to eliminate oneself if anyone felt this wasn't for them. The SIE (Self-Initiated Elimination) could be accomplished quietly by just letting the instructor know and Mr. Hubenthal would start the paperwork. It was a sobering revelation, but no one immediately showed an inclination to take the offer. It would appear the task for elimination would be with the instructors. In conversations with others the identity of certain instructors as very tough and to be avoided were brought about privately and it was our table and the students with Mr. Hubenthal that would be most affected by a change in instructors. We knew that as the ranks thinned out we would end up hopefully at another table, and not looking for another assignment.

Pinky spent a bit more time today in outlining what we would be doing today and cautioned us to remember that the T-6s were up in the air today and it would be very busy as there is one class that is finishing up this week and are getting their final check rides, before going to their basic training bases. I was to be first up to fly today and it would entail working on the stall series, pattern work and multiple landings, some touch and go, followed by at least two full stops. Flight time would be almost 45 minutes. Everyone from the table went to the assigned aircraft and took part in the required walk around. Pinky was trying to give us some tips on what to look for, not only on the aircraft, but the surroundings. Pick up wind direction, cloud cover and try to make a determination where you were going to look for emergency landing areas in the event of an engine problem. His last words to all of us were: "you must stay ahead of the aircraft. Think ahead".

My memory bank was working overtime as I went through the before starting engine checklist and then powered through the engine start, motioning the standby group to pull the chocks, holding firmly on the brakes. Releasing them I started to the end of the runway. I did remember to start an "S" turn, even though we were only a few yards from taking the runway. The PA-18 contingent (our class 56-H) was controlled on the grass runway by a light from what they called a mobile control. Red meant hold your position and yellow to taxi with caution. Finally, the green light meant you were cleared for takeoff. I was given the green light as I approached the runway, so I slowly taxied into position, brought up the power, glanced to make sure the green was still on and applied power, without any assistance from Pinky and more important, no conversation. Pinky had indicated to climb straight ahead, finally turning away from the traffic area and leveled at 4000ft, right on airspeed. Pinky wanted to go through the stall series, so I initiated the power-on, stoking the power and initiating a steep climb, slowly applying rudder pressure to counter the action of the propeller, until the aircraft started shaking. Putting the nose down and continuing the rudder action until we were at a safe airspeed and leveled off almost where I started at 4000ft. Pinky nodded and said to try the power off stall. I pulled the power back to idle, holding altitude, noticing the nose rising until the shaking got intense and recovered by pushing the nose forward, applying power, full left rudder and gaining control again. Pinky was pleased and said he would demonstrate some maneuvers and proceeded to show me chandelles and lazy eights, using the horizon as his reference point. It was like a half circle on the horizon. He was so smooth and I was mesmerized until he said to try the chandelle. It was flat and took so much room to get a turn that ended up on the section lines on the ground. What was to be done in 180 degrees I managed in 110 degrees, too steep, too fast! He just smiled and said we would work on that. We let down to the traffic pattern and entered flawlessly. It was not difficult for me to visualize a forty-five-degree entry to the parallel landing pattern. I had drawn on a piece of pressed paper a pattern with airspeed and checklist item to complete at points on the drawing. "Stay ahead" was drumming in my brain. Kept a decent downwind, rolled onto base and hit final a bit hot, but managed to get on airspeed by rotation. Touched down and applied power to go-around and found I didn't put in enough rudder and left the ground about 10 degrees off heading. I got back on heading and reentered the pattern. I was now in a group of other aircraft, doing the same thing as me, so established some spacing to make my approach. I stayed on airspeed as I noticed once again water mysteriously rolling out of my headset. Pinky said to stop on this approach, so after touching down and rolling a couple hundred yards I pulled off and started "S" turning back to the takeoff end of the runway. Pinky signaled for me to take the active again when cleared. I saw the very red light and then noticed another high wing PA-18 bouncing down the runway, finally leaping back into the air. I checked final and did not see any more traffic and was adding power when Pinky pushed hard on the brakes, showing me the red light still on. I slumped back into my seat as the light turned green, added power again and Pinky told me to continue onto the runway, pointed the nose down the grass runway and proceeded into the takeoff mode. It was fast, but before I knew it we were in the air again and leveling off to turn cross-wind. I was not quite ahead of the aircraft, but I wasn't far behind and turned downwind, on altitude, but low on airspeed. I managed to get everything right before turning base, losing the necessary

400 ft and turned on final for a smooth approach and landing. I was thoroughly wet and exhausted and was elated when Pinky indicated to park the aircraft. I pulled into the slot, shut the engine down and noticed Pinky furiously jotting down notes on his knee pad. Roland opened my door and I slowly exited my frame into the nice cool air. Pinky got out too, but only "to stretch" his legs, which he did by jogging a few feet with his seat pack firmly attached, allowing Roland to go through the drill of checking the exterior of the aircraft. I stayed as they both entered and took their seats. I stood by with the fire extinguisher as they started the engine, then pulled the chocks when signaled to do so and watched as they started out. I felt good about the flight and had a big smile as I entered the student area. I noticed Dugan was at his table, his flight suit totally darkened by sweat. There was not a dry spot on it. He laughed as I asked if it went OK. He nodded and said he thought it did and asked how my flight went. I said it was better than yesterday and sat down with my chute at my side on the floor. Dugan's flight paralleled mine in every way, but there was no attempt to do any acro. He was impressed that we had attempted them. The morning flight session ended after Charlie and Thurman had completed their rides. The critique from Pinky was much the same as yesterday as it was general and not specific, giving me the impression that all of us were at the same level and doing OK. He did point out that all of us had a decent day and that he was pleased with our progress.

The afternoon academic sessions were pretty much an extension of what we learned yesterday, with a brief time spent on personal hygiene, and for those who were married, a few comments on taking care of their wife. The housing for married students was somewhat marginal down town, but deemed adequate. Evidently experience had been that some wives had difficulty adjusting to, not only the area, but also to married life. Friends were few and far apart and they were cautioned to be aware of their present status. It seemed totally out of place for our current status, but I wasn't married, so it didn't have any bearing on me, but it was just an extension of the day. The time spent on flight characteristics was very interesting but was just a reiteration of some of our time in the aircraft. We received the training on proper exit position for bailout from the PA-18—interesting. Never thought we would leave one. Pinky only talked about emergency landings! With the conditions locally I thought I would choose an emergency landing rather than exiting the aircraft. Finally, I learned a lot about map reading and how to determine navigation check points. I noticed two missing seats in the class room.

It was obvious that the day's activity had emptied the level of energy for anything, but a chow hall dinner and some brush-up on the Dash-1 (that was the designation of all flight manuals). I decided I would take another look at the limited section on "emergency procedures". It turned out to be a quick read as I dozed off even before I started.

The next day started like most others with a weather briefing that indicated some snow for today and as we walked outside there was a flurry of the white stuff, but the clouds were so thin you could see round them and you could actually see the sun shining through holes. Pinky called them "sucker holes"! The ceiling was pretty high as we were at 3000-4000 in today's activity and we were well below the scattered clouds. The activity was a repeat of yesterday, however we did not do the chandelles or lazy eights due to no horizon to gage the activity. We did have one significant new area that started on the third day of flying, spins! Holy Toledo! What fun! You start with the power-on stall, lining up on a fence line on the ground and instead of starting the recovery from the stall, you pull the throttle to idle, kick in rudder and enter into what starts out rather flat, but after the second turn, counted by crossing the starting fence line, you are pretty nose down. Recovery was made when you completed the third turn by kicking in opposite rudder, stopping the spin and then adding power and pulling out of the now fairly, precipitous dive. I found I was good at this maneuver and looking to my right, I found Pinky smiling after doing one.

Pattern activity was to dominate each of the following days, but aircraft characteristics and control were areas of emphasis as the progressive time, per flight, in the air grew. With the increase, now at the most, three of us at Pinky's table would get flight time on any day. The first week had not seen any significant concerns from Pinky that we could discern. He had indicated that Roland and I would solo very soon as we had accumulated over four hours of flight time. On the sixth day of flying we were very stunned when Pinky announced that he was giving Thurman an elimination ride. Evidently Thurman has been having air sickness on every flight and Pinky said he had to complete this flight without any sickness problem or he would face a board for elimination. He would be the last to fly today. It was bright and sunny, and it would seem to be a good day for Thurman to fly.

Thurman had been hiding a "barf-bag" when exiting the aircraft on all-of-his flights and hadn't told anyone of us his problem. Pinky said Roland and I would fly first in preparation of going solo tomorrow, weather permitting. Charlie was a bit behind and would get a dual ride tomorrow to see if he was ready to solo. We had not lost a day to weather yet, but for us to solo the weather had to almost be CAVU. That is clear and visibility unlimited. Add to that no significant wind problems. After Roland and I had finished our flights Thurman met me as I parked the aircraft. Roland and Charlie were with him and we all watched as he started the engine and taxied away. The anticipation was unnerving as we all liked Thurman. He was definitely a bit immature, but he had always been serious in his approach to flying and had grasped the need to work hard. Every time I saw him, he was in his books, (actually thick pamphlets) on our classroom subjects. I guessed he had entered the Air Force right out of high school and then qualified for the AvCad program. He was a tall raw-boned, Oklahoma kid, not old enough to buy a beer in Blondells. He was intent on not washing out and told us that two of his friends had SIEed and didn't want to follow them out of the program.

Finally, we picked out their aircraft among three PA-18s in the pattern. The aircraft touched down and the power instantly went up for a go-around. That was good news as why would they shoot landings if he was going to be eliminated? They shot another touch and go before coming to a full stop and taxied back to the parking spot. As the right door opened Pinky looked at us and gave us a "thumbs up". We ran to Thurman's side as he exited with a big smile on his face. We were all very pleased that it had gone well for him. We asked him on the way back to flight operations after Pinky was out of ear shot, how it had gone. He looked at us, gave a whimsical grin and said, "I swallowed it"! We couldn't believe it! We would like to take him downtown to celebrate, but the cadets were confined to the base. They were only allowed to leave on Friday nights and Saturday, if there was no makeup flying. It would have to be enough to see the relieved cadet Chamblee, whose smile never left, relaxed at our flight table.

Roland and I were told that we were both going to go solo tomorrow. We were now on the afternoon flight schedule, so we both would have all night and all morning through our academic classes to worry about it. The weather was forecast to be for good weather tomorrow, so it would be a sleepless night! The reality is I'm ready to solo and Pinky knows that, but the thought of being alone was mind boggling! I had close to six hours in the aircraft and had not demonstrated any difficulty in any of the needed areas of emphasis. He has recently indicated in his quiet way that my performance is very good. I love flying, but creeping in, there is always the feeling that maybe I could use more time with Pinky. He has made it clear he doesn't feel that way.

THE CORD IS CUT

ugan was first in the shower and yelled as he exited that it was a good day to fly. He had gone to Blondells last night, supposedly to have a beer, but came in well after "Taps". The fact that he didn't ask anyone to go with him caused me to ask why the solo visit to have a beer. He had been talking about his girl-friend, Martie in Seattle since we arrived so what was up? There was no clear answer as Joe chimed in from the bathroom with some abusive comment. I quickly dressed and with Dugan ran to the chow hall. It was very cold! Temperature was in the teens, the sun was shining and despite the fur lined collar and my hat, my face felt like it was burning. The thought of my impending solo was the main reason I didn't feel much like eating, so grabbed some cereal and toast, orange juice and coffee. The class "group walk" to the "academics" buildings and the subsequent time in the classes was filled with thoughts of how to cope with various problems in the air. I was constantly reminded of the impending flying schedule as I glanced outside to a sunshine filled day and no apparent wind blowing in the trees. It was interesting that Roland and I were going to be the first to solo in the "Eagle" portion of 56-H. Dugan and Joe had indicated they were a flight away and others we talked to, said the same. Also, word was out that two of the aviation cadets had SIE'd yesterday afternoon. That cut down on two of the crowded five at different tables. Leaving class, we headed straight to the mess hall for a bite to eat, again I was not hungry so tried the tomato soup and grabbed some saltines and a glass of milk. I tried to make light of the impending solo, but Dugan kept telling me I would do well and it would be over soon.

When I got to our table in the afternoon, I echoed what Dugan had said in the morning. It was a great day to fly! The four of us waited for Pinky as he and Mr. Hubenthal were both out of the flight preparation briefing area. Finally, they arrived together and as Pinky sat down, he told Charlie to go to Mr. H's table as he would fly first period with him. One of the SIEs had been at one of the crowded tables, so you had to wonder if that student could have made it at a less crowded table!

The solo routine was explained to Roland and me. I would go first with Pinky and after some preliminary work we would full stop and he would exit. I would then take off and enter the traffic pattern to complete three landings. Each would be a full stop and taxi back until I completed the three landings successfully. Pinky would be in the mobile tower situated on the grass strip for the PA-18 to assess the approach and landings. He would give me a red light after the third landing if all were successful. I would then park the aircraft and he would repeat the procedure with Roland. After Roland he would fly a dual mission with Thurman, time permitting.

As we arrived at our assigned aircraft I felt a bit more confident and if Pinky detected any mental problem he would not let me go into the air solo. Everything was normal on the takeoff until Pinky pulled back the throttle and asked where I would put this aircraft down. I didn't hesitate to tell him "straight ahead". He quickly added power and muttered good choice to me. The rest of the short flight was a stall series and we entered the pattern for the landing. After stopping, I pulled off the runway. I taxied up to a point adjacent to the mobile control and Pinky got out of the now empty airplane except for me. He tidied up his side of the cockpit and fastened his seat belt and shoulder harness together, closed the door without a word and hustled into the broad windowed area to my left. I edged to the end of the runway, saw the green light and pulled into position. Power up, release brakes, bumping down the grass runway and all-of-a sudden, I was airborne. I was all alone, but I listening in my head to what Pinky always said, "Stay ahead of the aircraft". I leveled off, turned cross-wind on altitude, turned a good downwind on airspeed and watched carefully for the turn to base and started bleeding off airspeed and altitude to turn final. Right down the runway! Flaps down and all my check points for altitude were there. I touched down, exited the runway and pulled back to the end to get ready for the second of my patterns. As I passed Mobil control, I glanced over, but couldn't see into the raised area. Finally, I saw another green light and proceeded to go through the same drill. This time I was feeling confident. The climb to pattern altitude was interrupted by some prop wash from a T-6 that had strayed into the pattern. I bounced about for a couple of seconds and my grip on the trim wheel tightened. The turn to downwind was on altitude, but I was also a bit sloppy, not as intense on my turn to base, but as I rolled out on final, I was where I should be and nailed the landing. As I taxied back to the end of the runway I noticed another aircraft waiting for takeoff and saw Charlie in the seat. I hoped this was not a ride to assess whether he was on the brink of elimination and only hoped it was to expedite the flights for the rest of our table. Mr. H had his own two students that would fill slots at other instructor's tables very soon. At any rate I saw him takeoff and waited for the green light, which came as he lifted into the air. Once again, I came to a full stop in the middle of the runway, brought the power up and released brakes. I thought for a moment "this is fun", but quickly remembered to finish what I started. It was a good pattern, not as good as the initial one, but it was the first one where I remember looking around and I looked at the outside world. We had been cautioned about fixation on our flight instruments as you need to have your head on a swivel and make sure that the pattern does not contain other aircraft and even birds that can result in an accident. I was convinced I was the only aircraft in the pattern, but I did see the T-6 pattern was now occupied with two or three aircraft. I completed the pattern and landing, cleared the runway and looked to see a bright red light, so feeling I had just conquered the world "S"d my way to the parking slot. Roland stood by with the chocks as I cut the engine and opened the door. I jumped out, grabbed my parachute and saw Pinky strolling up with a nice grin on his face and stopped and shook my hand. Roland was busy loading his chute but gave me a "thumbs up" before he sat down. I stood fire guard and after they left I walked back to the student flight room. I felt nothing! It was over I kept telling myself. I walked into flight ops, which was almost empty. Thurman was at the table, looking into the air, saw me and asked how it went and I told him "great". He then went to talk to someone at another table, so I looked around, hoping to see Dugan or Joe, but both were gone. I just sat down, relieved and very happy that it was over.

The days of the PA-18 rolled on. We lost a few students, mostly through the SIE process, but a couple of student officers, one OCS student and three cadets were found not suitable for the program. Pinky said as the eliminations mounted, "We can teach anyone to fly, but we are limited by time and the lack of need in the Air Force pipeline". Charlie made it and his flight with Mr. H was not an assessment ride according to Charlie, it was merely an instructional one. He and Thurman both soloed after about their seventh or eighth ride. The tables were not vacant, but neither were they crowded. Mr. H had moved both of his students and there were no tables with more than four potential pilots. It was a lot easier to move around and not quite as crowded in the chow line. The empty desks in the class room were ominous and possibly foreboding to some, but I felt confident. Dugan had some moments due to his hard-nosed and loud instructor. (I'm not sure I would have made it with his instructor). Joe had no problem, or at least he never expressed a problem and he soloed the day after me, after his fifth ride. Dugan soloed the next day, so the week had been a success for our living quarters. Blondells would be in our sights for Friday night.

The program called for 18 hours in the PA-18, mostly dual, but everyone received a fair amount of solo time. I ended up with six hours solo and never extended my capability by doing restricted maneuvers as some boasted they were doing. I had a basic fear of extending my capability, not that I couldn't accomplish them, but why push the envelope? I worked to perfect my Chandelles and Lazy Eights. The last flight was a civilian check-ride. It was done by an instructor, not your own. Mine was with Mr. H. I had the distinct feeling that Pinky was intent on making sure I wouldn't experience one of the loud, intense instructors for that ride. He was a flying clone to Pinky. He was quiet, but firm and somewhat critical, but easy to fly with. We did the standard everyday flight items starting with the various checklist procedures for engine start. The takeoff was on the same grass runway, over the same terrain we had used for three and a half weeks. My log book showed I had made over 45 landings and almost 12 hours of dual time. This was a carbon copy of most of my flights with Pinky. Naturally he pulled the throttle back to indicate an Emergency and I instantly indicated the field straight ahead. Power came back indicating I could continue the climb. It was a cloudy day, but enough openings in a partial overcast to get above the low cirrus clouds that surrounded the field. There was no threatening weather in the forecast and finding an area to do the required stall series and limited acrobatic maneuvers (Lazy Eights and Chandelles) was not hard to do. Pinky's emphasis on these made it very easy to impress Mr. H with my ability to perform them. I only did one each and we retreated to the traffic pattern. There were so many check points for the grass field 45- degree entry that it was second nature to head directly to my entry point. As I set up a heading to the entry point Mr. H told me to use the paved runway. Some panic set in as I had only two landings on that runway. As I sighted the runway in my decent through a large opening in the clouds I had the sudden thought that I didn't know the direction of traffic. It had always been the same northerly active for the grass runway, but the paved runway ran mostly east and west. I looked to see if there was any traffic that I could follow. Finally, I did see a bright yellow aircraft going in an easterly direction at about pattern altitude. He must be on downwind I thought, so I set up a heading to be 45 degrees to the downwind leg. I had to be careful as my airspeed was almost fifty knots slower than the T-6. I forgot also that I had to make a radio call to enter the T-6 pattern. I spit out a request to enter the pattern, but was on interphone, not radio. Mr. H made the call for me! They cleared the pattern entry request and I leveled off at the proper altitude for a downwind leg. The tower called and told me to break out of the pattern as a T-6 had requested a straightin approach due to engine problems. I proceeded to do a 180 on my dog-leg, again requested, this time on the proper channel, entry. The T-6 landed safely and exited the runway. I rolled out on my entry heading, picked up a position which seemed appropriate for the downwind and turned. Mr. H pushed the stick further to the right and said, "your too far away from the runway". My wide downwind was problem, but otherwise everything looked good, so I adjusted my downwind and was careful to not turn too late for the base leg. The descending, right turn, only saw a momentary wings level as I had to keep the turn going to roll out on the final approach heading. The landing was made on the first 100 feet of the runway and I cleared the runway at the first turnoff as I was told by the tower to expedite leaving the active. I "S" turned all the way back to the PA-18 area and parked. Exiting the aircraft, I saw

Dugan about to enter the grass runway for his check ride with a tiny instructor known for his loud critiques, better him than me! Exiting the aircraft Mr. H was busily writing something on his kneepad, but he didn't express anything at the time. We walked wordlessly back to the flight center. The debriefing was short as he felt the ride went well and asked about my confusion entering the T-6 runway. He mentioned there were many ways to check direction of traffic including calling the tower. But he said I could have checked the wind sock as a last resort. He pointed out also that the pattern had to be more-narrow as the airspeed difference between the two aircraft is the factor to be considered as well as the short turn radius of the PA-18. You don't want or need an elongated base leg as you are possibly holding up other aircraft in the pattern. At any rate he was pleased, and I was happy to have made it through this first phase in my flying life. Looking at the grade sheet all scores were to the far right of the grading scale. I would be transitioning into a new aircraft.

THE TERRIBLE TANGO 6

With the completion of the check ride we moved to the T-6, the yellow Tango-six. When this class, 56-H arrived, we were told we would be the last class to fly the T-6. The following classes would fly the T-28. At the time it didn't mean much to any of us, however as time went on it was obvious we were very fortunate as the T-6 was an outstanding aircraft and especially as a training aircraft. Our class instructors knew the aircraft and had great faith in it. But there were other important facets about the T-6, as it was a most forgiving aircraft and we would discover that in the next five months. There was another change we experienced as we went into the T-6 as we gained some foreign students. It appears that most have flying experience but are expected to benefit from the Air Force program. Two of these new members to our class were from Italy and two more from Argentina and the final one was from Iran. They fit right in and all spoke English, although very rapidly especially when explaining what happened on a flight. An additional instructor was added to the Eagle flight to accommodate their addition. One Italian student established himself immediately when he inquired of us where to find the women. His name was Luciano

Bontalumi. He had dark, wavy hair and a perpetual smile and had everybody enamored with his fun look on life. They would be an interesting addition to our group, which now was diminishing by the day. At any rate the first few days in the T-6 were more of an orientation of the aircraft, studying the flight manual and getting accustomed to the fixed procedures simulator and the use of the checklist for every phase of flight, from walk around to engine shut down. The stationary "simulator" was a trainer type cockpit with instrumentation located exactly as that of the T-6 G. It was more to accustom oneself to the cockpit and the location of instruments. Over and over we went through a process to familiarize ourselves with the location of each of the items on the checklist. It was somewhat boring to go to the simulator building and either sit in the trainer or watch as someone else would go through each checklist calling out each item as they pointed to the spot where it was located. We finally graduated to going to a parked T-6 and repeating the process in an actual cockpit. Finally, what seemed like an inordinate long time, but it was less than a week doing this dry training that we were scheduled to "fly" the airplane. Pinky had spent time in those early days explaining how to get out of the aircraft if the situation called for it, but emphasized that an "emergency landings" in this area were a good choice. Within two days of this speech about staying with the aircraft in the event of a problem, one of the classes ahead of us had a student put one down in a nice plowed field, gear up. That's another thing that complicated our thought process, we now had a retractable gear to contend with. What's next? Also, instead of sitting beside the student, the instructor now sat behind us. Each position had a carbon copy instrument panel and similar capability to control the flaps and lower the gear. The canopy was a roll back type, independent for position at both front and back cockpit. It was funny, as leaving it open seemed more normal and there was nothing in the checklist that prohibited it, but the practice was to close it for flight. We were again dealing with a "tail dragger", so we must "S" turn during our taxi to and from anywhere. The lack of forward vision was more pronounced in the T-6 as you could not see anything forward through the engine cowling taxiing straight ahead. When the engine was started a plume of smoke would exit from the exhaust tube and would envelop the person standing fire guard. The aircraft excited me.

We had heard a little from Pinky about his exploits in WWII but we heard more through idle conversations with some of the other instructors, including Mr. H., that Pinky, a former Navy pilot during WWII, lost three Navy F-8 Corsairs and actually put one of them down on a beach on a Pacific Island, so he knows a thing or two about landing or leaving a sick bird. It also means that he had to make a decision at some point to leave two of those aircraft for one reason or another during flight. From that time on I would watch Pinky put on his chute. The leg straps could not be too-tight and he would walk with a necessary, slight bowed motion after arranging his leg straps, something I adopted. Pinky never seemed upset about anything and never uttered a swear word for any reason, even when it seemed nothing was going well. His patience was incredible; and it was obvious he took our training personally. He knew how to cajole and praise, talk when needed and remain silent when not. I would experience that on my first Tango six ride as he introduced the aircraft to me during the initial phase of indoctrination, talking checklist items, engine torque characteristics during takeoff and immediately after takeoff, talking in a calm voice, urging me to address the aircraft, become a part of it and don't let it take control. Assessing the need to plan ahead and in the event of a loss of power on takeoff you should be looking straight ahead for your place to land, play with whatever airspeed you have and don't trade altitude for airspeed as the instant you put the nose up you are going to stall and "splash" (his words). Flights up to this time had always been less than an hour. This first flight would extend that by at least another half hour. It was a revelation as we first learned how the use of flaps and the raising of the gear affected the trim. If there was pressure on the stick, trim it out. Learning to stall the T-6G, the approach, shaking characteristics were similar to that of the PA-18, but more severe. The process for the power on stall was merely to set the power, place the nose in an steep climb attitude and wait for the shudder. The recovery was simple, kick in rudder to keep the nose straight, push the nose down on the section line and add power. The power-off was similar, except you kept power-off as you pulled the nose above the horizon and as the airspeed diminished continue the nose high attitude until the stall occurred. The same recovery was used. Pinky emphasized the recovery involved, keeping the nose down until you see the fence lines clearly on the ground below. Everything was well defined as each acre of land was sectioned off in clear patterns. Keeping the nose straight would allow the pilot to recover using nose down and power up. After the initial demonstration and subsequent attempts on my part, Pinky blessed my work and said I was ready for the next demonstration. He put the nose up in a stall attitude and cut the power to enter a power-off stall, but as the aircraft started the familiar shuttering he held the nose up and suddenly it fell off to the right and we were in a spin. Pinky was calling off each turn as he passed the section line on the ground he started from. After the call of three, he jammed in left rudder and added power as he centered the stick and we were in a controlled dive. As the power built up he started pulling back on the stick and calmly leveled off. It was exhilarating, much like being in a roller coaster going down, but faster! The PA-18 spin was a "lark", compared to the T-6. He advised in the dive that you had to be careful in the recovery as the sudden use of the stick to pull out of the dive could result in a high-speed buffet. We climbed back to 6000ft and he proceeded to talk me through entering the spin. As the T-6 veered to the right and entered the spin my right leg was locked on the rudder pedal. I started to count the turns across the line below. After the third turn I released the pressure on the rudder pedal and applied pressure to the left pedal, added power and again I was in a straight down dive, gathering airspeed. I made my second mistake when I yanked back on the stick, trying to pull out too early, only to experience a high buffet that Pinky had warned me of. Pinky calmly pushed the stick forward from his back-seat position and told me "slowly", without raising his voice! After the level off my first mistake was explained to me, when seeing the third turn I should have abruptly applied opposite rudder. I had drifted 20-30 degrees off heading in the recovery. He was a perfectionist and he intended that I would perfect the most important phases of flight; stall and spin recovery were at the top of his in-flight items that I needed to master. He proceeded to show me another spin, where after inducing the spin he took his feet off the rudder pedals and the plane recovered itself. All he had to do was pull out of the dive. He said once again, "the aircraft was very forgiving". It was a confidence builder to be sure. As we flew back toward the field he was one not to waste airspace so proceeded to start demonstrating maneuvers I had seen before in the PA-18, the lazy eight and chandelle. It was great fun to establish airspeed and arc over the horizon doing those simple acrobatic moves. I love this airplane! We descended and as we entered the pattern Pinky called my attention to the "wind sock" that sat alongside the runway. It was fluttering a bit and was parallel to the runway. He said the sock was a "fifteen knot "one, in other words if it was extended straight out, the wind was at least 15 knots strong. Of course, it also gave a great indication of the direction relative to the runway. The sock became a check item as I entered the pattern on subsequent flights, more to detect a cross-wind than to check velocity. Once established on my first downwind I recalled my last flight experience with the PA-18. The altitude was the same, but that was all. The pattern was much wider due to the airspeed of the T-6. The first landing was made by Pinky from the backseat.

You could tell he was pleased to be out of the PA-18 as his Navy background in tail dragging aircraft really came into play. He touched down smoothly, tail first on the first hundred or so feet of the concrete then let the main gear touch. He explained that in "tricycle" gear aircraft that's how you should land. Navy pilots always landed tail first as they were always of the mind, they were catching the "hook" on carrier landings. That was explained to me by Pinky over-and-over again, until I'm not sure I could ever try to roll-on the runway using the main gear at touchdown. It was a good technique, but don't let the nose get too high. I shot three landings after that all were reasonable. I had to remember I was a bit higher in the air now in the T-6. My first round-out was low and I skipped the main gear but recovered after the bounce to put the tail down where it belonged. Comments from the back seat were close to "I told you so"! The following two were much better. After the full stop and getting back to the parking ramp I was covered in sweat, but it felt good. I opened the canopy, mainly to dry off, but the cool air was welcome. The flight time was at one hour and twenty minutes, the longest I had spent in the air. When I pulled my chute out of the aircraft, I was the first to admit I was more than tired, I was ready for a long nap. Too bad academics were still a needed exercise today. Crawling out of the aircraft I felt I had accomplished something significant.

As a senior in high school I worked part time for the father of a friend of mine who owned a rehab facility for aircraft. He would take old aircraft and make them like new, mostly bi-wing PT-19 and PT-17 type. Most of them were converted into farm dust-spraying aircraft. Some were sold to other countries as training aircraft. One day he had me go to the local airport in Hawthorne, California to meet him as he was going to San Diego to pick up an aircraft he had just bought and would fly it up to Hawthorne. It turned out to be a T-6 he had coveted for some time. It had belonged to a marine and it had been outfitted with current instruments and was in excellent condition. He let me sit in the front seat and look at the inside of the bird. I thought at the time it was beautiful, but never had any idea I would someday fly one just like it. Today I did!

Naturally the ground school now concentrated on this new aircraft and the engineering surrounding it. Also, the psychological training took on a new aspect of flight, but so did the intensity of such things as weather. It was getting warmer and spring was close by and so was the Mississippi River. We were told how thunder storms were spiked by the river and how they would grow into monsters to be avoided at all costs. The knowledge of the growth and identity of the hazards of these storms were implanted in our brains. The cumuliform cloud and its three phases would be something I would never forget. The weather at Malden had changed from snowy type weather to more of a cold rain. Day temperatures were now in the high fifties and even low sixties. I had hung up my fur collar blue flight jacket and now used a green thin flight jacket for flight, but mostly just wore flight suits as they were comfortable and easy to get into. I stuck the thermals in my drawer and switched to thinner socks. To make it even better we were now allowed to wear our flight suits to class. We were still losing students, not to the SIE route, but to flight problems. There were at least seven who had not survived the PA-18 and already we lost a student officer and a cadet in the T-6. We heard from others that the other half of our class at Laredo was also losing a like amount, of students. Every table was down now to around three students, with one exception, Pinky. All four of us were still doing well and surviving the new aircraft. Thurman had conquered his air-sickness and Charlie, though being flown with by Pinky more, which could be an indication he might be struggling, however he says he is having no problems. We all knew it would not be long before we would be farmed out to another instructor as that had long been the plan from the beginning. There was no doubt Pinky liked being an instructor and it showed after good flights as well as bad. A crooked smile would sneak out when we were being debriefed whether it was a good flight or a bad one. The difference was if he spent time on an area that he felt was sub-standard, then we would get a comment about working on that tomorrow. We knew Pinky would move us only when he was sure we would do well with some of the characters at other tables. There were a couple I absolutely didn't want to go to, one being Dugan's loud and sometimes abusive instructor. Dugan did OK though as he was like a rubber wall, everything bounced off. Charlie would never survive him.

Each day brought a new challenge. The second dual ride was an introduction to real acrobatics. Pinky would demonstrate the roll, the barrel roll, the half roll and reverse, the Immelmann, the loop and variations, such as the eight-point roll. He would then take them one at a time and I would work on them. The key to every maneuver was the entry as you would start on a very visible section line on the ground and work with it or around it. The roll was easy enough as it was fast enough that as you rolled through it your line on the ground was something you came out on, right roll was the easiest, but you also had to use rudder pedal to combat the torque of the propeller. Left roll required more rudder to control your heading! The barrel-roll started with a slight dive off heading and using the horizon as a reference for position above and below it you did a complete circle around the section line starting thirty degrees off heading and ending up back on the section line. The most difficult for me was the half-roll and reverse. When I was upside down I could not control the nose and when coming back up I was always off the section line heading. Pinky would demonstrate again and again, still I would not be on heading on the return. Every day he would say "We'll work on it". The loop and Immelmann were very easy. It was a matter of controlling airspeed throughout, with pressure on the stick. For an Immelmann you would merely have to roll out on the reciprocal of the heading you started on at the top of the loop. With the farm land below you started on a section line and on the dive of a loop you would pick it up as you were going "downhill". The Immelmann was named for a combat maneuver used by the Luffwaft during the first WW, I believe. Of course, every flight we would go through the stall series and spin until Pinky was assured, I could master them as we went forward. It was obvious that acrobatics were a secondary thought of his as on each dual ride we would always do the complete stall series and spins were always the first item we did after getting to altitude and it was only then that we would go to Acrobatics. When they were good, he would spend more time on acrobatics; if they were bad, then one or two barrel-rolls would be the extent of being on your back for that ride. Then it would be pattern and landing activity, an area in which he was intense in his evaluation of. I would know if he was pleased with a pattern and/or landing based on the clicking of his interphone, meaning he was about to add something to my actions. Silence meant the effort was noteworthy.

I don't ever remember a euphoric comment about any particular flight activity. His priorities were on those things that could kill you if you couldn't control them. On the third dual ride we were cruising to the designated acrobatic area which was well removed from the activity around the airdrome. We were level at about 6000 feet. There had been a pause in conversation, when suddenly the throttle came out of my hand and moved to the idle position. Silence! We had never talked about an engine out at altitude, it always been on takeoff and low pattern altitude. Suddenly I knew what Pinky wanted. Make-a-decision on what you intend to do. We were at a safe bailout altitude, but we were also at an altitude where our glide factor could play into a safe return to the field. I did an immediate 180 back toward the base and set up a clean glide speed, exchanging altitude for distance. I told Pinky of my intentions and then said the thing he wanted to hear. "I can make a better decision when I get to a lower altitude on suitable emergency landing spots or bailout." The power immediately came back up and he said, "OK, let's get to the acro area." It was times like that where the aircraft and you became a unit working together and you knew that you were in control. It made the flight a sound effort, demonstrating to Pinky I was staying ahead of this flying machine.

The following dual rides were much the same, more and more, demonstrating progress in all Pinky's necessary areas of competency and more. Landings and pattern work became more intense. Minor deviations from airspeed or altitude were met with a gentle hint or a bit of pressure on the throttle or stick. He was relentless on perfecting my work. I became a super critic of what I was doing. I wanted to please him and welcomed the many silent moments of flight as I knew I was doing well. We still worked on my acrobatics without too much negative comment, but when he would critique a maneuver it was more of "let's do that again" and then an "OK". If he talked about stalls or spins you knew you didn't do it to his satisfaction. It was satisfying to me that Pinky had little to say about my pattern work on the next two dual rides. Pinky was no longer giving group critiques. He would talk to you coming in from a flight, and if not finished, then join you in the Parachute storage area for a mention of things he saw while you both hung on your parachute rack. If he was in a hurry and left to fly another student, he would catch you when he was done with that student. If he wanted to talk further he would take you to a vacant table, but he did that with only Charlie and Thurman. Ford and I seemed at about the same point in our progress as our conversations with Pinky were usually over before the chutes were hung on their racks.

I also found I was a bit more energetic, participating in flag football games between the officers and av-cads. I was also more prone to go into town for dinner as Kelly, Dugan and I had become regulars at our little restaurant in town. People who frequented the place would smile and even say hello when we came in and the receptionist knew our names and seemed pleased at our arrival. On more than one occasion we also stopped at Blondell's for a beer and conversation with some of the regulars. Dugan spent most of his time talking to Blondell!

A T-6 SPECIAL EVENT—MY SOLO

As we completed just the stall and spin part of our dual ride during the fifth dual ride, Pinky said to fly to the Dexter grass field. The instructors used it as an auxiliary field on occasion to thin the traffic out at Malden. It was in-close-proximity to Malden and a mobile tower had been placed there some time ago. Spring was upon us and the weather had turned to that point where the severe winter weather was finally over, and the terrible spring weather had not begun. The runway was well defined despite the grass nature of it. The mobile tower there was manned by one of the instructors in the "Hawk" class of 56-H and although they did have ground to air communication capability, most of the flying was controlled by the Red-Green light method to not interfere with traffic communication at the Malden field. I had shot a couple of approaches there on a previous flight, with a touch and go, so knew checkpoints for the pattern. On final Pinky said: "make it a full stop". On the ground he instructed me to taxi adjacent to the mobile control and stop. I pulled to a stop, looking right into the massive window of this mini tower, which you could not see into and set the brake pedals. The wind sock was the first thing I noticed. It was limp, no wind. "I'm getting out here" Pinky said on interphone. "OK, I want you to shoot three full stop landings, after the third full stop pick me up right here". "Use the green light to take the active and after three landings you will get a red light, meaning you need to return here and pick me up." He grabbed his parachute, fastened the seat-belt and shoulder-harness together, crawled out on the wing and leapt off dragging his chute. Stunned to silence, I watched him walk to the mobile control, turn and wave and disappear through a door. He knew I had sweated the solo in the PA-18, so to preclude a sleepless night he came up with this solution. I was the first at the table to solo so it wouldn't work on any of the others, but it sure worked on me. I was momentarily paralyzed, but realized I had to move. Everything was perfect, there could be no excuses as there was nothing but blue sky and the wind sock couldn't utter a ripple. There was no traffic here yet as most of the period was in the initial morning time frame. Sobering to the circumstances, I released the brakes, added a bit of power and started to move to the takeoff position. Being alone I didn't know how to act, usually there was something to say or I was reading the checklist aloud. After I arrived at the pre-takeoff position 90 degrees to the grass strip I looked back to see a green light. I put my head into the cockpit, finished the checklist and peeked up to see the light and it was still green, so I relaxed my shaking knees, which were locked as I was holding the brakes to the floor and released the brakes. It was apparent this setup was pre-planned as there was not another aircraft in sight. I took the runway, applied power as I was heading in the right direction and rolled along to takeoff speed and was immediately airborne, by myself. I sucked up the gear, raised the flaps and climbed straight ahead to pattern altitude and turned cross-wind. I was nervous, but now I didn't know why. I had landed this aircraft at least fifteen to twenty times on previous flights in the T-6 and had 79 landings in my logbook in the PA-18. I entered downwind on some altitude, close to what I should be on, but thinking, I wonder if Pinky is watching from mobile? What do I have to do now? Gear! Oh yes, put the gear down. Two green lights, down and locked! I watched carefully the area below me and was certain that Pinky had a set of binoculars trained on my yellow bird. His intense, watchful eye would know if I was on altitude and heading and so I took a good look at my pattern location to make sure I was positioned on a proper downwind. After a slight pause I turned to my base leg, gear was down and locked, green gear light. OK I'm on base to final, losing altitude and airspeed, milk the flaps to 20 degrees, continue the turn, roll out at 800 feet and looking straight down the runway and drop the rest of the flaps and let airspeed stop at final approach speed. Everything is green, round out was made, but too late and a slight bounce, but the recovery was good. Pinky wouldn't like that! I rolled to a stop, cleared the runway and taxied past the mobile control to the end of the runway. Looking back, I got another green light and repeated the first process down the runway. I was thinking it was hot, so for some reason as I approached level-off I opened the canopy. The refreshing air was a sort of a wakeup to what I was doing. I was really soloing the T-6! Having the canopy open was a new experience, not that it was forbidden as it was not, as it was just a roll-back canopy and didn't affect airflow across the fuselage. It just seemed to free up any apprehension I may have had. On downwind I lowered the gear, started the flaps and closed the canopy before turning base for the second landing. I'm not sure Pinky would approve of the canopy being opened, but then again, I know he has opened his on occasion, probably to throw out his gum wrappers, as that was his only "vice", chewing gum. I set the power and dropped the rest of the flaps. It was a good final approach and I touched down tail first, a landing he would like and that I'm sure it pleased Pinky. I was feeling good and sort of waved to the mobile control as I passed by for my third and last attempt. Again, the green light greeted me, and I accelerated with a little more emphasis, rolling around to the takeoff heading, power almost already full forward and bounced, happily down the grass runway. On this takeoff I became aware of a pain in my right leg. Keeping the nose down the runway had caused me to sort of lock my leg on the pedal and it was the first time I had realized it. It was more of a cramp, so as I pulled up the gear and flaps I reached down and rubbed my calf, felt a knot and placed my foot flat down on the floor. It went away instantly! I opened the canopy again and found I had extended my takeoff heading a bit, so turned cross wind and picked up my check point for downwind and turned. As I got to the mid-point of the runway I again dropped the gear and set the flaps, fully prepared for landing. Everything was in the green for landing and as I turned final for what was to be my last approach I Thought I had done fine up to now, so don't screw it up. Looking down the runway I remembered my canopy, so reached with my left hand and closed it. It was another very good tail first landing. I was really, really, happy! I rolled back to mobile control, set the brakes and waited for Pinky to appear. After a couple minutes he exited the little control shack and waved for me to go on. I held up my gloved left hand with three fingers extended. He answered that with two fingers as he extended his arm in the air. Had he not seen three landings or did he not like the first one and want me to have three like the last two. I hesitated, but he was re-entering mobile control, so I didn't have much of a choice. I released the brakes, put the power forward and once again went to the end to receive a green light, but it was red. I looked up the approach end to see another training aircraft on final. After he touched down, the green light came on. The T-6 on the active was going around on a touch and go. I added power and aggressively trailed him into the air and for the first time experienced the turbulence caused by another aircraft. It was not severe, but it did surprise me as everything had been calm up to now. This situation had been mentioned in class many times as well by Pinky after previous flights. The PA-18 didn't present a problem due to its little prop and subsequent rotation, which doesn't trail the spinning air like the T-6 and much larger aircraft. The rotation of the prop creates vortices of air going back and they do dissipate with distance. We were told it is not severe in smaller aircraft, but it can cause accidents from larger ones. I would have to space myself if he was staying in the pattern. I sort of hoped he would leave, but he didn't, so I extended my takeoff heading to make sure I wasn't too close to him in the pattern. I turned finally and when I got to a position to get on downwind he was far ahead of me. I didn't open my canopy this time as I was too involved in watching the other aircraft. Can't do two things at once! I completed the pattern and approach. When lined up on final I had pegged my airspeed and as the ground rose up to meet me I gently raised the nose and made another very good tail dragger landing. I was getting very adept at the tail first process, with the main gear smoothly following. As I started down to mobile control I saw Pinky on the grass waiting. His chute was on and he had on his ear phones. I stopped and he crawled over the rear of the wing, opened his canopy, unfastened the seat belt and shoulder harness and crawled in. In seconds he was on interphone and said: "OK, let's go". I was about to tell him about the number of landings, but he was giving me directions to go back to Malden and land. He made no comment of anything on the short trip to the field so I would have to wait until we landed and to top it off I was tired, in fact exhausted! After landing we got out of the aircraft and he paused to take off his chute and place it back in the seat. After being refueled Pinky had a flight with Roland, so told me to wait at the table for when he returned. I did watch as he filled out the flight log, putting a one-hour-forty minute-flight down and six landings. He did see the first landing! He didn't like it I guess. He was a perfectionist, no doubt about it. That little bounce was too much for him and he knew I could do better. I decided I would not mention the four unless he brought it up. Critiques with Pinky were usually very short as he usually said what he had to say in the air. I've seen him privately talk to Charlie and Thurman, but he has never done that with me. I was very satisfied with myself as I wended my way back to flight ops. As I entered I saw Joe Kelly, with a big smile on his face and a cigarette in his hand (he was one of the very few who smoked, including the instructors) and he proceeded to tell me he had soloed. I gave it a minute and told him

I did too. We both laughed and I told him about the four landings. He said it only took him three and of course we could talk about that at Blondelles tonight. Dugan was nowhere to be seen, so we wondered if he was on a solo flight, but at any rate we would have a beer or two tonight. This had been a great day and I don't think I will be flying tomorrow, unless heaven forbid, Pinky says to go solo. Hopefully not!

The roommates took off for the town of Malden after academics were finished. A light rain had begun and there was indeed a need for a jacket. We piled into Dugan's Chevie for the ride into town. He was a bit miffed as he did not solo today and in fact was told his ride was below standard and would need an additional dual ride before soloing. We went to our restaurant on the corner and by now were well recognized to the point we were welcomed by name. Joe was a master of conversing with the locals and it had rubbed off on Dugan and me. After our meals we walked the short block to Blondelles. Dugan and the barmaid had become close and were more than mere acquaintances, which was obvious when she blew him a kiss from beyond the bar. Joe and I let out a whoop as Dugan went to the bar and received three cold beers, which he paid for as Blondell laughed at an embarrassed student pilot. It had not been a good day for him. This too shall pass!

The saga of Robert Donald Dugan and his solo was indeed a long-awaited affair as his Friday, hopefully last dual ride before solo, was on the same day as Thurman soloed and now Charlie was the only one left at our table to cross that barrier. I had shared my concerns about Charlie with Dugan and Joe, so to be among the last to solo was a mental barrier for Charlie as well as Dugan.

His big frame was suddenly very sullen, and we would have to bear with him for the weekend. Friday night at the local beer establishment could be something he needs. Monday is a long time off. Mr. Hennig was his instructor and he could be heard above the engines roar when delivering his critiques of what he termed a poor flight. Friday's dual ride was not met with that type of harangue, so we knew the solo was on tap. Dugan seemed OK with the weekend wait, but we will wait and see how that time goes. On a different note after his solo Thurman was notified by Pinky he would be going to another instructor's table, bringing our table down to three and leveling each of the nine instructor tables to that number. Twenty-seven student pilots. We started at 39. Roland and I both wondered why Thurman and not one of us, but we were pleased to stay, even though we knew it won't be long. I sort of thought Pinky wanted the two of us to stay as-long-as he could keep us, as he was a born instructor and loved doing his time in the air. There were still the four foreign students at their table. They wouldn't wash out, but they wouldn't be going to a basic base for further training. That was made clear to us when they arrived! Wash outs would eventually allow Mr. H to empty Pinky's group and we were apprehensive as to where we would end up. Meanwhile Dugan was verbally given the go ahead by Mister Hennig to go solo the next flying day, which confirmed our assumption of the quiet Mr. Hennig after Dugan's flight. That would occur on Monday. He would have the weekend to think about it. Pinky scheduled me for a dual ride and Charlie was to make his solo effort before my ride. Outwardly Dugan seemed very confident about his impending jump in class to the solo ranks, but Charlie was outwardly very nervous. Monday would be in the afternoon flight schedule so the two of them would have to wait through the weekend and a morning of classes to do their thing. Some can handle the anticipation better than others. I was glad I didn't know ahead of time that I would have my solo ride when I did. Even now I like my security blanket riding with me, even if he says so little, I don't even know he is there. I do feel I think like Pinky because he expects so much from us that you begin trying to anticipate his next move and sometimes do it without thinking or his nudge.

DUGAN'S BIG DAY

Monday began as a cloudy, misty day with visibility going to be fairly-limited, threatening a solo-fly day. There did not seem any likely hood that the morning "Hawk" flight would get any flying in. Dugan was vexed, but Charlie seemed pleased his day might not happen after all. In the weather class during our first session in the morning, the weather instructor said we were experiencing some spring type frontal passage and that it should be clear in the afternoon. You could see the knot in Charlie's face as he heard the news. Dugan smiled at me, but I knew he was also experiencing the feeling we all do before something significant happens to establish your status in a special category. Half way through the morning you could hear aircraft starting engines, so at least dual rides were taking place. As we wandered to lunch we didn't need to wonder about the solo flights as it was perfectly clear. The misty day had become an unrestricted flying day the green flag would be up. After lunch we marched to the flight shack and found the door closed. We always had to be cleared to enter by one of the instructors, but there was no one poking their head out telling us to enter. We waited at least ten minutes before a blue shirted instructor named Mr. Bostic opened the door and motioned us in. There was no indication for the delay to enter, but the group of instructors must have had something important to discuss. When they had that meeting it was usually to discuss students on the cusp of being eliminated.

As we got to our table Pinky told Charlie to get his chute and mentioned nothing about the delay. They were going to go fly dual and then go to Dexter for his solo landings. Charlie looked like someone being led to the gallows, his small, thin frame sinking under the weight of his parachute. I would meet Pinky for my dual ride upon their return, so at about an hour after their launch I should start out of the flight shack. As they left I saw Dugan still sitting at his table, waiting for his instructor to make a move. I watched as they talked and finally the instructor smiled and as much as if to say "are you ready" Dugan nodded, and they departed. Thurman was now at a table where all three students were aviation cadets and he was very engaged talking to two others who seemed much older than the rest of us, but I knew the upper limit for age entering pilot training was twenty-six so guessed their period as an enlisted man was a fairly long time. Being 21, most people seemed older than I was, however most of the student officers were my age, Kelly was a bit older, Dugan was three months older than me and I don't think Thurman was even close to twenty yet. Some of Thurman's cadet buddies looked his age, but most were older looking. Despite the age of the now up to this point successful pilot training group it was obvious that this was a much smaller group of pilot hopefuls. Those remaining in eagle flight were guys who at the beginning you could tell really wanted to fly and talked about it, not in a boastful way, but with a determined wishful tone. Their personalities were such that they stood out as they went about this risky business, happy to be here and focused on remaining. I knew most of the officers from pre-flight at Lackland AFB and at that time you could ascertain physically they had the attributes for managing this flight rigor process. One Don Duncan had convinced me to go to Malden. He was from Saint Louis and said it would be a good choice. He was sitting at his table waiting for his last dual ride. He was married to a woman who was a professional dancer. She was touring with a group and he was living in the barracks next to me and Dugan. After waiting inside for a reasonable period-of-time I got my chute and walked outside to sit in one of the benches adjacent to the parking area for the T-6. It was now a nice peaceful day with only the smell of AvGas interrupting the fragrant spring air. I wondered how Charlie and Dugan were doing, hoping all would go well, but knowing that if Charlie completed his ride successfully, I would be hearing about every little thing that happened to him during his three landings. Roland was very tolerant of his boasting, but I would sometimes just not listen. My roomie, Dugan, on the other hand, never complained or talked much about his flights and would merely acknowledge he managed to complete the process that we all had to do. I looked at my watch and saw the little hand at two and the big hand at twelve and walked toward where Charlie and Pinky would park. It wasn't far as the T-6 parking area was right in front of the two flight shacks. Roland had shown up and walked with me to greet the hopefully happy Charlie. We waited as two aircraft were taxiing in, sashaying right to left, one veered to the right down the ramp and the second Tango six continued toward us before turning into the parking slot that was where I was told to meet them. The engine shut down and the chocks were inserted by the crew chief and slowly the two pilots emerged from the cockpit. Pinky had that "always" look and a beaming Charlie stood on the wing grabbing his chute out of the front cockpit and then hurrying down to the ground. Pinky came down and said they would have to get a fuel truck before we flew our dual ride. I said OK and proceeded to go back to the bench I had left previously. Pinky told Charlie he would see him after our flight and we watched as Charlie, all gestures and mouth in constant motion, walking with Roland back to the flight shack. Pinky sat down and we both took in the fuel truck as it stopped adjacent to the wing of the silent T-6. The driver was pulling out the large and long refueling hose and proceeded to fill the wing tanks, first on the left wing and then pulling the hose under the aircraft, proceeded to work on the right wing. When finished he twirled the cap and placed it on the fuel cell. The cap had a flange on it to use for tightening it and when finished it locked into the cap to indicate it was locked. Pinky signed a sheet given to him be the line crew chief and motioned me to get to the aircraft. As I watched, Pinky gave a final check on the two caps to make sure they were cinched tight. While we sat there Dugan was passing on the other side of the parking line. I waved and gave him the question look, shrugging my shoulders and raising my palms and he responded with a thumbs-up gesture. I was very pleased for him. Other than being a WWII veteran and a Navy Pilot I didn't know much about Pinky and I didn't learn any more today as we talked about flying and things to remember and keep in mind while in the air. It was all-important to understand what can happen in an aircraft. It was not a car you can stop along the road if you have a problem. I was very fortunate to have him as an instructor. He was the consummate tutor, but also, he was a very private person to have around when trying to become what he is. A pilot!

The flight days were much the same, with some variances, but Pinky didn't change. On the dual days it was always the same. Takeoff was followed by a climb to altitude and initiating a perfect stall series. That is if you missed one you did another until it was perfect. This was followed with a spin on a section line—three turns, rolling out with a full recovery. If he didn't like it, you did it again. Time permitting you were able to practice your acrobatics, but it was always those you didn't do well before and after many futile attempts at the half roll and reverse he would indicate we'll start there tomorrow. Pinky, on one occasion told me to do a fourth turn in my spin. I wondered why until I entered the fourth turn and became aware as he told me to recognize how tight the turn had become as I fought to recover as it was completed. His purpose was to demonstrate how difficult the recovery could be if recovery was delayed. On the other hand, one day he had demonstrated how forgiving the T-6 could be by taking control of the aircraft, entering into a spin and when in the initial stages, one full turn, took his hand off the stick, the control column now oscillating from knee cap to knee-cap and the aircraft stopped itself as it ended in a steep dive toward the ground. Before too long dual days would become more dedicated to back seat instruments. Pinky had warned us of the impending change of flying venue.

Tomorrow would be a solo day. On solos I would practice what I liked. I would climb to a safe altitude and open the canopy. It was funny because I had the idea that the closer to the ground I was the safer it would be. Anyway, I would do lazy eights and Chandelles, rolling from one horizon to the other. I would do a loop and maybe an Immelmann, but very seldom would I practice any rolls. One solo day I was doing lazy eights at altitude with the canopy open. I must have gotten distracted, which is not a smart thing to do while flying as I had entered the first turn and climb to the left using the horizon when suddenly I was in an abrupt power on stall and seemingly about to go vertical to the ground. I jammed the stick forward as I fell off on a wing to initiate a recovery and evidently the abrupt nature of my attempt to rectify the odd position, I had allowed the aircraft to be in caused an interruption of fuel flow to the engine. It stopped! I mean dead stopped, like totally not running, the propeller was vertical in front of me and all I heard was the wind or more likely airflow of 160 plus knots, going across the fuselage and around my open canopy. It was eerie to say the least. Wings now level and the nose in a semi-glide toward the ground. I was overcome with the absence of the sound of an engine, however a serene feeling accompanied this silence. Thoughts ran through my mind. What would I tell Pinky or the accident board, or both? Better yet where would I land this frame? I began looking for fields I could use to put it on the ground. Would they wash me out? And then, with the nose down in a controlled shallow dive, the propeller started to turn, slowly and the engine sprung into life. A satisfying roar, like I never heard before. I was flying again!

What a feeling and yet on reflection the silence of the moment or was it more, as it certainly was not long, was an experience I will never forget. I was in another world for that time. I didn't panic, but I certainly was terrified for, at the instant I saw that inactive propeller, what should I do. Whether it was instinct, good luck or limited experience and good instruction that made me react the way I did, I didn't know or care, but it was obvious to me I did fine. I never got to the point of even thinking about leaving the aircraft. I was firmly in the seat and in control. I decided to stop my activity in the acrobatic area and spend the rest of the period shooting approaches and a final landing. I wondered about telling Pinky and decided not to. I handled it myself and it would be my secret, at least from him. When arriving back in the area I made a series of patterns and low approaches, before my final full stop. I felt good about myself and did think I would ask someone in the know, another instructor perhaps, about fuel cavitation. Not Pinky as he would know instantly I had experienced it on a solo ride! The civilian mechanic for the aircraft asked me if the aircraft was good for a turn around and I answered yes as I returned the after-flight report on the Dash-1 to him with one landing and an hour and thirty minutes of normal flight recorded.

I have begun to enjoy these solo flights, climbing to altitude, going to the acrobatic area, opening the canopy and feeling like I own the world. I have to admit, I'm a bit more careful than I have been as I stay ahead of the maneuver I want to do. I do not attempt those I dislike or should I say, can't do well, but simple rolls I have now found to be really fun, maybe even two or three in a row and when I end up off heading I just shrug my shoulders and say "I'll work on that". When you feel the aircraft yawing into the propeller you know you have lost the fence line. (Boy am I glad I didn't go to one of those bases where there are no definite property lines to follow). I do like to enter the pattern and fly approaches due to my misguided belief of thinking it is safer flying closer to the ground. On retrospect it stands to reason, the higher you are the more likely you are to arrive at a logical decision. My solo flights are fun, but not adventurous. While on those flights in the acro area I have watched other obvious solo flights attempting a maneuver that is restricted and falling into a recoverable condition, but think what happens if you can't recover? Bailout and elimination in that order.

CHECK RIDES

Everyone is to have check rides and the first one occurs at sixteen hours in the T-6. they are given by the flight commander, or his assistant. That meant we would share Pinky from day to day as Mr. H cannot possibly give everyone that check, so Pinky pawns us off to fly solo, or go with another instructor for a dual ride, something I haven't done to this point. From that point on the forty hour and final checks are administered by military check pilots. When the first check came due for our table, Pinky of course, assigned all his remaining three students to Mr. Hubenthal, his good friend. Of course, we go with this check pilot who is fully aware of our level of competence as the two leaders of eagle flight are seen talking together constantly. When I flew that ride I felt like no one was there as other than greeting me and giving me instructions on what to do and where to go it was like Pinky, very quiet, with perhaps a word or two directing the next item to check off as accomplished. The first deviation from normal flight was right after gear-up and I had turned away from the traffic pattern, Mr. H pulled back the throttle and told me to find an emergency landing spot. I quickly sounded the reaction items in the engine out, emergency landing checklist, leveled the wings and put the aircraft in a controlled glide at a proper airspeed and selected a fine plowed field directly ahead and revealed my intensions. He immediately put the power forward and directed me to the acrobatics practice area, where we followed the same routine I had been doing for almost a month with Pinky. He only asked me to do the barrel roll and a chandelle, nor was any mention of the difficult half roll and reverse made. I was instructed to do all the stall series and a three-turn spin. All would have made Pinky smile! We then returned to shoot a touch and go landing, followed by a full stop landing. Both patterns were flown pretty much on the money and the full stop was a picture-perfect tail dragger. Two landings and an even hour plus ten-minute flight and it's over! I am so used to longer flights now and it just seemed odd to be up for a mere hour and a few minutes flight, however I'm pleased it was over and Mr. H, like his assistant flight leader, had little to say other than I passed and he did say I did a fine three turn spin.

A few days after the sixteen-hour check and a series of solo rides Pinky decided to take me for a dual ride. It was a Friday afternoon and I was the first to go up. Roland was told yesterday he would be going to another table next week but didn't mention whose table. Charlie was going to get a dual ride after I was finished. I was thinking about a date I had with a girl who went to a "Teachers College" in Cape Girardeau. I had met her on a weekend that I drove there with Duncan. He knew the area and so we just were going to have lunch, walk around town and come back before dark. There was a friend of his wife that went to school there who was going to meet him, and she brought her roommate with her. The room-mate was a thin, cute brown hair, blue eye girl, twenty years old. We hit it off and I asked her for a date. She gave me her dormitory phone number, so I called the next week and set up a date for this Saturday. I wasn't too keen on coming back late at night on the southeast Missouri two lane, winding roads so we agreed to meet at the same place for lunch. It was on my mind, but it wasn't going to interfere with this ride. Pinky had said something about more acrobatics, meaning we were going to work on all the rolls especially the half roll and reverse. It was not long after taking off when we were cruising at about four thousand feet northeast of the field, when over the headset an abrupt sound emerged like a voice in distress. It was guttural and strained! Then there was a call from another voice saying something to the effect that there was an aircraft flying erratically, explaining that the aircraft was in climbs and dives, falling off in uncoordinated flight. The first voice repeated its guttural call, more like an indistinct uttered groan than a word. Another aircraft, an obvious instructor, gave his location, saying he had sighted an aircraft going into steep dives, followed by a recovery and momentary level-off, then climb, followed by another dive. We were fairly close to the location and Pinky said, "let's see if we can find them". I turned to head in their direction, all the time listening to the reports from a now observing instructor pilot whose voice was strained with apprehension about the fate of the aircraft he was watching. There was at least one call stating that the aircraft in question was going in and after a pause that had everybody, who was on the frequency, holding their collected breath, stating that he pulled out. More calls were made reporting the severity of a dive or call that he surely would not make it. Altitude, or lack of, seemed to be the greatest concern. The now close instructor aircraft started talking to the stricken aircraft, calling out the tail number and asking the pilot to respond. The tower was now responding with the identification of the pilot flying that aircraft. It was Lieutenant Dick Coyle, a student in 56-H. They began calling his name, crying out, Lieutenant Coyle and Dick, hoping for a response. The observing aircraft picked up the call and finally there was a somewhat readable answer that was more like a "wa" if that makes sence. It was accompanied by a reported rapid recovery from a steep dive. Pinky said, "there he is" in a significant raised voice and I could see the two aircraft, one well off to the side of another T-6, gyrating with small climbs and dives to a sort of level flight, like being on the final part of a rollercoaster ride. It was apparent that Coyle had passed out for some reason and was now coming to as his voice was more coherent and he was responding to the other aircraft trying to talk to him. They asked him if he understood a request to fly straight and level and he answered "roger", but he said he couldn't hold on to the stick as his hands would not open or close. Pinky was the first to say, "he has hyperventilated"! This was something we had learned a great deal about in our classes and the quick in and out of breathing could result in this condition, passing out and losing the use of your extremities. The tower called and said the flight surgeon was coming on the air to talk to him. The hours in the classroom talking about the physiological aspect of breathing too fast flooded my memory bank. Coyle must have panicked over an in-flight situation he more than likely put himself into and passed out. I remember the spin Pinky started and took his hands off the stick, with the aircraft recovering on its own. Could be that he did something similar to my loss of power, when my engine cavitated, due to a maneuver that got out of control. I briefly thought about my engine stopping and my reaction to it. He may have panicked and passed out, with the aircraft self-recovering, thus the climbs and dives with the throttle in a fixed position. Dick was now more responsive and had the aircraft in control, however he was flying away from the field. I knew Dick Coyle. We had both gone through pre-flight together, a really, nice guy. He was from Kentucky and was very athletic and a perfect candidate for flight training. He always professed a great desire to be a pilot. I was watching and listening and hoping something could be done to get him safely on the ground. The discussion was becoming clearer as it was obvious he comprehended directions now from both the tower and the close accompanying aircraft. The flight surgeon had him pull out a "Barf bag" which was in a pocket in the left side of the cockpit and breathe into it, holding it to his face. After a few minutes of that he was having him breathe at a regular rate, sometimes holding his breath for a few seconds. Coyle was asked if he could turn the aircraft back to the field. He responded that he could still not use his hands to grasp the stick but would lock his wrist on the stick and try. The chase bird was telling him to add power as he was getting low on airspeed and was pleased when there was a positive response. Coyle started a shallow turn and immediately was losing altitude. We were at fifteen hundred feet and the chase aircraft had said they were at twelve-hundred. He had Coyle level off and add more power. Once stabilized Coyle was asked to once again to start a turn to the right. The tower was now calling for all student solos to return to the field and land immediately. The flight surgeon was very calmly asking the condition of Coyle's hands and the response was he could not open them. As the turn continued a decision was made to try to land him on the grass field instead of the main runway. Coyle completed his turn and was now heading in the right direction. Pinky and I stayed a safe distance above and to his right side. There were a series of hurdles to overcome, but at least Coyle understood directions and was maintaining a semblance of controlled flight. It was obvious that discussions were going on about landing gear up, but that was not going to happen. The gear would be down for landing. They had also decided to milk the flaps down incrementally to keep his nose from rising too rapidly. He acknowledged the need for nose down trim and said he could manipulate the trim wheel. Pinky suddenly said we should land so I headed to enter the pattern for a full stop all the time listening to the conversation with Coyle and his now joined wing man. As I pulled off the runway we stopped to hear Coyle being told to drop the gear. I was wondering if he could, as you had to forcefully pull the gear handle down. He apparently did what he was asked and responded the gear was down and it was verified by his accompanying aircraft. Now flaps. It was remarkable that he was able to accomplish these procedural items, maintain control and fly the airplane, using only his wrists. We parked and watched as Coyle planked his T-6 on the grass runway and rolled to a stop after a turn to the left toward a fenced off area, but short of it. He had been told to shut down the engine immediately after landing. Fire trucks surrounded the location and an ambulance door opened as individuals jumped out and crawled on the wing to retrieve Dick from the cockpit. It would be his last solo and his last Air Force training ride.

It was determined that Lieutenant Coyle had indeed suffered from hyperventilation, panting like a dog, thus cutting off circulation to his extremities. After a very short stay in the base dispensary he was back to normal. He would stay overnight. The following Monday Dick met a Flight Evaluation Board (FEB) and was eliminated from the program. Some small satisfaction should come from the fact was there was no damage to his aircraft. It was normal flying the next week, but with a new awareness of our own personal vulnerability! Both the flight line instructors and the class room teachers spent a lot of time retraining us on how to prevent or stop hyperventilating. It was something we all were made aware of and the compensation needed to prevent it. Who knows maybe Dick was the reason for many of us making it through the training? Pinky even brought in a barf bag to demonstrate how to use one in the event we felt stress in the cockpit and started to have any symptoms of the problem. I still had not mentioned to him about my loss of power and my reaction to it.

I ventured along the two lane highway through "the boot", as it was called, of Missouri on Saturday morning. It was a great day and I was happy to be getting away from the base and the recent memory. It was hard to shake the sound of Coyle's groans and I knew I would have to forget the incident somehow. The freshness of the day was a good start. The date was for a late lunch along the Mississippi River at a small restaurant that I was introduced to a couple of weeks ago by Dave Duncan's friend. I would pick up Cathy at the dorm where she lived. She was a junior at the Teacher's college, very bright I think and fun to talk to. She was a bit frail looking, but talked of running as a hobby, so maybe it was too many miles. At any rate I was looking forward to the date. You could smell spring in the air and the trees were getting green, so time was passing, and the memory of cold, icy, sometimes snowy mornings was a distant memory. There was one other thing and that was the "Spring Thaw". The river would be very high and hopefully not a problem as the café was right on the river. I arrived at the dorm to find Cathy waiting outside. She said it was too nice of a day to hang out at some window waiting for me. She had a lot of faith as it was a good hour's drive from Malden. We drove to the river to find the little restaurant high and dry. She laughed when I told her I was worried about the spring thaw and she said the river never got near the restaurant in the three years she had been here. Cape Girardeau was a very nice town, quaint maybe, but definitely-not a big city and most definitely laid back, in time. It was a good relaxing time and she seemed to enjoy my stories. We walked along the river on a manmade trail, white fleecy clouds interrupting the sun for quick moments and the slight breeze which had a freshness about it, but it didn't dull the pleasant retreat from the apprehension of the next flight. She told me her father was a mailman in a suburb of Saint Louis, her mother a housewife and she was an only child. She also disclosed that she always had a summer job in a shop close by to her home and going to school was her first time away from her family. I enjoyed her company and we agreed to do it again soon. I left as it was getting dark and found my way back through the back roads to Malden and found the dual room abode totally empty. No Dugan or Kelly to share my day with. Oh well I had a good book to read.

Pinky walked in one afternoon and said he and I would go cross country on a navigation flight, so he pulled out a very used map that he had used for many previous flights. He spread it on the table and pointed out a triangular path from Malden to Cape Girardeau to Fayetteville Arkansas and return. I was to prepare a similar map for the flight tomorrow. Our navigation classes had gone through map preparation and how to identify objects from the air using "dead reckoning" procedures to fly the proper path to a destination. All students had to do one dual navigation flight prior to the forty-hour check, then sometime before finishing our hundred and twenty hours at Malden there would be two more Navigation legs, both solo. I stopped by the flight planning center by the small tower and picked up the right map and spent that evening drawing lines from Malden to each check point, putting the heading on each leg and annotating features to use on each leg, such as towers, roads, rivers and other predominate items to identify the route and make sure I was on course. I put down radio frequencies to report to various Aviation control areas as we hit each check point. Each leg also had the time and distance from point to point which I could refine when given the winds aloft, prior to the flight. I was pleased with my map as I showed it to Pinky the next day. He examined it intently and showed me how to best fold it to put on my flight board, which fastened to my left leg.

I knew Pinky would expect me to do all the navigation and

he would be along for the ride. What seemed like a big feat when thinking of it was a lark as taking off and leaving the flight area for Malden aircraft was like leaving the roost for a free, non-involved ride. No acro, no spins, no stalls, just staring and looking for items I had marked on my map. It was a different type of ride as we left familiar landmarks, picking up my outbound heading and headed somewhat southeasterly to our first turn point. There were a few clouds in the sky, but nothing seemed to be building and as we approached the river there was a bit of turbulence. I looked for the Teacher's college campus and saw it as we started a turn south to Fayetteville. My estimated time enroute was off by a couple of minutes. Cape Girardeau looked even smaller than I thought it was as I drove through on my trips there. This was a twenty-four-minute leg, going to Fayetteville, so I picked up the outbound heading, somewhat paralleling the river. I was mesmerized by the size and especially the width of the river. There were many islands, maybe more like sandbars in the middle and large ore carrying boats going south. It was muddy and you could see the current was fast from the air. Maybe the spring melt was an effect? I would rather be flying. I had the canopy open and the smell was of fresh blossoms, even at 2500 feet. Pinky said the spring brings thunder storms that form on the river and then move west and south and the weather forecast that was given to us before takeoff is very important. Severe weather is common in this time of year, causing many times the solo navigation flights having to be cancelled and flown another day or picking more westerly navigation points to follow. Today, however was a very good day. Visibility was forever and ground check points were easy to find.

The features around Fayetteville were easy to spot and passing the VHF station and watching the needle start to rotate signaled the turn back to Malden. We climbed to 4000 feet into a bit more turbulence and tiny puffs of clouds. Pinky said he had the aircraft and turned to fly over the top of a thin layer of clouds. He touched the top and we were in a washer board environment bouncing up and down in a gentle fashion. It was fun and Pinky was having a ball! He said that was one of the many fun things about flying, topping this thin cirrus layer and watching the puffs wash over the wings. Suddenly we were in the clear again and he gave the aircraft back to me. Where were we? I glanced furtively right and left, looking for some ground reference point. We had been off heading for only a few moments, but it was long enough to take away the reference points on my map. I was on the proper heading to Malden and I still had time to go on this leg. I didn't say anything and neither did Pinky till finally he asked. Which way did I take you off course? I responded to the right! And he said, if you went to the right then you must correct back to get on course. To hold the destination heading from right of course will take you past your destination to the right. So, it wasn't all play after all. It was another "Pinky Lesson"! I turned ten degrees to the left, now looking only left to find a reference point. Pinky said nothing. After about five minutes I spotted one of the items clearly marked on my map, a tower of significant height to stand out from the wooded world below. I turned back to the heading to Malden. As I hit my time en-route figure, the field appeared directly in front of me. I would be a couple of minutes late, but no problem. I asked Pinky if we could ask for a straight in approach as we were on a heading close to final approach and he said that was a good idea. Seeing no traffic to hinder us, I made the call, requesting straight-in and was cleared. I started a descent and leveled off at 1200 feet, took the power back, lowered the gear and then flaps and landed. I was enjoying my flights now, but I always had a sense of fear when scheduled to fly solo. Instruction was meant to present you with situations and train you to react positively to them. Two lessons I learned today, I hope I don't forget either!

The flight room was now down to twenty-two students. Pinky said Charlie and I would go to another instructor after our forty-hour military check ride and Clyde M. Pinkerton would then be able to be of more assistance to Mr. Hubenthal. It was apparent that Pinky loved instructing. He was very much at home in the air and the fact that he was able to get all four of the students assigned to him to the forty-hour mark was something no one else had been able to do. His patience with Thurman, who did leave early, and Charlie was the only reason they made it. Roland and I never had a make-up for any maneuver and we both soloed at the minimum time so we probably would have made it even with some of the recognizable hard-nosed instructors in the Eagle flight. There were a couple of washouts I think would still be here if they had had Pinky, but that's speculation. His attention to detail on the critical elements of flying was where he stood out and excelled. It would be tough to leave him, but it was inevitable, and I knew it.

The reputation of each of the military check pilots was well known and of course your thoughts about that ride were such that you were hopeful to get one of those considered to be easy and friendly. They were the ones who had remembered going through this phase of training and would overlook some slight deviations in the check-ride. Word had filtered down on the traits of those and how to react to their routines. Then there was the one who stood out as someone looking for a problem and was over-critical of the flight effort of the student. The Captain who was the commander of the small (six pilots) group was considered a "Santa Claus" and everyone was hoping to get him. The other five ranged from being "good" to a first lieutenant, named Van derSluis. He was the one everyone wanted to avoid. The civilian instructors were even critical of his record for failures of students on the forty-hour check. As I got close to my time in the T-6 for the check, Pinky would fly each dual ride as if it were a check ride with Lieutenant Van derSluis. He knew the routine that this difficult lieutenant usually took, and he would try to emphasize each portion of the check as if it was the one facet of the ride you had to do well. The takeoff, the climb to altitude on airspeed, the stall series followed by a precise three turn spin and recovery were all critical. He would go from one to another with no real pause between those flight maneuvers. In the acrobatics portion he thought VanderSluis would only do a single loop and a barrel-roll to complete that part of the check but said, he might do a chandelle instead of the loop, but always the barrel-roll. I was only hopeful that any check pilot wouldn't ask for a half-roll and reverse, especially him! In the traffic pattern altitude and airspeed were of course important, but most of all don't over-control the aircraft on final. It seems Lieutenant VanderSluis was giving a ride to another student two classes ago when on the landing, the student over-controlled a minor bounce that resulted in a ground-loop that sheared the gear and caused severe damage to the aircraft. Needless to say, VanderSluis is very sensitive to this phase of the check. I had never had any problem with landings, but Pinky explained the ground loop was actually a common problem with the T-6 and almost all bicycle gear aircraft. There was no way to demonstrate this problem and now that I'm aware of it I resolved that because I have never ground-looped the T-6, I shouldn't worry about doing so.

I reached the forty hours and knew I would be scheduled for that must-pass flight soon, so it was no surprise that on nice sunny Thursday morning as I sat at the table with Charlie, Pinky came out and gave me my check-ride slip. The slip was the passport to the military flight check section where I was to give it to the clerk and wait for a pilot to select my name and run me through the first in a series of challenges I would have to face in this selective process to become a pilot. Before I left Pinky said that if I got Lt. Van derSluis to remember that he would more than likely give me the emergency landing right after takeoff so make sure I announce to land straight ahead. I grabbed my chute off the rack and I walked briskly to the outer door of the military flight check building. It was a great day for flying, however my heart rate couldn't care less, my palms already sweaty. Dropping off my chute on the convenient rack outside I went through the door and into the outer room of the military check area to find another four students waiting, all looking like I felt. The clerk took my slip and placed it in a pile in a tray near the door. I joined the others and sat down, and the conversation was more of adjusting to where we were than about our upcoming check. The others were all in the graduating class and were getting their final checks; I was the only forty-hour check ride student. There was no discussion on who might be your check-pilot. My thought was that someone had already been assigned to give us our check. The first military pilot to come into the area was the Captain and he immediately changed that thought. He smiled as he reached into the tray and extracted a slip, looking at it, he called out a name. The selected student who was called, smiled, got up and walked out the door with him. This was a random thing and the Santa Claus had already left. A silver-bar lieutenant entered and did the same thing, grabbing a slip and calling out a name. There were three of us left and Vander Sluis had not appeared. Maybe he wasn't flying today! They all didn't fly every day, did they? There were only five of us and there are six instructor check pilots. Again, a lieutenant stepped into the room, picked a slip and was joined by another waiting student. Almost instantly Lieutenant VanderSluis, who I had never seen before, but his name rag was obvious due to its length, stepped into the room, grabbed a slip and called out "Dugard" as he opened the door to the outside. I couldn't believe it! Why me? I stood up and he motioned me to follow him. I grabbed my chute from the stand outside and got in lockstep with my forty-hour check pilot. He muttered where our plane was parked and looking at the slip he picked up, said "Forty-hour Check"? I nodded yes as we walked without another word to a T-6 parked on the outside of the row of planes about fifty yards away. Reaching the aircraft, he grabbed the maintenance records and shared the information with me, while asking leading questions on the meaning of the various marks, such as "red-cross, red-slash and red-dash". I answered to his satisfaction and he told me to do my walk-around and he would follow. It was a rudimentary process, making sure all areas were in pre-flight condition. No oil leaks from the engine, tires and struts free from impediments and the wheel-well clean and unencumbered. Finishing, I grabbed my chute as VanderSluis crawled into the rear cockpit. I followed and placed my chute in the seat, sat down and fastened my seat belt and shoulder-harness, put on my headset over my Eagle hat to find him already talking. I got the last part of the message and it was to start the engine. I checked with the mechanic, now fire guard and he indicated it was clear. After starting the engine and going through the pre-taxi checklist I looked to find the crew-chief had already moved forward to the left side of the aircraft and was pointing to the chalks at his feet and clearing me for the turn out to the taxiway, motioning with his arms over his head to come forward and then dropping his left arm down to signal a turn to access the taxiway immediately adjacent to our position. As I applied power I was careful to go straight out to insure the tail wheel did not get cocked, which could happen if you turned too abruptly. Once on the taxiway, I carefully "S" turned to the takeoff end of the runway. The lieutenant had not said anything since I started the engine. I called tower and requested permission to take the active. I was feeling OK but tried to remember all of the instructions about being ahead of the aircraft. Go through the pre-takeoff checklist and saying it loud and clear so he is sure to hear me. Call for clearance to take the active runway. What had Pinky said about takeoff? Don't be in a hurry. Having been cleared I got into position, and instantly cleared for takeoff. I pushed the brakes to the floor, held them, advanced the power, stiff legged the right rudder pedal and brought up full power. I released the brakes and start down the runway, slowly the tail began to rise to the level wings position. I was on the center-line of the runway, got to takeoff speed and gently raised the nose. I announced the first item of the after-takeoff checklist "gear-up" as I felt the gear locking into position and green lights coming on, the end of the runway passed below me and I started the flaps. I had a clean airplane and suddenly the power was yanked back, "Emergency landing" I heard. That's it, waking to the command, I said to myself "right on schedule". I started calling out the reaction checklist and looked out and picked out a field about a hundred yards away and said, "plowed field, straight ahead". The power came forward from the back seat and I thought I heard an utterance of praise. It was definitely a confidence builder for what was to come. That was over and I continued my climb as he called out a familiar heading to the acrobatic area. I was calling out and clearing myself like crazy, to make sure he knew I was looking before turning. On my sixteen-hour check ride with Mr. H he said I should let him know when I cleared turns in any direction, and I remembered his words. When we got to a safe altitude for stalls and spins he had me go through the power-off stall first and it was perfect. I started on and ended up on the section line I selected below. We climbed about two thousand feet and turned away from the field. After leveling off at six thousand he wanted the power-on stall. I was adjacent to a good section line and picked a spot on the horizon to fly to. After the stall to the right, he wanted one to the left. It was more difficult to the left as the engine torque worked to keep the nose to the right. Pinky had worked that for me so many times that I sensed I must be doing well as most do not do both or ask for power off to the left, as it seldom happens in a prop aircraft. After "ace-ing" it, I was instructed to do a three-turn spin. As always, a section line appeared ahead of the aircraft that I would use to line up on and use for reference. I rode to line up on that section line with a slight turn to the right, pulled off the power trimmed to achieve a power-off attitude, felt the shudder as the stall approached and kicked it into a spin to the right. It was flat to begin with, but slowly steepened through the second turn and then in an almost seventy percent nose down, I hit the section line for the third time, jammed in left rudder, totally arrested the spin, and slowly completed the recovery straight ahead. As I leveled off I added power. Again, I knew I heard some guttural sound like "good" but couldn't be absolutely sure. We climbed back to altitude and he told me to do a simple loop. I cleared the area, started a dive straight ahead and hit the loop airspeed. Power was set and I had to maintain that airspeed while watching the horizon and as I approached vertical, glanced at my magnetic compass to find the heading I was on and maintain it until I could pick up the opposite horizon on the downside. At the top of the loop I saw my airspeed was a trace low, so pushed the nose down a bit. You must remember that when you are upside down the horizontal stabilizer works opposite to when you are level. The airspeed came back to where it should be at 240 knots and stayed very close through the bottom of the loop. I was a small degree off heading when back straight and level, but it was as good as I could do. When stabilized and after a short pause I knew he was writing down information on his knee pad, so I kept the heading I was on. It had been maybe two minutes, but it gave me time to assess where I was at. He had not asked me to redo any maneuver, so they were either good or not. I was pleased with everything I had done so far and so would Pinky be. The sound of the lieutenant's voice snapped me out of my thoughts and now while just tooling along he asked me to do a barrel-roll. I was not surprised but realized this could be the start of all the various rolls. I liked barrel-rolls and usually did them very well but knew merely minor errors will kill a good roll. The roll had to complete a circle of sorts on the horizon, so entry and final wings level can't be the beginning or end to a flat roll. I announced I was clearing for the roll to the right and turned to enter with the dive to the left, set my airspeed and smoothly lifted it to the inverted state, nose up while pushing down on the stick and completing the roll as I dished out slightly at the end. There is a constant cross-check on the roll, outside watching the horizon and back into the cockpit to manage airspeed. Again, I waited as he was not talking. I was hopeful he would not ask me to do the dreaded half-roll and reverse. Finally he said "OK, let's return to the field, enter a normal traffic pattern for a full stop landing". Relieved, I rolled back toward the field and started a descent to establish my forty-five- degree entry to the downwind leg. It would be the traffic pattern and the landing now and I would be finished. By now in the time I had been flying approaches to the runway at the field I knew every check point student's would use to insure they are properly set in the traffic pattern. It was a bit early for pattern work for most as we would enter a little less than an hour on the first flights of the morning. To my surprise the pattern was fairly, crowded, and I then remembered there were other flight checks going on so made sure my separation from other aircraft was substantial. I notified tower of my intentions and was cleared for entry and an approach and a full stop landing to the main runway. There was a T-6 about to turn base, so my separation as I entered the downwind was good. I made sure I was announcing the clearance from other aircraft as I turned. Adjusting my airspeed for the pattern I was caught up with the quiet that surrounded me. There was seemingly no engine noise and a total lack of instruction or conversation from the back seat as well as direction from the tower. I was in a world of my own! As I got adjacent to the end of the runway I dropped the gear. "Down and locked", I announced! I started the turn, dropping flaps, continued through base leg and rolled out on final, right down the centerline. I was feeling some pressure on the stick and realized Vandersluis was applying it. The closer I got to round-out, the more pressure I felt, now the rudder pedals were stiff from another source. He was bringing the nose up. I continued to positively hold on to the stick and I was also firmly planted on the pedals. The touchdown was a "squeaker", a perfect landing and roll-out. He actually paid me a complement, saying, "good landing", but I knew he made it! His bad experience with a ground loop had psyched him out. As the tail wheel touched the surface and we slowed down, all the pressure left the stick and the rudder pedals. I turned off the runway, stopped to finish the after-landing checklist and "S" ed my way back to the parking slot. After leaving the aircraft and walking back to the military ops center he turned and said, "Nice ride, you passed, I'll finish the paper work and send it to your instructor. I wondered to myself, no critique? I said thanks, turned and started back to the flight shack. I was on cloud nine as I walked the block, I was actually looking for someone to tell about the check. This is a big moment, I've passed the first serious step to getting my wings, even though it's during this primary phase it's a military check! It's a point where many don't make it. I knew as I entered the almost empty room that Pinky and Charlie were obviously out on a dual ride. Thurman was sitting at his table with a rugged looking cadet named Hill. He glanced up, but turned away before I could tell him, so I put my chute on the rack in the next room and sat down. I knew Kelly was on a solo ride today and I forget what Dugan said he and his instructor were going to do, but I'm sure it was a dual ride. Because the ride with Van dersluis was fairly short, actually right at an hour and ten minutes, I wouldn't have to wait too long for others to come back from their flights. I suddenly realized that tomorrow Pinky would more than likely send me to another table. The thought burned at me as I knew all that I did on the check ride was due to the preparation that Pinky had provided me with. His emphasis on stay ahead of the aircraft was something I did during my check. There was never a time I wasn't prepared to do the next item that Vandersluis told me to do. I was totally prepared for that ride and it was with the toughest of the check pilots. I did have to reflect on the landing. I'm sure it would have been just as good without his help. Anyway, I'm happy. I wanted to tell someone about my ride, however the few people there were not in my circle of friends. It was a bit frustrating! After a short period of time the room began to fill with other of today's first period flyers, but no Pinky and Charlie. I knew that one or two others had completed the forty-hour check, but neither Roland nor Thurman had, and Kelly had told me he would get his, the next week. Dugan hadn't been told yet, but it was close as our flying time was about the same. One of the hot-shot aviation cadets was supposed to get his ride today, but he hadn't come back into the ready center. Roland finally came in from his solo flight and walked through the room as I was toying with one of my flight manuals. He still had his chute on his shoulders and proceeded directly to put it away. Pinky and Charlie finally entered and as they saw me Pinky, in his usual nonchalant way, asked how it went and I responded with a smile and said it went great. "He said, I passed!" Pinky asked who the check-pilot was and I said, Vandersluis, and he smiled. I proceed to tell him about the flight, from the emergency after takeoff to the final landing and the fact that Vandersluis made the landing. He laughed and shook his head back and forth. He was very pleased, and I was happy. Roland appeared and heard the last part of the conversation and reached over to shake my hand. I walked outside as Pinky began to talk to Charlie about their ride. I didn't want to get too excited as there were about eighty hours left in the primary program and a great deal yet to learn.

I had seen Dick Coyle before he cleared the base. He was very subdued but was pleased to be going to "Navigator" school. He would be tested again for any problems, but they determined as I surmised, he had gotten into a serious flight situation and panicked during the recovery. Again, my stationary, vertical prop came to my mind. I will admit to having a sense of fear and anticipation every time I go solo but know I have overcome something significant as I reacted to a situation in a measured fashion and feel I will act appropriately again if I have to as my confidence is rising. Pinky lost three aircraft and survived, one he put on a beach (Talk about an emergency landing). He had to punch out of the other two. I want to keep everything I fly in the air!

Friday passed without any changes and it was not until the following Monday that Pinky caught me as I entered the flight room and told me I was leaving his care. He walked me over to and introduced me to my new flight instructor. He was a diminutive individual, known for his loud voice and hurry-up character. He had two students left, both of which I didn't know too well but heard from others they were good students. Of course, this meant that my new instructor had washed out two additional individuals, neither of which I had an occasion to have a relationship with. His name was Mr. Maxon, he was about 5'2, had a small round face, wore a hat over a bald head and didn't seem to have the capacity to smile. Pinky had told me Maxton too had been a Navy pilot, more than likely a by- the-book instructor, so something about him would at least be similar. I didn't know if the choice of a new instructor was up to Pinky or if it was just a matter of attrition at the table. At any rate there would be an adjustment on my part. I had the feeling though that he liked Mr. Maxon and made the choice.

Mr. Maxon didn't say much to me the first day at the table as he flew a dual ride with one of his surviving students, a lieutenant named Dick Butterer, a nice guy from Pennsylvania, tall with red hair and freckles. He lived off base as he was married, so I didn't know him too well, but he was easy to get to know. I was alone at the table as the other student went on a solo ride but found Dugan at his student table and we shared what little we knew about my new instructor. Bob said he heard that although somewhat loud, he was liked by his two students that were left. Dugan's table was right next to Maxon's table so spent time talking with the residents at Maxon's table. Maybe he was trying to make me feel good, but I would go with that. Bob was told he was to solo the next period, so I left him with his thoughts. I knew that I would find out more about Mr. Maxon tomorrow as he indicated he wanted to ride with me before I had a solo ride. I carried the thought through the rest of the day that I would have to make a good impression with my new instructor on that ride tomorrow, otherwise it could be a tough haul through the last months of primary. It was the old saying "first impressions are lasting".

The next day started with a bang the night before! Dugan and I celebrated his solo yesterday with a beer at Blondelles. We had taken two cars as Bob was going to stay awhile and I wanted to get back as we were in the morning flight schedule. I don't know when Dugan came in as I didn't hear him and when I tried to wake him up it was like raising a walrus from the dead. We finally got into our now very diminished flight group after breakfast and prepared to march "route-step" to the flight line. Joe called roll and there was one missing. It was our Italian exchange pilot, Luciano. As we started to leave we could hear his voice calling for us to wait. A car had pulled in by the barracks area and Luciano was jumping out, flight suit in hand, scarf around his neck, boots in hand and now running to catch us. He fell in at the rear, smiling and gesturing with arms flying in all directions and stopping periodically to try with little success to get his flight suit on over his trousers. The car he was in was now turning away, not before we all got a good glimpse of the blonde driving the convertible, top down, speeding away. We had all heard that Luciano was a good pilot, very accomplished and liked by all due to his light-hearted approach to our daily activities, but now we had the impression he knew how to find his way around in this country! At any rate the comments and the laughter continued until we arrived at the flight operations shack. The green flag was up outside, and the door was open. A head appeared motioning us in. We hesitated a bit to allow Luciano to finish putting his flight suit on over his trousers and tee-shirt. He adjusted his scarf and put on his "eagle" cap and we all entered to find our tables empty of instructors. We sat down as Mr. H and the others entered. Mr. H then addressed the group, congratulating us as everyone in Eagle flight had successfully passed their 40-hour check ride and he said it was gratifying to the instructors to have passed this milestone in the program. Loud clapping ensued and Pinky walked to my new table to show me the results of my ride with Lieutenant Van der Sluis. The grading sheet was scored 1-9, nine being the highest. I had a 76 out of 82 on the eight separate graded areas, with nines on takeoff, emergency landing, stalls, spins and approach and landing, yes, he gave himself a nine on his landing. There was no grade less than the seven for the barrel-roll, the rest were eights. Pinky had a great smile on his face as he said he hadn't seen that kind of grade from the tough lieutenant ever. My new instructor was non-committal, but I knew Pinky had shared the results with him before giving me the slip with the results on it.

He nodded as we began our day. He was like Pinky as he merely stated which each of us would do that day. Naturally we were going to have an assessment ride, but he didn't call it that. I sort of felt it was another check ride, but I didn't feel that kind of pressure. He indicated we would go through the routine maneuvers with some time spent on acrobatics. He must have seen my grading sheets from Pinky, or Pinky told him my acrobatics was the weakest part of my flying or why would he mention that specifically? I gathered my chute and followed him out to the flight line. He was really, small! Even his hands were tiny. I couldn't help noticing them as I glanced at the seat-boosting pad he carried for use in the aircraft. He told me to do the exterior check as he climbed into the rear seat, adjusting the pad he carried, placing it behind his chute. He was telling me to hurry up as I walked around the yellow bird. I jumped on the wing, adjusted my chute and got in. He criticized my S turns as being too compressed and time consuming. I hadn't gotten to the end of the runway and already he's cited me for nothing of consequence. He made me nervous. There were no further problems during the takeoff and climb out to the acrobatics area, although he was talking the entire time. Watch this, watch that, clear right, did you see that other aircraft. It was my substance time as he asked me to do a stall series, power off, then power on, followed by the three-turn spin, through all of which he made comments and all of which he was not necessarily, critical of. He surprised me when he said something good about the spin as I pulled out right on the heading I started on. I knew the acrobatics would start soon and was hoping we would just do the simple things but knew the instant he chose to do the chandelle, rather than a loop it would be the hard side of those maneuvers. After the chandelle he said to do a simple roll. I did and came out off, O-Oh heading. He demonstrated one and it was perfect. Do another he said. I did and it was better, so he followed with "Do a half-roll and reverse"! My breath vacated my body as I found a section line to start on. I rolled to the right pressing on the left rudder pedal as long and as far down as I could, but as I got upside down, my foot was free and as I rolled back, I was easily ten degrees off heading. He was not happy! He demonstrated one. I fixed my eyes on the heading shown on the magnetic compass. It didn't waver! How could he, being at best 5'2, hold that heading constant as he went topside down? He had me do another, same results. As I rolled out, I glanced in the rear-view mirror as I wanted to get a facial reaction and couldn't see him. Odd I thought as I often would glance back and could always see the guy in the back. He said, "I will show you one more". As he steadied the aircraft on heading, I wondered what he could see if I couldn't see him, so I looked back along the inside of the cockpit open area back to his seat. As the roll started, I saw Mr. Maxon almost prone, stretched out, pushing the rudder pedal all the way forward and not losing contact from the laying down position. No wonder, he was looking at the compass, not the horizon to complete the roll and in that position, he was able to freeze the heading as he completed the last half of the roll. I almost laughed, but contained myself as he said, "Ok, Let's see you do it right this time". I carefully bottomed my seat, stared at the compass and did the first half, holding tight with my foot on the top pedal which I could now depress all the way to the "fire-wall" and transferring the pressure to the other pedal as I completed the reverse, right on heading. Good, he yelled and some other remarks that floated over me as I brought my seat back up to see out of the aircraft. He must have seen me drop down, but if he did, he didn't say anything. Suddenly I felt vindicated as I finally did that maneuver right. Up to now I didn't get the fact that my height was insufficient to complete that maneuver, without "cheating", to make contact with the rudder pedals. We proceeded to do a set of lazy eights and a barrel roll, the latter he was not too pleased with as he felt my entry was forced and off heading but said to go and enter traffic. I flew the pattern, as always, very well. It was tight, on altitude and airspeed. Turning final I knew I would be on line down the runway. I touched down tail first and rolled to a stop, taking the first exit from the runway. I taxied in the "S" fashion to the parking area, pulled in to the spot directed by a crew-chief, shut down the engine, grabbed my checklist and left the cockpit. Mr. Maxon was already on the tarmac, back-pad in hand, slapped on an eagle hat to his balding head and motioned to start on our path going to the flight shack. He was very complementary about the ride and made a comment about my Navy instruction on how to land an aircraft. Tail first of course! There were no further comments, but thought it was a good ride. I made an impression and felt I was lucky a second time as I felt I got someone I could fly with as it was an extension of Pinky's type of flying. That was a good thing as there was over two months left in the T-6 and familiar methods of instruction are a path to success. Mr. Maxson was also a very soft handed pilot. There were no jerks when the airplane moved under his direction. He too, liked to fly and instruct. I will benefit from being at his table. I may even learn to like the series of acrobatics that I've avoided up to now. One thing is for sure, though I will not practice the half-roll-and-reverse solo!

A different sight emerged the week after my first flight with Mr. B. A new aircraft appeared on the ramp, the T-28. As indicated before, 56-H was to be the last class to fly the T-6 in training and the class ahead of us at Malden, 56-E would graduate in two weeks, the end of May. The next class coming in the beginning of June would be in the T-28. There would be some T-6s leaving in the next couple of weeks and by the start of the new class the T-28s would take up at least half the ramp. I wonder how Pinky and Mr. Maxon and the other ex-navy pilots will react to a tricycle gear? Not a problem for me yet and I'm sure it won't be a problem for them as I believe they can fly anything.

The class was progressing very well and there have been no washouts since the forty-hour check. Word has it that the graduating class will be getting their final check ride the next week. I've met a couple of the student in 56-E and they are mostly going to single engine school, although some chose multi-engine. I'm more inclined to go single myself when given the choice. Instructors can designate a student for multi-engine and despite the student desire they will go multi-engine. I don't think Mr. B would send me to the B-25 training, anyway I hope not.

A tragedy occurred today in the graduating class. One of the student pilots on a solo flight lost an engine and attempting an emergency landing five or six miles from the field. He plowed into something hard and was killed on impact. Any accident is tragic, but this one was especially so as it was his last flight before leaving for his next training base. It does stop the day to day thought of immortality. Since Dick Coyle's incident there had not been a hint of a flight problem and now a fatality. The fatality was an aviation cadet so many of the AvCads in 56-H knew him, even though he was in another class, graduating ahead of them. It's very sad and a sobering incident which has an effect on everyone, especially those who fly.

The T-28s continued to roll in and were now a dominating factor on the flight line. The "E" class instructors were all in a checkout process of the aircraft, so we now have them to contend with in the sky around Malden. They are a lot bigger and it seems strange to watch them taxiing as they don't have to do the "S" turns and they sit much higher than the T-6 which really seems small now. Sort of compare the size of the T-6 to the PA-18. 56-H students who go to single engine basic flight will have a chance to fly them as they are the lead-in to the T-33 Jet trainer. For now, we will still have a lot of flight activity before we get to that point. My trips to Cape Girardeau were over as Cathy's out for the summer and is now back home in Bellevue, just outside of Saint Louis. It's about two plus hours to get there but it's a nice drive, so the trip there is not a problem. I usually stay at a close in motel and spend the night. She knows her way around so movies and café eating is usually the date and then I drive back Sunday afternoon. A really, great, turn of events happened as we went to a night club that Cathy got a couple of tickets for and we saw Nat (King) Cole one night at a nice venue in downtown Saint Louis. He wandered through the tables while we ate and stopped at our table for an instant as he was singing. He had a baby-blue suit on that clashed with his slicked back hair, but he can really sing! We also did see a couple of outdoor concerts, making the trips very worthwhile. The drive was pleasant as going south it paralleled the Mississippi River. Some good things had to end though as Cathy and I both realized I would be finished at Malden early in August and I would be leaving for other places, so we made our goodbyes in July. I would be dateless for the rest of my time at Malden.

With summer came the merciless hot weather and there was no air conditioning in any of the facilities at Malden therefore there was no escape from the heat and humidity. Minimal clothing was the uniform of the day. A flight suit and a t-shirt were the basic dress during the ten hour day on the base. It was hot and the weather was anything but pleasant. Thunderstorms plagued the afternoon flight schedule and rain was a frequent companion every day, but it usually arrived late in the late period of flight. In the morning after suffering through a humid night just lying in bed hoping for a breath of air and sweating into your sheet, no covers, waiting for the break of day so you could get up. Once up it was still and relatively clear, but you could feel the heat beginning to rise. There was little wind and walking to eat breakfast you knew that the chow hall would foster no relief. Grabbing at coffee and orange juice and slipping through the line I would grab a piece of toast and throw it on my plate waiting for the hot SOS (you can figure that one out) to be thrown on it. It was a staple and despite remarks about it, it was easily the favorite food in the morning, whether going to fly or to the academic building. Flying in the morning was a treat as you didn't have to contend with the turbulence stirred up by the coming thunderstorms as they danced west to meet the still air over the Malden training facility. Morning flights were special during the hot days of spring and summer. Once in the air you could see the clouds building to the east, almost like a ridge forming along the mighty river. You knew that they would soon grow to wondrous heights. The weather classes had given us intense lessons on the three-stages of the thunderstorm, growing cumulus clouds to heights above forty-five thousand feet and the final anvil shape of the final stage appearing. Evenings we escaped to our favorite eating place and then Blondelles, the former was air conditioned, the latter was just a cool place to go. Dugan's time with Blondelle was always a factor in going there, however it was a nice place to have a beer and it had become a hangout for many in the class. Luciano came often and usually with a different girl. He was always laughing and was in the middle of any conversations about flying. He was the one who disclosed the story about the Argentinian student, who started after the PA-18 phase with Luciano. It was said on his first dual ride with his instructor. He was told to do a barrel roll and he proceeded to astound the instructor with a series of rolls and other maneuvers. When asked he told the instructor he had hundreds of hours in the T-6, flying them as a primary aircraft in his homeland. The instructor suggested that he just be given solo time to finish the mandatory training as he couldn't help him further.

A frequent sight on the flight line was having a T-6 start engines and students standing behind and to the side, opening their flight suits getting the wash of the engine to cool and dry them down. Also no one seemed to hurry to get out of the occasional morning rain as it was another way to lower the body temperature and of course, taking off solo and opening the cockpit was another way to beat the heat. It was oppressive to say the least! My flights with Mr. Maxon were always much the same. He and Pinky were from the same cloth and their emphasis on every flight was identical. "Stay ahead of the aircraft" and fun time with him was trying to outdo him on any maneuver. He taught me how to snap roll the T-6 and how to shake someone off your tail with a myriad of maneuvers. He was a fun instructor and he would even smile after some of our dual rides, especially when I was in the back seat for instrument training. When solo I was actually afraid to practice some of the standard things, but I had no trouble at all snap rolling the T-6, or doing continuous rolls to see how many I could do before entering a vertical dive. Something Mr. Maxon could do far better than me. He could do five and I was stuck at four, seemingly my limit, so each day I would seek to get five. I tried, but It never happened!

THE NAVIGATION LESSON

The day solo navigation leg was going to be flown by the entire class one afternoon. We were to go to Cape Girardeau turn to Paducah Kentucky, then to Fayetteville Arkansas and return to Malden. We would take off at a two-minute interval to start the nav-leg. Everyone was busy drawing lines on a map to make sure we had visual sighting for our "dead reckoning" venture. I didn't need any help drawing mine and was diligent in again citing items that would reveal a location to me. I felt I was ahead of the game because I had great luck on my dual navigation ride. I had noted headings and time point to point, (ETE) on each leg. I used a clip to secure it to my flight suit leg pocket and could easily adjust it going from one leg to another. I had become friends with a friend of Cathy who worked at the radio station in the Cape Girardeau area. It was about a mile or less from the town and away from the river. I had told him I would fly over his station one day and buzz it, so all my planning for the flight included a minute or two where I would fly over the station, do a couple of 360s well clear of the tower and then proceed to Paducah. I was toward the end of the sixteen flyers doing the navigation flight so once in the air and with my map, perfectly folded with my time and distance very illustrated I picked up the heading to Cape Girardeau. The clouds were in the distance, but our weather briefing had said we would not be affected by the weather for the flight. As I approached the river it was clear, and everything looked calm enough. I could see the road paralleling the Mississippi and the ore boats going in both directions. It appeared a bit misty, but the visibility was quite good. The tops of the clouds were definitely in a growth process, building to the east, but far enough away to not be a threat to flight. I refolded my map to show heading and distance to Paducah with the estimated time based on my groundspeed along the route. As I approached the outskirts of Cape Girardeau I turned to the radio station, a slight bit to the left off heading and away from the river. I could see the high antenna of the station from a distance and proceeded to start down to a lower altitude and leveled off at about five hundred feet and circled the station twice, wagging my wings like a fighter pilot. I knew it might end up having the takeoff behind me getting a bit close, but I felt a little increase in my airspeed would negate most of that. I did see a couple of people on the ground outside the station as I flew off. I again rearranged my map to show the heading to Paducah as the map had turned as I looked out of the cockpit checking the station. It was about a twenty-five-minute leg. I took up the heading from my map, cruised back up to the planned altitude and flew on. That was fun and I wondered if that was the friend Of Cathy that I had told I would buzz the station that I saw outside. I was not paying a great deal of attention outside the cockpit to sight visual pointers on the ground but was firmly on the right heading to Paducah. After about twenty minutes I started checking my map and looked ahead to see signs of the large city. I was running into some cirrus clouds that were somewhat masking portions of the ground, but I had a clear view ahead. My time had expired and there was no Paducah. I flew ahead a couple more minutes and was beginning to panic. What would they think if I got lost on my navigation leg? Worse yet what if I ran out of gas? As these thoughts ran through my mind I heard a voice over the en-route radio frequency we were flying on, "do you know where you are"? A bit stunned I hesitated for a moment as the voice then said, "look out on your right wing". I looked over to see a smiling Pinky, canopy open, tucked close into me. As I saw him, I shook my head, still too surprised to respond. After a slight lapse in exercising my mike button he gave me a heading to Fayetteville, dropped down and turned his yellow bird to the right. I followed and picked up the heading he gave me and as I finished the turn to the right there was Paducah, Kentucky in the distance. I had not learned the lesson Pinky gave me on our dual navigation ride when he deviated off course to experience the ride on top of the cirrus clouds. He adjusted his heading to compensate and I unlike my mentor, blindly took the same heading I planned for, instead of coming back to my intended flight path or adjusting my heading to compensate for the deviation. I had gone off course a good five miles to buzz the radio station and then took the same heading from there that I planned from the city. I did not adjust therefore I would always be tracking to the left of my planned route. Then, the cirrus clouds on my right towards the end of my timing had masked Paducah and I missed seeing it. If not for Pinky I might have been in a real fix. Fortunately, the instructors were positioned at each of the turn points to catch any deviant student pilot. They were flying above the planned navigation altitude and would circle and seek any distinguishing yellow T-6s as they passed below and made sure they were where they should be. If after a two to three-minute break and no aircraft, they would search to find any lost soul and set them straight. Fortuitously Pinky saw me. What a sight! A smiling Pinky tucked in on my wing, I will never forget it. I held my heading very steady to Fayetteville and the now clear skies allowed it to be picked up almost after my turn to the proper heading. after that final point in the leg it was a matter of following my intended heading, a simple route back to the sparsely populated lower portion of Missouri. The towns were not well defined as they all looked the same and they were sparse, but the rotating beacon, even during the day, was a dead give-away so finding Malden was a snap. It was good to see a familiar place to land. I flew a visual approach to final and I landed without any other incident. After parking I walked back to the flight shack. Some of the other students were there including Dugan and Joe who were among the first to start. They asked how it went and I said "fine, no problem." Only Pinky knew and he wouldn't tell!

INSTRUMENT FLYING

It came accidently out of a discussion we were having at the table with Mr. Maxon when he mentioned the fact that we would be starting our instrument training in the coming week. It would be a big portion of our final weeks at Malden as we would be getting twenty-five-hours "hood" time. He explained we would be flying from the back seat using only the cockpit instrumentation and tracking to various locations using radio range identification procedures. It was the aftermath of hours of instruction in the "Morse Code" in our classroom on range procedures. We would now have to identify stations by heir three letter designation, broadcast in Morse code and then track to them and identify station passage. To know station passage you had to know the difference between an "A" and an "N". One was a di-da and the other was a da-di. Four cones extended out from each station two were "A" and two were "N". It would work in a fashion that as you tracked into a station you would hit what they called an "aural null", where you would not hear anything for a few seconds and then hear the opposite signal indicating passage. You could not wander off your track as to do so you would miss the "null" and the station. Once in the air, under a hood, which covered the entire rear cockpit you were taught to first find and then tune in a desired station, intercept a predetermined radial. There are 360 of them and the reciprocal of the radial would be your heading to the station. Once on the desired radial you would track to the station. Then you had to identify an "A" or "N" quadrant you were in as the "null would be identified as you left one quadrant to another, picking up the "Morse code" designator on the other side of the station. Mr. Maxon did a lot of demonstrating, but it was tedious work when you were doing it without any help. I had difficulty on the first three attempts, picking up the radial I was supposed to fly inbound. When told to pick up the 270-degree radial to Cape Girardeau my first tendency was to fly a heading of 270 degrees catching myself and picked up a heading to intercept the radial flying 90 degrees inbound. It's easy to miss the aural null and you really have to be quick to hear the change from "A" to "N" or vice versa. Fortunately Mr.M was very patient and you knew something was wrong when you would hear a sort of a sigh or heavy breathing on your head set and he would say: "do an identification turn", meaning you missed the station and had to fly a ninety degree heading off the radial and then pick up the beacon inbound to the station, trying again to identify station passage. It would involve that ninety degree turn, followed by a two-hundred and seventy degree turn to track back to the station. I got very good at the abrupt maneuver! Some of the fixes we flew to were off a VOR, much easier to identify than the radio range as station passage was immediate and there was no problem in knowing when it happened. Once done in the air we would proceed to the Malden fix and pick up a landing system for the base. There were two types of instrument approaches, one and ILS (Instrument Landing System) and the other a GCA (Ground Controlled Approach). Both were very tedious, and it was never over after one approach. Two and three at the very least with the hood coming up at minimum approach altitude and Mr. Maxon making the landing. It was nothing to land with my flight suit totally drenched in sweat. It was the most exhausting time I experienced in my training since my first days in the PA-18. Slowly it became easier to figure out intercepts and tracking. Of course, the ante was raised as we got more proficient, we were then made to establish ourselves in a holding pattern on a specific radial to the station and then fly timed legs in a race-track pattern, holding until you were cleared to leave the fix. The timed legs usually were two minutes on each side of the track but could be more. The clock used for timing was small and had a sweep second hand and was now part of the instrument cross-check making the pattern an arduous event. You had to depress a small button to get the sweep hand going and when you were fully engaged in holding a heading and staying on altitude that button became a difficult spot to find. I was always pleased to be told to come out from the hood when cleared from whatever instructor I had, as others would fill in to complete the hours needed for everyone, then sit back while they landed the airplane. It was a grueling experience, but one needed to finish the entire program. I was very happy when Mr. Maxon signed off on my proficiency in instruments in what he called his personal check ride. I never received a "pink" slip during any of the phases, but to go through instrument flight without one was considered rare. Most students had at least one, Dugan had two and Kelly had one, so it was an accomplishment. Another square completed on this long path to being awarded silver wings.

THE MYSTERIES OF NIGHT

We started these two new phases of flight well into the last six weeks we would spend at Malden, the first was that introduction to flying under a hood and being subjected to instrument flying and the other would be changing our routine to night flying, starting with some solid dual rides, with lots of pattern work and multiple landings and a short navigation leg. It would culminate with a night cross country. The dual rides were informative and enlightening, as the sight of a runway rimmed with lights and the use of colors to define taxiways from the runway and approach lights leading to the actual runway were all eye-openers. Another interesting new visionary sighting was the torch coming out of the exhaust tubes of the engine, a fire that was obvious, but not seen during the day. I didn't find any great problem with the change from day to night, except the emphasis was on the takeoff and landing phase of flight. We were restricted from doing anything other than short navigation legs and pattern activity. The preparation prior to our rides was a briefing in the ready room with only red lights, making it very surreal and mysterious. The red light did not affect your night vision and thus protected your sight during that time. Everything looked funny, like there was an aura around everybody, but when walking outside to go to the aircraft, everything was very clear. For the first time you could see that exhaust of the T-6. When approaching the active runway, the flame was very apparent coming from the exhaust tube extending from the side of the engine. It did give credibility to the power of the engine. Then in the traffic pattern it was very easy to spot aircraft due to this signal from each aircraft. Also, the wing tip (passing lights?) red and green really came into view. The afore mentioned runway lights made it easy to establish runway parameters, even though you could not see many of the check points we used during the day. The landings were a bit different as the last stage as the runway seemed to leap up to you and did cause late round-outs for many, but those of us who were among the students of the tail-dragger instructors it didn't affect us much. Rounding out a bit high we just sort of fell the last few inches, (maybe more) making it a very firm landing. At least we didn't launch back into the air. This did not cause concern for Mr. Maxon! I would end up getting some solo time at night. The solo rides were a bit boring as I spent most of my time cruising around the dim areas below, constantly keeping the military rotating beacon in my cross check. I did spend a lot more time in the pattern, making low approaches to the runway, but found as more students started their solo flights the pattern to the single lit runway became very crowded and the downwind leg stretched a considerable distance. I became content to make one low approach at the end of my flying time and then one full pattern for a full stop.

The night flying cut into our trips downtown for dinner and a beer or two and had to be content with chow hall food. We were still involved in classes, so it made for a long day as our schedule called for mornings in class, the long break and then to the flight line for flying. If you were not scheduled to fly, you still were at the flight shack for three plus hours, mostly a boring time. You could only learn so much about an airplane and most of the aircraft and flight material was now covered so well in class, you didn't bring those books to the flight shack. Most of us had a novel or two that accompanied us to our table and those were passed around once read. Mr Hubenthal and Pinky as the two men in charge were around, sometimes willing to share time with us, but they too were getting students checked out for the night routine.

NIGHT CROSS-COUNTRY

The cross-country navigation leg was to be the same as the day dual ride. There would be no student-instructor night dual ride. The student preparation was the same for our day solo ride, but now we had the night vision procedure, and because we were in mid-summer we didn't start our takeoffs until after 2000 hours (that's 8 pm) also they switched our academic schedule to afternoon classes, but they were shorter and we were finished well before 1600 hours We could actually sleep in as there was no formation before we started class. Dugan, Kelly and I went into town for breakfast one day and did a little shopping afterwards. Kelly, with his outgoing persona and his rugged good looks was a hit in every store we visited. It seems he knew a lot of people (women), interesting! Night navigation made the towns stand out due to the lights, however there were no landmarks, other than water breaks from land that stood out at night. The radio station tower lights I could see easily but passed up any chance of deviating off course as I had learned my lesson. When I turned at Cape Girardeau the Mississippi River with the snake like lights of the city running along the banks made for an easy turn point. But the most impressive part of the night flights was the stars above.

Our celestial navigation classes were among the most interesting as certain stars and pointer systems to use were almost masked by the amount you could see. Stars were so bright and clusters of stars so common it was very difficult to pick out many of the prominent ones that were obvious in our night classes where we identified those most used in visual navigation. There was no moon on the night of our cross-country, so the prominent navigational stars were still very, obvious above all the ground clutter. We had had only rudimentary star identification, but the big dipper (Ursa Major) and the north star (Polaris) were two I knew and easily found. The river had a similar pattern as each-and-every boat, tug, barge and whatever had lights, not in clusters, but spotted in various positions on them, many searching the water around them, skimming the surface for possible obstructions in the surging river. Of course, all of them were moving, some upstream and some had a destination far south, maybe even New Orleans. The lights were doing a dancing tango along the dark background of the water. It was very impressive to see, but all too soon I had to make my turn to Paducah. Just using the pattern of lights in the towns made it easy to stay on course, even though I kept the planned heading steady as displayed on the compass going to my turn point to Fayetteville. I could actually see another T-6 occasionally due to his signature exhaust. And then I could pick out the running lights(red and green lights on each wingtip), further identifying one in front of me or behind me when making a turn to the new destination. Fayetteville was a large town compared to the others and was obvious well before my carefully planned time had elapsed to turn. Going to the final-destination would be a bit different.

Malden is a small town and the towns around it all look similar. There was no distinguishable pattern of their lights. Even a degree or two off heading would make one of the other towns around Malden look like my landing point, but the rotating split beacon on the tower at this military location made it easy to see from quite far away. Seeing the split in the light made it easy to pick out to the right of the scarce lighting of the town. It was a very welcome sight for a student on his first foray at navigation at night. I started my decent to the base early, keeping my eyes focused on the beacon. The runway lights reached out identifying the place to go to. Reaching pattern altitude, I easily found my forty-five-degree entry to the downwind leg. It was then that I realized there were other aircraft around me as the torching identifier of other T-6s in the pattern became obvious. Looking to my right I could not find one that would keep me from entering the pattern, so started my left turn to parallel the runway. There was an aircraft well ahead of me and I spied another on final approach. I spaced myself from the immediate aircraft in front of me and then waited until he was on final to start my descending turn to the base leg, hoping I hadn't stretched the downwind for aircraft after me. I continued the turn to final, picking the approach lighting to the runway directing me to my touchdown point. It was a very euphoric moment as I was about to start my round out, preparing for touchdown. This time I did not "splat" on landing. I felt the tail wheel touch and let my main gear follow for a sweet completion of this necessary item in our night program. I had logged over an hour more at night as a solo pilot. And always felt flying at night was a most satisfying and enlightening part of our training.

THE LAST DAYS

The final days approached. We were to finish with a hundred and twenty hours in the T-6. My solo time had built up to a point where I felt really confident in flying the aircraft and if you didn't count the instrument time, I had an equal amount of solo flying as I did dual. I still did not do any of the restricted maneuvers that others boasted about, but I had mastered in my own mind, the basic control items that without handling them you could kill yourself. I had fun, but I was not dangerous, and I witnessed others that not only boasted about their folly, but I have seen them in the air, falling out of a loop or Immelmann maneuver and end up in a dangerous position close to the ground. I was told by some that buzzing the loose cows was fun but being an animal lover and not in the business of endangering my own tail, I stayed at a safe altitude during my primary training days. Now, I was ready to take the next step. As we sat in the ready room one morning in mid-July we were given a formal military piece of paper. It asked to select the type of aircraft we wished to fly in Basic. It had two blocks clearly outlined: one for Single Engine and the other Multi-Engine. There were two signature blocks below that, one for the student and one for the instructor. Next to the instructor block there were two other blocks: Agree and Disagree. I signed my name and marked the "single engine" block. The others at Mr. Maxon's table did likewise. Mr. H collected them all and we went back to the business of flying for the day. The last two weeks flew by and during that time we received our assignments, Dugan Kelly and I all would go to Laredo, Texas for single-engine jet training. I was surprised that Charlie Englehart would also go there, but who was I to judge, maybe Charlie hit it up with his new instructor after he left Pinky, which didn't happen till well after he passed his forty-hour check. Even though he had the Captain Santa Claus for his forty-hour check, who gave him some low marks, he was not turned down for single-engine. There were some who chose multi-engine, one, I knew whose wife felt it was safer. I heard that one student officer, an OTS (Officer's Training School) graduate selected single-engine, but his instructor didn't agree. They had a meeting with Mr. H over the instructor's decision and Mr. H gave the student a ride and thought he was ok to go to single engine and so he did. Others willingly chose the multi path and were happy with the choice. Chamblee was a no-brainer, as after his initial problem with air sickness in the PA-18, he had no further difficulty with any parts of the program and would go where most of the AvCads went, the single-engine route. None would go to Laredo, an all officer program. Roland was one who always seemed to float through the program with his wide smile and willingness to listen to anyone, he also,was going with me to Laredo, Texas.

The new class came in the week after 56-E left, it was 56-K, they would not begin flying the T-28 for at least three weeks, but their instructors would be, as they were converting their talents to that new, silver aircraft. We would at least know that those flying that aircraft were very qualified pilots. The airspeed they would be flying in the pattern would be a bit higher and the same difference on final. The T-6 crowd would have to extend their pattern to keep it safe. Most of the instructors for our class seemed reluctant to leave the T-6 as they had built up a comfort zone for it and knew every sound it made. The T-28 was a new and strange animal to them.

THE FINAL CHECK

All that was left was the final check ride with a military check pilot. It was a week where all of us would get that final assessment to go forward. Fail this and everything would change. Few had ever flunked this ride but there had been some we heard about from instructors, so make sure you don't think this as a walkover. It's not. It was assumed that the final check by the military section would be a necessary coverage of the many procedures and maneuvers we had been introduced to since starting in the T-6. We should not have any trouble proving we were ready to go forward, and yet there was the thorn in the bush that could always appear, so the worry mat comes out and we anticipate the flight with a feeling of dread. What if I draw Vandersluis again? I would hope I was just as good a second time with him. At any rate the anxiety rate went up and discussion was all about that subject as we prepared for this final check ride. Our trips downtown had diminished as the schedule had caught up with us and we were plagued with afternoon thunderstorms that seemed to roll in as we finished our flying or class activity. They were fierce, with heavy rain, lightning and sometimes hail which would bang off the roof of our shacks and threaten the windshields of our cars parked close by. The rain would cause waves of water to roll across the narrow roads and the farmland around the base became like a giant pond. You wondered if anything could survive the flooded fields, the hail would surely destroy anything growing in those seemingly barren areas. The humidity was uncomfortable, the worst in the realm of discomfort. It was morbidly miserable as everything seemed to cling to you. There was no way to find relief once the storms hit the airfield. They had caused numerous delays in our flying throughout July, the morning flying sessions survived somewhat and maybe the early first hour or so in the afternoon, but the red flag was a familiar sight after that and the call would go out for all aircraft to RTB(return to base). Even with all of the delays and cancelled flights somehow, we were in a position to get our checks as July turned into August. I sat in the lobby of the military check pilot shack with four others awaiting someone to come and pick out our names for the check ride. This time the Captain stepped into the room and picked up a slip and glanced around and looked as he called out the name. Lieutenant Dugard! I was pleased and relieved as I was the first to get selected that day and suddenly it was a beautiful morning. The ramp was still wet from last night's storm, the air was steamy, there was no wind and the heat was just beginning to rise, but it was a perfect day for my ride. After all the preliminaries and a brisk walk around the aircraft I placed my chute in the front cockpit as he was chatting with me about where I was going next. He was pleased when I told him single engine. He talked about Laredo as we taxied out to the takeoff end of the runway and only stopped when I lined up for takeoff. Once airborne and almost a thousand feet in the air he gave me the emergency landing call. It was well above the need for a straight in approach so I looked around. I spied a nice level area to my right, somewhat muddy and water obvious in low spots, announced by intensions and turned to lineup, set my airspeed and started my decent and he applied power to end the drill. As I started my climb he started to discuss the fatality that happened in the 56-E class and saying sometimes in those level looking fields are objects you can't see until it's too late. He said that mud and sitting water can be a factor in surviving a landing in even a plowed field. He told me to keep the nose up and be right at stall speed when you are about to splash. That was comforting!

We climbed to altitude and he said to set up for a stall series, which I did and easily accomplished the two of them. He asked who my instructor was and gave him both Pinky and Mr. Maxon. He said he thought both were excellent teachers and I agreed, although I never thought of them as teachers, but they certainly were. The spin went well and as we flew to do some acrobatics, he asked to take control of the aircraft, which I gratefully gave to him and he proceeded to do a simple roll to the left and then right. He said: "match that". I had never been challenged liked that but took the aircraft back and did one to the left and then right. He thought they were very good. I told him how Mr. B and I tried to do as many as possible before the nose went through the horizon. He took control again and did four, I did the same. He laughed and said: "do a half-roll and reverse". I bottomed my seat, fastened my eyes on the compass and started right, stopped when upside down, stomped on the rudder pedal, pushed the stick slightly forward and rolled back to the left, maybe I drifted a degree or two off heading, but it was good. I popped the seat back up and waited. He did not comment but wanted me to do a loop, so cleared the area above and did the loop. He said: That's enough, let's get back to the pattern, so I turned the aircraft back to the field, set up my entry, flew one pattern and landed as a good navy pilot should, tail first. Taxied back "S" turning all the way and parked. As we exited the aircraft he said: "good ride and good luck"! It was over! I ended up with a hundred and twenty hours and ten minutes in the T-6G. I also had logged an incredible 235 landings in that aircraft.

The last two days were sad as we had to say goodbye to our instructors and I felt that difficult, even knowing they would start with a new class in just a few days. Mr. Maxon was sad looking, and Pinky had that perpetual crooked smile on his face as they shook my hand. Once I had been with Mr. Maxon for a significant period he became very involved in my well-being and in the end his table of students had bonded with him and he was genuinely happy when we did well. Pinky had been a "father figure" to all his students. Joe, Dugan and I made a last visit to our favorite eating place downtown and they were genuinely sorry to see us go. We had been on a first name basis with most of the help and they always lit up when we came in. It was more than being merely customers of their restaurant as it was a sweet friendship with the owners and the waitresses. They were like family. Our final beer at Blondelle's was just that. We had a beer and said goodbye. Even Dugan just walked away. There were no tears as we left, but there was a feeling of emptiness and loss. Tomorrow there would be a completion of preliminary flight training ceremony, with the awarding of our completion papers, then a pickup of our flight records in the morning for both Eagle and Hawk flights. We should be done by 1000 hours and then we would start two weeks of leave and travel time before we reported to Laredo, Texas. It was not going to be a farewell to most of the others in 56-H, just a short break and new duty station until we got to the next step before getting our wings. Leaving the tar-paper hut and the familiar grounds of the facility we had spent almost six months was not difficult. The shaking of the hands of Pinky and Mister Maxon was more difficult as it was obvious, they felt they had a stake in us and our success in this road to a flying future and they felt our departure very personally. As a recipient of their skills and wisdom, I definitely felt a loss as I turned away from those two after saying goodbye and receiving our departure package, only to be approached by Mr. Hubenthal, who held out his hand and had a smile on his face and said the words, "good luck". I did shed a tear and felt no shame as I walked to my fully loaded car.

HOME

Leaving Malden in the middle of the day I intended to drive straight through to my home in California. It was a distance, but I was confident I could make the trip. Leaving Missouri was just a matter of going southwest but getting away from two lane highways was a bit more difficult. I found a four-lane highway in Arkansas and looking at my map I picked up at the gas station in Dexter I found Route 66 and it led me to the Oklahoma turnpike. I was impressed and I didn't even mind paying the toll. I drove into the night and hit the outskirts of Las Cruces New Mexico, where there was some highway construction. Not the least bit deterred, as there was no traffic, I ignored the warning of a speed limit due to the construction and shortly was pulled over by a local sheriff. As he walked forward I pulled out my California driver's license and waited for him to come to my side. I showed it to him and he told me he would have to cite me for speeding in a construction zone. Even worse I would have to appear before a judge. It was 11:30 at night! He told me the court was in session, so I could follow him and pay my fine now! Really! Upon arrival there was no one there but the Judge and a court clerk. The sheriff introduced me as a military person, with a California driver's license, going home on leave. He also told the judge I was very cooperative. He read that I had exceeded the limit by 30 miles an hour. I expected the worse. He then added that there was no traffic. The judge was sympathetic and cautioned me to keep it under the limit while in New Mexico. I told him I would. The fine was reduced to ten dollars plus five dollars court cost and I could pay it in cash, which I did, thanked them and promptly left. I carefully drove through the rest of New Mexico. The rest of the trip was uneventful, but I was thoroughly washed out when I got home. I had been on the road for almost twenty hours and knew I would never try that again. I had almost two weeks to recover before reporting to Laredo for "Basic" flight training. It passed by quickly and I was very happy to see this break come to an end. It was not the same, people were different, and they really weren't interested in what I was doing. My family was happy to see me and it was nice to sleep in my own bed and eat home cooking but I was ready to start the next stage with friends who had a common interest that I could talk to without boring them.

LAREDO AFB

Going to Laredo I had computed my drive and the time it would take, so stopped at a motel in El Paso, not wanting to go through the effects that I felt on the trip home after leaving Malden. I had driven the length of Texas before, going to San Antonio, but the additional miles to Laredo seemed endless. From my early morning departure to well after the sunset I was driving in Texas. I signed in late on a Sunday night at Laredo AFB, Texas. I was assigned to a first-floor room in the student barracks and was given a paper with my instructions for the first day. It would involve a check-in and welcome to the base and to the 3640th and 3641st training squadrons. The 3640th would be the training squadron for 56-H. Tomorrow morning the incoming students would gather in the base theater for this indoctrination. Directions to the theater were included and it showed that the theater was across the parade ground from the barracks. I must have been among the first to sign in on this last day before the beginning of our first day in single engine jet fighter training. The first screening had been made and I was anxious to begin. The halls were empty so despite being hungry I decided not to try and find a place to eat off base and just settle in for the night and finally felt I belonged in this environment. I discovered Dugan in the latrine in the morning. He was in the adjoining room, separated by the latrine and said he got in from Seattle late last night. We walked out of the barracks together, dressed in our short sleeve summer uniform and both of us agreed we needed to eat and set out looking for the student mess hall on our map. It was close to the theater and we could smell bacon cooking as we got closer and were ready to settle in for the first meal at our new base. I asked how Martie was. He responded that she was fine and that was that. The short walk was interrupted by constant hellos to Malden graduates, but there were also many who came from the other two primary bases, Mariana Florida and Mission Texas, some I recognized from our pre-flight days at Lackland. Strange how things worked out as going to Malden was a great move for me as I had a great pair of instructors and a wonderful experience in the boot heel section of Missouri. In conversations with those who went to the other primary bases I didn't get a feel that they were as fortunate as the Malden group. I asked about some of those who went to other bases for training, quite a few washed out and others chose multi-engine training at Lubbock. As this was the only single engine training base offered to officers in this class, I should run into a few who made it through primary. I had made a few friends who I had played flag football with from our training barracks, a couple who had been in my graduating class from Loyola University.

The mess hall was only partially full and the line for breakfast was empty. Once again SOS with coffee hit the spot. Finishing our morning meal and now fully awake and ready to go we walked to the theater. The now large group sort of intermingled outside of the theater and in the lobby as you recognized someone from Lackland, saying hello and acknowledging the fact that they made it to this juncture of training. As the doors swung open to the interior of the theater, we entered looking for a seat. The darkened theater was a relief from the start of a warm and humid August day, as it was very cool inside. We sat down about halfway to the stage in the first two on the left aisle seats. Joe Kelly rolled in, walked over the two of us, smelling of "stale cigarette smoke" and plunked down next to me and Dugan. There were more moments of recognition, sharing stories of how they got here and how they spent the time between the two training bases. Once settled there was a sound of silent murmuring and a feel of apprehension. The call to attention stopped the chatter and the sound of the assemblage snapping to a standing brace was followed by the echoing sound of a group of senior officers walking down the center aisle to the stage. Once in place a call of "At Ease" sounded out as the group came to an attentive seating silence. Everything started with an invocation, given by the Base Chaplain, Major Lewandowski, a short, squat guy with a booming voice. The Base Commander, Colonel Milton Adams followed and spoke warmly about the base and its environs and welcomed us to the training wing. The commander of the Pilot Training Group, Colonel William Samways then gave us a pitch on the daily regimen and the fact that the city of Laredo was a great neighbor and Nuevo Laredo, the border town across the river was very available, but be careful. He was followed by Major Robert Allison, the commander of the 3640th Pilot Training Squadron. He gave us information on the mechanics of the program such as time in aircraft and the updated requirements for graduation. We would be divided into the two training flights "A" and "B", much like the "Eagle/Hawk" at Malden. The names of those in each of the flights were posted in the foyer to the theater and we could check those rosters when we left. We would assemble after the noon meal and march to the flight line in the same summer uniform we started the day in to meet our instructors. Our days would be divided like they were in primary, with flying one half of the day and academics the other half, switching every other week. We then received some more words on the local area and the base policy on border crossing into Nuevo Laredo. The Flight surgeon cautioned us on some of the problems with the prostitutes across the border, followed by another plea to be careful, although there was no history of problems with the local merchants or night clubs and there were no "off-limit" places presently. We were finally finished with the introductions and as the group of senior officers left the theater we stood at attention until we heard the call of "dismissed" which sent everyone into the lobby to find out what flight they were in. It was only after the crowd thinned out that Dugan, Kelly and I got close enough to find out our destination. Dugan and I were going to "A" flight, but Kelly was in "B" flight.

The bachelor students in 56-H all ended up in individual rooms in the barracks complex with a shared a bathroom. Everything was close by, including the gym and across the street from my room were a pair of three wall handball courts. It was something I wanted to try but outside activity was something I would wait until a cooler time period. The chapel was about a block away and the mess hall was situated at the end of the barracks area. Being it's August and right on the Mexican border it was very hot, so after a quick lunch we marched to the flight line sweating through our short-sleeved summer uniform. Both groups were together and as both training squadron buildings were next to each other, when we arrived we just went into whichever one you were assigned to. It would be the last time we went as a composite group until graduation. In fact, for the most part we didn't cross paths much unless we met at an eating place downtown or took in a local movie. Trips across the border would comprise most of our entertainment as the food was good and the music was fun to listen to.

Dugan and I followed the crowd going into "A" Flight building. It was an open room with individual tables and chairs around them. Everyone just picked a spot to sit down and waited for the appearance of the Flight staff and instructors. Shortly after our arrival the flight commander, Captain Charles McDade, known in flying "call sign" parlance as "Spitfire" appeared with a trio of lieutenants, who he introduced as assistant flight leaders. He proceeded to tell us about the training regime we would undergo and was the first to tell us we would be on the morning flight schedule this week. He familiarized us with the various areas we would be using, such as Personal Equipment, which was where we were to pick up and have our parachutes fitted. He then called out the instructors from an adjoining room and introduced them to us. Most of them were second lieutenants like us and many of them had recently graduated from pilot training and this was their first assignment after they received their wings. A couple of them looked very young, but most, when introduced were trying to mask any hint of inexperience. Most of the instructors would have three students but some would have four. As they went down the list our names were identified as being assigned with an instructor. I would be with 2/Lt Darwin (Doug) Anson. He was tall and very laconic, didn't say much, but seemed nice enough. Each instructor had given their group a name to identify themselves from one another. Our group was known as "Shotgun Flight". My two table mates were Dick Clark from Minnesota and George Fong from New York. Charlie Englehart, also in "A" flight was in "Badger flight and a good friend, Bobby Dantzler was in "Gaydog" flight. Dugan went with an instructor named Helmut Meining, a former WWII German pilot. His flight was "Deadeye". Roland Ford, my tablemate at Malden went to a 1st lieutenant, named McNew, whose call sign was "Scotty", turned out to be a native Texan. We had a short get to know meeting and then we were all released to get settled in our new quarters and base. We would all have to have new identification cards and base tags for our cars to take the place of the temporary card we now had. Most of us spent the rest of the afternoon at the "Pass and ID" section of the base, getting new ID cards and automobile stickers for the windshield of our cars to identify we belonged on the base so we wouldn't be stopped every time we entered the gate. It became obvious there would be little time during duty hours to do anything but fly or go to ground school initially for the T-28, followed by the T-33, along with classes in navigation, weather and other assorted subjects. There was much to see outside of the base as it was a short ride to the border and crossing over was just a matter of parking in a convenient lot and crossing the foot bridge into Nuevo Laredo. We were cautioned not to drive into Nuevo, instead park on this side as it was safer and walking over the river bridge was fast and no hassle as we just showed our Military ID cards as we get to the Mexico side. There would be time later to explore the area and we decided today was not that time. We were told about an excellent steak house in Laredo, just outside of town and decided to go there for supper. It would become our favorite eatery as the meals were gigantic and the steaks were the best. It was an all-white exterior building and as you entered you saw waiters with white hats and aprons to continue the trend. All the tables had red checkered table cloths to add to the atmosphere. The name of the place? "The White House".

THE TERRIBLE T-28

The next morning after an early wakeup and breakfast we marched as a group, "A" Flight, 56-H, to the flight line. It was supposed to be a very warm day and the smell in the air was unfamiliar, however it was one we would get very used to. It was the smell of the standard Jet fuel, JP-4, used in all Jet aircraft presently on line. Also, there was a sound that was a bit strange, but also one we would embrace as we progressed to flying the base trainers. It was the power unit for the aircraft on the flight line, which were needed until the aircraft were on their own power. Once the Jet engine was started and power came up to idle, the unit would then be disconnected and shut down. The sun was glinting off the array of silver skinned aircraft, lined up and down the ramp, row after row of T-28s and T-33s, waiting for the instructor and student population to get them into the air. The T-28 looked like a proud little girl, resting on her tricycle gear and standing a bit taller than the Low-slung T-33s, with their tip tanks looking like something that doesn't belong on their sleek bodies. It was hard to imagine that we were now in a phase of flying that would hopefully launch us into even more complex aircraft, it was a bit mind boggling. We finally arrived at our training squadron operation center. A tall lieutenant motioned us inside and naturally we followed. Like all training squadrons it was a room occupied by many long four to five chair tables, a rack for hanging coats and an area set aside for flight manuals and Air Guides. There were also boxes of red "A" flight ball caps, all sizes. We were told to grab a hat and that would be our uniform hat for our time wearing of our flight suits until graduation. We all pocketed our blue service hats and placed the new, in my case, a size seven, ball caps on our heads. On key, our instructors filtered into the room and my instructor, Doug Anson seemed out of place, taller than most and an unsmiling face, not necessarily "all business", but more bored. He walked to an unmarked table and motioning to us, he directed the three of us to the table, assuming we would know it was his. We stumbled to find a chair without sitting on one another. There were a couple more introductory remarks from Captain McDade and then he told the instructors to take over. Doug asked a few basic questions of each of us, but nothing deeper than were we all single and where did we come from. He then put on his sunglasses and told us we would walk out of the building and do an exterior check of the T-28 and if time permitted, we would go to the simulator building and do a cockpit checkout of the aircraft. He sort of laid out a schedule for first flights as he looked at our flight records from primary. As he perused them, he indicated Lt. Clark would get his introductory ride in the T-28 first thing in the morning, followed by me and then Lt. Fong. It didn't occur to me, but then he said he liked to do things in alphabetical order. Each ride would be about an hour and would be mostly confined to pattern work after some brief activity at altitude.

Our first introduction to the new aircraft was that walk around of an aircraft sitting outside of flight ops. We crawled up on a wing and gazed into the cockpit. The instrument panel had all the standard instruments, circular in pattern, but there was also a couple of vertical, rectangular ones. I would have to ask about them. Of course, all of us had seen the T-28 when it arrived at our primary flight schools, but few of us had taken the time to look at it, me, included. It was much bigger than the T-6, whose tail always sat on the ground and this silver beast had the tricycle gear which meant no more "S" turns while taxiing, and it was a shiny new aircraft and that was good. After the walk around, Doug took the three of us to the simulator building. Walking in to the cool inside of the simulator building we were introduced to one of the two T-28 simulators. The cockpit was identical to the one in the flying aircraft and another unpowered simulator box was next to them for us to practice instruments familiarity and the position of handles such as flaps and landing gear, using our checklists of course. The 41st Flying Training Squadron had the class ahead of us in the T-28, so we would be sharing simulators with them. That class is close to going to the T-33. We could use the training box without a scheduled time, however the simulators were scheduled from the flight operations center and that was done through your instructor when you started in the instrument portion of our training. There was a lot to learn and with any new aircraft it would rush at us day by day and flight by flight. Mumbling about what we have seen, we walked back to our new instructional home.

When we arrived back in the operational center, we found inside cloth bags and a stack of paper and some three ringed binders in three separate locations on the table. Checklists of the T-28 were also stacked neatly, starting with the walk around, interior, starting engines and all the others through the after landing and engine shut down checklists. This in essence, was our dash-1 and essential items we would need to become very acquainted with for our new aircraft. We were anxious to get into the Dash-1, but Lt. Anson said that would have to wait for this afternoon when we will be introduced to the airplane in our engineering class for the T-28. One of the checklists was outlined in red, titled "Emergency Procedures". I'll check "engine out" first, just to make sure I can restart one as I don't want to put an aircraft down in this desert, surrounding the base in south Texas. The other checklists were more of a blue, flip-type and would fit in the lower leg pocket of a flight suit, convenient to access in the airplane. Our immediate task was to put the papers in the proper order in the proper binders, something that would start tonight. They even provided a canvas bag to hold the diverse group of the new "reading material". No going off base for dinner tonight.

THE ACADEMIC WORLD

Our first day in the academic world was to be an eye opener. We were met at the academic section by a Lieutenant Harris, who was to be our T-28 Engineering instructor. Our greeting included a blue bound, large, flight manual which he informed us would be required reading over the next four weeks. Tests on the contents would be a common occurrence as well as verbal quizzes to test our knowledge of critical items covered in the many paged "novel". Our second class in the afternoon was another "introduction" to navigation by Lieutenant Watson. This time the title was "dead reckoning". Pinky had introduced me to this form of navigation but didn't call it by that name. I had used and misused it during my navigation flights in primary. I would have to admit this was interesting, as according to Watson there were many other things to be used in addition to the normal identifiable items such as rivers and such. The use of terrain features and other facets of seeing where you are going were much greater when explained as a prime method of getting where you are supposed to go to. He was, no make a mistake about it, a southerner and spoke in a folksy twang that was easy to listen to. He instilled in me the need to make a readable map, that was folded in a fashion that it could easily be turned to see the next segment of your route and highlighted in a way that those very seeable terrain features and discernable objects were clearly marked and annotated. It was a good start to our introduction to this new aircraft and our need to know everything required to fly in them.

Lt. Anson did not mention it, but we actually did not immediately start flying the next morning, instead we were taken over to "Personal Equipment" to get a back-pack parachute fitted and assigned, this was a change from the "seat" pack we used in the T-6, along with our very first "brain bucket", the hard helmet that would be worn for all of our flights during "Basic Flight Training" and beyond I assumed. The six-striped sergeant who issued my chute was a grizzly veteran who as he was cinching and pulling the straps until I thought I was going to explode, looked at me and said, "I hope you never have to use this, but if you do you will really like the tight straps." He then took out the parachute information booklet from a small pocket on the upper left side, checked it and indicated unless I used the chute, it would be good through my graduation date. I smiled and said thanks. I walked into the next room where others were being fitted for their helmets. I waited until a two-striper motioned for me to sit in the chair in front of him. I did so as he started opening a large box and pulling out a very new white helmet, wrapped in cellophane. He started placing fitting elements in the helmet, first on the crown, then on the sides. Once finished, he put it on my head. He was quick to recognize he needed more padding on the sides and grabbed a couple of thin ones for the sides and one more for the back and pasted them on top of those already inside. Satisfied he put it back on my head. It felt firm enough and he was satisfied as he picked up another box and pulled out an oxygen mask with bayonet prongs on the side. He attached the left side to the helmet and told me to hold the little device on the bottom in to open the flap inside, so I could breathe while he adjusted everything. He attached the other side and started pulling the little straps until it was very snug on my face. Once satisfied, he started attaching the microphone to the side of the helmet and then plugged it in to a console in front of him. He asked if I could "read" him and I shook my head up and down to confirm. As I took off the helmet, I thanked him. He smiled and motioned to the next guy in line. Going through the fitting and installation of the padding for the helmet was even more time consuming, but necessary as the last thing you needed during a flight was an ill-fitted helmet. When finished and leaving the room we were given a new helmet bag to place it in. On the inside was a large pocket and on the outside another one. Wondering what we were supposed to place in these pockets didn't last too long as before we left, we were issued a set of flying gloves and another pair of sun-glasses. (We had received glasses and gloves during primary, but it was good to get new ones). We were also given another flight suit to go with the two we already had. They were somewhat stained and worn, but still wearable. We were told to bring in our flight suits to the parachute shop, where they would sew on our new squadron patch and for me my "brown bar" rank, plus stenciling a name tag to be placed on the left breast and another on our helmet bag. When finished we were told to walk back to the operation center and wait for our instructor to talk to us. I joined Clark and Fong at the table, but never saw Doug again that day. Released, we walked back to our barracks to prepare for an afternoon of Harris and Watson. Of course, after lunch, I was joined by Dugan, who talked about Herr Meining, his German instructor. We compared notes and I was pleased with who I had, despite his funny and quiet, stoic demeanor.

The flying began with an introductory flight, mainly to learn how to start the engine and follow the checklist items. All three of us stood on the wing and observed as Doug went through the starting engine checklist, showing us location and position of the handles, gages and buttons. They had all been an assignment for last night from Lt. Harris, familiarizing two pages dedicated to the forward instrument panel and the two side panels. Knowledge of those was a pre-requisite for flight. After going through a dry session Doug brought his long frame out of the front cockpit and crawled into the rear and Dick jumped in the front after placing his chute in the seat. Fong and I stepped out to act as fire guards while the engine was being started and found it wasn't necessary. There was an airman assigned to do that. We gratefully backed away and watched. A special mix of fuel is used, called AvGas, for non-jet engines and the exhaut created by the radial engine is a bit choking and has an acrid smell, unlike the distinct aroma of the JP-4 used in jet engines. I learned it was a high grade kerosene, not the gasoline we use in automobiles. We stayed through the engine start and the taxi out from the parking slot to the main taxiway, then they disappeared into a sashaying group of aircraft heading to the end of the runway. As aircraft took to the skies we lingered on the flight line, knowing we would join in the measured feeling that we were starting in a new phase of flight. The instructors were not much more experienced than we were, some had just graduated from the same program, their wings hardly out of their boxes and pinned on. We were no longer among WW II tested pilots, now we were stepping into aircraft with pilots with barely over 500 hours, more than half of that from their own training. It was a sobering moment, but then we regressed into our shells and waited our turn to test our flight skills in a new aircraft, shiny with tricycle gear, but I was already missing the yellow, tail dragger and my skilled instructors. I ducked back inside to grab my parachute, deciding I would wait outside for their return. It was a warm day and outside was better than looking at my dash-1 for the umpteenth time. Fong, his usual non-communicative self, stayed inside. I didn't have to wait long as Doug and Clark turned into the same spot they left, barely 45 minutes ago. The engine shut down as I walked to the right wing of the aircraft. Clark was removing his "brain-bucket" and had a satisfied smile on his face, then crawled out on the wing. I swung my chute up and joined him and proceeded to place my chute in the now vacant spot and crawled into this seemingly large cockpit, trying to survey all the instruments at once. It was mind-boggling. I was interrupted by a yell from the back seat to "plug-in". I strapped my helmet on, fastened my oxygen mask on and reached for the microphone cord, plugged it in to the helmet and heard the soft voice, telling me to read the "starting engine" checklist so we could get going. I looked out to see Clark was well clear of the aircraft, so I proceeded to go through the proper procedures and pushed the engine start button and the twin blade prop rotated and the noise came right through my new helmet.

I taxied out following the directions of the airman who was positioned in front of the aircraft. As I got on the taxiway I was the only aircraft and was moving right along, when Doug hit the brakes, thrusting me forward in the straps of the shoulder harness. He then said something to the effect that there was a limit to taxi speed. I adjusted the throttle and set the pitch of the prop for takeoff as I now dawdled along to the hammerhead. Once in place I was going through the "before takoff" checklist, saying each item as I performed them. Doug said nothing until Mobil Control cleared us for takeoff. As I pushed the throttle forward Dougs voice came over the interphone, telling me it would be a good idea to close the canopy, which I did. Nice way to start with a new instructor.

Doug flew with all three of us on a Thursday morning. Laredo is hot in the summer and it was August! Takeoff distance is affected by heat, but we were too dumb to realize or at least consider it. I found the aircraft heavy and powerful. Sitting in the front seat and seeing everything in front of you while taxiing and on takeoff was a delightful change. The pressure on the left rudder pedal on takeoff was a real challenge and the climb out was impressive. It was a definite step up from the T-6, however I missed the ability to open the canopy in flight. To do so in the T-28 would more than likely result in a very angry instructor and a bent vertical stabilizer. It was above all a student oriented aircraft. I was finding that my instructor was much like Pinky as he covered the basics and maybe a bit more, but was very into himself, saying little except what he felt was necessary. The new aircraft engine seemed more powerful than the engine on the T-6, which it is according to the Dash-1, at 800 horsepower it has almost twice the thrust potential of my little old training aircraft. The power was overwhelming. I was holding on as we pushed down the runway. Doug said nothing until I rotated for takeoff, but it was not a word it was pressure on the stick, cautioning me to not over-rotate, a cardinal sin, but once the gear settled into the well and I attained the proscribed climb speed, everything fell into place. Doug instructed me to turn south and level off at four thousand feet. I pulled the throttle back to settle on cruising speed, overran level off, but adjusted back to the right altitude. The surge of the aircraft surprised me as my slow adjustment of the power led to a spurt of speed that I didn't anticipate. I quickly pulled back on the throttle and found a niche to this new aircraft. Doug said, "I've got the aircraft" and I quickly removed my hands from the stick and off the throttle. Instantly I was upside down as he was doing an aileron roll and out of that came a split "S" as I was jammed back in the seat. Leveling off he said, "you can take it now." I was still trying to settle back to normal flight as he was telling me about maneuvers that I should anticipate doing on my solo flights to become acclimated to the T-28. He suggested I try a stall series, power on then power off, followed by a spin. The instinct of doing that series, taught by Pinky was instantaneous, and I started a steep climb, not touching the throttle until the shutter started and the right wing fell, now adding power with the nose down and bringing the wings level. I was born to do this! The stall was much more severe than the T-6, both power-on and power-off.

The spin to me was violent and recovery was a brute force effort to overcome the spin as the stick had to be held tightly and recovery had to be swift. The major change in the spin was to only do two turns, not the standard three in the T-6, as the aircraft tightens to an almost vertical position and is very difficult to recover. Also, unlike the T-6, if you let loose of the stick it would beat your legs to a pulp and just tighten up, whereas to release pressure in the docile yellow bullet, the aircraft would recover itself. I thought to myself that I didn't need to practice the spin anyway. Acrobatics were another thing as the introduction to the simple lazy eight and chandelles seemed more defined, and easier. The simple roll was not simple as the heaviness of the T-28 made each aspect of the roll more definite with the need for pressure to combat the torque of the engine, especially inverted. The nose seemed to be more prone to dive down. This was an 800 horse power engine. the Navy version was 1200 horsepower, so I can imagine their angst over doing basic maneuvers.

Doug talked me through the first landing and of course I wanted to keep the nose high on round-out. Without his pressure I might have drug the tail of the aircraft. It was a definitely different experience; this was a new aircraft! Once on the ground the need for rudder pressure to stay straight on the runway was not too great and was easy to manage, of course the throttle was in the idle position, so it made sense I just didn't anticipate it. Parking was easy as you could see directly ahead to follow directions of the crew chief in front of you. I could see Lieutenant Fong was waiting anxiously with his chute so unstrapped as I shut the engine down. I followed the checklist and exited the aircraft. Doug crawled out of his seat and said we needed fuel to continue with his desire to finish all of us today. He called the crew chief over and told me to go inside. I left and felt the heat of the Texas day as I put on my red "A" flight hat and headed to the flight shack. Entering I spied Dick Butterer sitting at a table. He and I spent time with Mr. Maxon at Malden so stopped to say hello. Married, I didn't have a chance to see him most of the time. He was chatting with a guy named Gerry Gable and both happened to be at the same table as Roland Ford. They were McNew's "Scotty Flight". Gerry was from Minnesota and although he was a bachelor, living in the same barracks I was, this was the first time I met him. He and Dick were talking about hunting, something I had little interest in, but my coming in from my first flight changed the subject. Neither had been up yet and were waiting for Roland to come back from his first ride with McNew. I told them I was impressed with the power of the airplane but didn't feel comfortable with the flying characteristics yet. Gerry asked some leading questions about flying in general as I must have given him the idea I was a bit apprehensive. He was insightful as I have had moments where I questioned my desire to be a pilot. I had a feeling I would become a good friend of his as he had a genuine set of characteristics I admired. After a few minutes their table mate, Roland and Lieutenant McNew walked in terminating our discussion. Funny how a discussion with someone tests your resolve to do something. I learned a bit about myself and was determined to complete this journey to become an Air Force Pilot.

I learned quickly about the T-28. It was not the "forgiving" aircraft the T-6 was. I became very adept at pattern activity, spending much of the dual time with Anson shooting landings. It was seldom we spent a great amount of time practicing the basic flight items I learned at Malden. We would do stalls and an occasional spin, a few acrobatic maneuvers, but mostly it was landing this new beast. In the first three flights in the T-28 I felt a need to never relax and to quote Pinky "stay ahead of the aircraft". We did enough acrobatics to know that in the spin it was all you could do to keep your knees from being whipped as the stick would gyrate round and round. You never wanted the T-28 to tighten the spin too much as it would be a dangerous situation that would lead to an unrecoverable one. Doug emphasized the recovery had to start early. I wasn't attempting to count turns as I had to do in the T-6. First and foremost, there were no section lines to count in southern Texas, it was only desert, so it was a matter of feel and when you could sense the tightening, you recovered. Again, I knew I would not have to practice spins as I was very confident, I could recover if I ever got into one unintentionally.

With all the practice I was able to overcome my tendency to keep the nose too high and did well on my landings. After the forth flight Doug told me my next flight would be a solo one. It would encompass three graded landings from mobile control after an overhead pattern entry, with pitchout to a downwind. This was a new concept for us to fly. On regular flights there would be no more 45-degree entry as on the first flight we were shown the pitchout as you came directly into the runway at higher than pattern altitude, pitched right or left to parallel the runway descending to downwind altitude and then level the wings momentarily and continuing a descending turn to base and final.

It was a fun approach to landing and expedited the flow to the final approach. The major difference for the solo flight was it was that after takeoff you climbed to altitude and practiced what you were taught, then came into the pattern and when you were to the pitchout point, declaring you were an "initial solo at pitch" student. That would key the mobile tower to observe your three full stop landings. When taking the active for this flight you would announce that you were an "initial solo". Doug need not be there to observe the landings and if not, he would get a report from whoever was in mobile control that day. That duty was rotated from instructor to instructor, when one of the other flight staff was not utilized. I had a feeling Anson would be in Mobil Control as I began to figure out his makeup and approach. His demeanor was not as casual as he tried to make it appear.

T-28 SOLO

I t was an afternoon flight, very hot and very humid with some plump clouds on the horizon. I walked out to my aircraft, accompanied by Doug, the hot breeze hitting me in the face and my new parachute clinging to my back, the straps were digging into my shoulders as the sweat was rolling down the knave of my back. It was a bit hazy from the humidity, but the visibility was good. Reaching the aircraft, I climbed up to the front cockpit, and placed my chute in the seat, then hopping down to check the aircraft 781 I felt overwhelmed. There were no red "X"s, and it had a full fuel load, it was obviously cleared to fly. I performed the walk around inspection and paused to remove my sweat filled baseball cap and shoved it in my bottom flight suit pocket before I got in. Doug, always silent, said nothing before I climbed in. I went through the before starting engine checklist while he watched. He stood on the wing as I cranked the engine and when it roared into power he exited and bid me well—silently with a nod. I felt confident, still I was very nervous, but not as much as I had been in primary with the PA-18 and the T-6. I closed the canopy and turned out to the main taxiway, now feeling the welcome cool air filling the confines of the cockpit. I casually looked around and was caught with the amount of activity going on, other aircraft moving, crew chiefs directing traffic, bread trucks attending to needs and none really concerned about my solo. It was only me I realized as I taxied slowly to the end of the runway. Upon reaching the hammerhead I was number two for takeoff. I set the brakes and watched the T-28 in front of me take the active as I went through the before takeoff checklist. A voice filled my helmet," shotgun student you are cleared on the active and hold" and as I rolled on the end of the runway, I announced I was an "initial solo". There was no response, but finally "runway aircraft, you are cleared for takeoff." I was cleared to takeoff! The thought filled my mind, alone? I applied power and carefully pressed on the left rudder pedal to compensate for the surge. I was right on center-line and released brakes. I rolled a bit farther than I had anticipated, but later remembered it was at the hottest point of the day and I had a full fuel load. Feeling the freedom of runway friction, I was airborne, I put the gear handle in the up position and watched the green lights come on. I started the flaps, milking them to the zero- degree level and started my climb straight ahead, then I initiated a right turn to the south to get free of the traffic pattern. It was like a runaway train as I pulled the nose up to maintain the dash-1 climbing airspeed. I still had the idea it was safer closer to the ground, so I leveled off at around five thousand feet. I was not about to do stalls yet and I had told myself I wasn't about to or did I have a need to practice a spin so I was limited to tooling around to kill time and burn fuel. Simple acrobatics were something I could do so started with an aileron roll. That went well and so tried another, then I decided to do a lazy eight and proceeded to do an elongated eight across the horizon. Pinky would have laughed at how flat it was! I decided to do a chandelle, Oh, that was better! I kept the nose in the right attitude, climbing and turning position as I rolled out after 180 degrees. I was intrigued with the desert around Laredo. There really wasn't much around the two border towns so I ventured southeast, trying to pick out anything that wasn't brown. I did a few steep turns surveying what was below, essentially nothing. Finally, my thoughts went to entering the pattern for the pitch pattern for the first full stop landing, so I turned back toward the base. I wished I could open the canopy! I had killed about 35 minutes and it would take about another ten to get back in position for entry. I ventured back in a smooth thirty-degree bank as I didn't want to overdo anything. I would learn later it was more fun to make those turns steep, to the extent you could feel the pressure in your gut. Those fat clouds had grown some but didn't seem to be an immediate problem. The haze from the heat, combined with a slight wind raising dust was masking much of the visibility, but finally the runway came into view. I positioned myself for the pitchout pattern, lining up down the runway. I checked my airspeed and it was good. I hit the end of the runway as I called "initial solo". Putting what I thought was a good steep turn as I looked to see if there was any traffic close to me. As I finished the turn to downwind I heard a call aimed at "the initial solo", "breakout and reenter the pattern". I added power and started a climb back to traffic altitude as I heard Doug's voice "That was a candy-ass turn"! My perceived bank was not acceptable, and it was taken as non-aggressive enough for a single engine pilot. I ventured back to the proper overhead altitude and positioned myself inbound to the pitch point. I was now very uncomfortable as I knew that Doug and everyone who heard the breakout call would be watching. As I crossed the approach end of the runway I paused and then yanked the stick into a left turn. I knew I went beyond forty-five degrees and I felt the pull on my body throughout the turn. My vision dimmed for a moment, but I was grunting to stay visually alert. As I rolled out, I heard what I thought was a clapping sound. If there was anyone in front of me, I couldn't see them as I had partially greyed out, but I was level on downwind and it was time to lower the gear and start the flaps. Gear down, in the green as I continued my turn onto the base leg. It was obvious I would have to keep this turn tight due to my pitch. There was not going to be a momentary rollout and I just continued the turn to final. The final approach in the T-28 was so much different as it was steeper and then suddenly, quicker than you think, you are in the round-out so flat as you could see all of the runway in front of you, a floating sensation and then touchdown. The screech of the tires as they touched down let you know you have arrived and now bringing the power to idle. I rolled to the first available taxiway to exit the runway and start back to takeoff for the second landing. I stopped at the "hammerhead" and called "initial solo" again and was told I was number one, but to hold for traffic on final. I looked out to see a T-33 coming in followed by a T-28 not too far behind him. I decided to open the canopy. Mistake! It was so blinking hot outside and the aircraft had been cool, despite the sweat I had built up and suddenly it was like a furnace. I quickly closed the canopy, but the damage was done. I would have to sit and wait for the air-conditioned cockpit to return. I had to wait through three aircraft on final, but finally was cleared for takeoff. As the power came up I could feel the cool air rejuvenating the climate in the cockpit. I would be in a closed pattern, so would fly the normal pattern at 1200 feet. Once off the ground I raised the gear and set the flaps. I turned downwind and flew the normal pattern and made my second landing. It was good and I was happy with my turn to final, I was able to go wings level for an instant to see the runway. I went through the same routine for my third landing and was lucky as I did not have to wait on the hammerhead, having been cleared as I approached the runway for the third takeoff. Flying the last pattern, I had a great feeling of being alone and liking it. Everything went well and by the checklist. The last two approach and landings were the best and I felt very good as I taxied back to park.

It wasn't relief it was something else, but I was happy I would not have to be an "initial" anything for a while. Funny, I didn't notice anything on the return to the parking slot, except what was in front of me. After engine shutdown I crawled out as I saw Doug and Dick Clark walking to an aircraft for a dual ride. He couldn't possibly have seen my last two landings! Dick smiled as he thrust a "thumbs up" and Doug sort of waved. "Fame is a fleeting thing", but I had soloed the T-28!

FORMATION FLIGHT

My dual proficiency rides with Doug were few, as I spent over half of my flying time as a solo pilot. I did get to the point where in the dual rides I loved flying formation. When first introduced to flying on the wing of another aircraft I was surprised at how exhausting it was. Trying to hold a position using one item on another aircraft as your key point to maintain position and both aircraft being subjected to turbulence, minor movements of the lead aircraft and your own jittery hand is the most sweat producing flying I had experienced. Once dual qualified I spent flights in a solo wing position. It was fun, but it was also tedious work. The T-28 was a stable platform and once engaged it was a matter of concentration on position. You had little concept of the difference between straight and level and turns and after over ten or fifteen minutes involved in that close quarter flight you were completely drained. On one memorable ride as a solo I was flying the wing of Anson and Fong as the lead and Clark and a Lieutenant Jim Hudson, a solo student from "Doulphin" Flight, in a four ship. We had taken off about a minute apart from the base and our join up was catching Anson and Fong who started a slight turn to the south and each of us would increase our angle of bank until we were all in position. As the number four I had the steepest angle of bank and had to really move out to gain position. Once slotted on the left wing of the lead, as two and three were on their right wing, we started our climb to a safe altitude. Once level Doug directed me to change over into the right wing, making the formation an echelon right. This would be a position when arriving back to land we would be in for the pitchout to land. Doug, then had number two, Dick Clark to take the lead and he and Fong, who was having some problems with formation flying, would drop back to number four, making me number three. Clark assumed the lead and Doug now wanted Hudson to drop over to the left wing and resume a "finger-tip" formation. It was the first time I was sandwiched between two aircraft, so any moves lead would make I had to try to not deviate as it would have an adverse effect on poor Fong trying to hold position. To make it worse there was just enough rough air to make us bounce a bit. With a helmet full of rivulets of water, now escaping down into my oxygen mask I was becoming more aware of the conversation going on in the open mike between Doug and Fong. Trying as I might I was almost reacting to Doug's directions to Fong, making my position moves from the platform Clark was flying almost counter to what I should be doing. Fortunately, after what seemed like a long time Doug called out to "go loose", meaning we would drop back a bit in order to relax. After the return of feeling back in my arms I was instructed to take the lead and Clark was to assume the four position. Clark dropped down and I saw him pass below me. I was now the lead and thinking this would be good I heard Doug instruct everyone to pull in tight. Now back in "finger-tip" mode

I was the object of the others attention. Doug told me to turn back toward the base and what is common in formation flying, everything must be done slowly and gently and now knowing I'm the only one with forward vision I would have to make sure I was clearing the area ahead for the turn. Looking down to my compass and direction finder I slowly initiated a gentle bank toward the station, trying to keep the pressure on the stick constant. Picking up the heading back I called a roll out on heading to the base. This was the most tedious thing about the flight, as I knew they were all tucked in and very close to my aircraft. Once level, Doug called for another position change. I was to fall back to number four, He and Fong assuming the lead again, bringing us back to our starting positions. He then placed us into echelon right, preparing for our entry into the pattern. I looked at the entire formation as we approached the initial and saw a very tight group and waited for the first aircraft to start his pitch. In order we would start our turn as we saw the belly of the aircraft in front of us. Once completing the one-eighty degree turn to downwind, gear would come down and wait for the aircraft in front of you to turn base leg. After that turn, flaps would start and then the turn to final, now in trail for landing. Always anticipating "prop-turbulence", you made sure that your wings came level as you touched down, rolling out and turning off the runway we taxied back to our parking slots. I learned my lesson in this Texas heat and left the canopy closed making the most of the few air-conditioned moments until I shut the engine down. I would most definitely need to start tomorrow with a fresh flight suit. In the debrief, Anson seemed pleased, but didn't get euphoric. He spent most of his time talking about the changes we made in position and cautioned us that there was no hurry to make those changes and once done to tuck it in.

I was ready for a trip to the "White House" for a big steak and a pitcher of beer. I would have no trouble finding someone to go with me. It was Friday and there would be no trouble talking Dugan into going. Lieutenant Hudson excused himself and he returned to his group. It was then I noticed Doug had cornered Fong and was talking to him. I was not in a position to ever see Fong in a particular slot as he was always behind my position, so wondered how that was going.

It was an eventful evening as four of us went to the steak house for dinner. Dugan found Kelly, who had just returned from academics, when we got back to the barracks and I had enlisted Gerry Gable to go, so after a shower and changing into clean clothes we all jumped into my 1954 Ford Victoria, drove into the outskirts of Laredo and arrived at the White House. After being directed to a table, covered with a red and white checkered table cloth and four place settings, which included a large steak knife we ordered a large pitcher of beer. The waiter wanted to know if anyone was interested in their large (24 ounces) steak. If you finished the entire steak it was free. Dugan decided he was going to order that steak, the rest of us ordered steak, but something we knew we could finish. I think Dugan's mistake was having a baked potato and a salad as he could not finish that large piece of meat. He was literally down to the last two or three bites and just couldn't finish it off. Of course, he was drinking beer with the rest of us, but not too much. The suggestion was made to go over the border to Nuevo Laredo, seemed like a good idea so we left and took the 15-minute drive to the border. I parked in a safe parking lot on the U.S. side. It was one where there was an attendant and for a small fee, he would make sure your car was not bothered. It was still early, maybe nine or nine thirty, with still a hint of light as we crossed over the bridge to the Mexico side. There was a pedestrian gate at the end of the bridge with a uniformed individual standing there. We all took out our Air Force IDs and flashed it at him as he opened the gate and smiled as we passed by but said nothing. I had been to Tijuana a few times, so was not surprised at the streets of Nuevo Laredo. Once in town there were a lot of kids pimping, soliciting and others begging from the "gringos". There were many road side stalls with different kinds of items for sale, some just trinkets, others some apparently nice pieces of clothing and blankets. We strolled along and spotted a cantina and decided to walk in. We were hit with some loud, but entertaining "Flamenco" brass being played and an almost empty bar. We ordered a cerveza from an English-speaking bartender, who asked if we were from the base, funny how we stand out. He said there had been a few more from the base in earlier and indicated this was the place to have a good time, good music and girls. The music was catchy and somewhat fun to watch the group of five, dressed in traditional Mexican dress playing trumpets, but loud wasn't a fit description. After one cerveza we left and went back across the bridge, knowing we would come back. The car was found unscathed and we returned to the base, ready for the quiet and relaxation of a weekend.

Anson was a good pilot and a quiet instructor, never getting excited about anything in the air. He would get frustrated from time to time and with me he found an area that caused him some grief, as I had some difficulty with the loss of engine emergency landing procedure. He would demonstrate this procedure on almost every dual ride after our first four or five rides. It was all about hitting the "high Key and executing a couple of 360 and lining up on the runway without power. I was either too long our too short. It finally clicked enough for him to feel I could do it properly, but I knew he felt uneasy with me on that procedure. In most dual rides he seemed very satisfied when I would demonstrate an ability to perform all the required acrobatic maneuvers, plus the stalls and spin. There was no secret to becoming efficient in the simple acrobatic work as the horizon was the key. You used it to measure any roll. The barrel-roll being the most difficult to do well, as you wanted to etch a perfect circle on the horizon, half below and half above on both halves of the eight. I would always start with a diving turn to the left and then bring the nose up, while turning to the right, inverted at the top of the roll and continuing pressure on the stick, remembering that on top pressure on the stick was reversed. Forward pressure kept the nose up, otherwise you would fall out and make a loose circle. Continue the roll until you come below the horizon, pulling up to complete the circle and not giving away any altitude. The other rolls were very easy. It was a problem doing the Immelmann well, but it was really only a half loop, rolling wings level at the top, completing a 180-degree turn. The problem was on roll out and ending up with a perfect change in heading of that 180 degrees. It took a smooth roll out. The "Lazy Eight" you just painted the eight on the horizon, making sure it wasn't flat. Chandelles were sort of half of the barrel roll, going inverted at the top and rolling out, going the opposite direction. It was fun and especially playing with the tightness of the half loop. Doug had said a sure way to get someone off your tail was to keep it very tight and do it in the clouds. I had been taught well how to stall an aircraft and recover from them. After a series on my first and maybe the second dual rides Doug never asked me to do another series. I didn't need to be reminded of the need to recover from a spin quickly as I had experienced the tightening spin too many times and the concept of counting turns was not employed at any time. It was if you were in one you recovered quickly! Doug did insist that we do one each ride. Because of the severe warnings of stall in the aircraft it was easy to recover, just be aggressive, stay away from the spin!

INSTRUMENT TRAINING

I spent nine hours doing instrument training trying to hone the skills I had learned in the T-6. I had little trouble flying under the hood and rather enjoyed it. I was a good instrument pilot and was told so by Doug, when he was in the mood to speak. There was more than a couple of hours spent in the simulators in the instrument training building doing homing and tracking solutions. After an hour in the "box", you have had enough, but it was the first time I did penetrations and holding patterns, so it was a way to know what you were supposed to do when in the air. Also, the "box" could be "frozen" to discuss mistakes. When everything stopped the top would come up and the first words out of Doug were usually "do you know what you did or where you are?" He would bring me back to the point where the mistake was made so I could do it right. Because of those training sessions I had no trouble passing a check ride in instrument flying. Unlike primary, the check rides were given by your instructor. Doug said nothing other than "you passed" and filled out the sheet for me to sign.

THE AIRPLANE

I learned to not particularly bond to the T-28. I always felt it was heavy. It was an easy pattern flying aircraft, very responsive and easy to land. In the air it didn't have that easy feel of the T-6. I never had a mechanical problem with the Tango-6, but on more than one occasion I had oil leakage across the cockpit wind screen in the T-28. I t was very disconcerting to say the least and detracted me from trying to work on various items during a flight and it always resulted in a single approach and landing. It did limit what you could do on a training flight. You did not declare an emergency, but when you did inform them of impaired forward vision, they would tell you to fly till you felt compromised as they wanted you to get the required flying time. On the other hand, flying in formation was one way to not waste the flying experience of a solo ride as you just tucked in to the other ship's lineup points and stayed locked in. Looking at an angle right or left kept you from looking at the oil, sloppily running across your windscreen and up, over the canopy, then when finished with the formation activity a single pitchout and turn to final was all you needed to do. You would be peeking around the rivulets and spots as they gather together to destroy a clear view of the runway ahead. It was called a "cross-control" landing. It's handy to know how to land that way, however, you don't want to push your luck! Sometimes the bounce you endured smoothed the blurred view ahead and allowed for the next landing to be better. Fuel leaks also happened frequently, and they were the cause of many students losing valuable practice time. Most of the leaks were from the cap on the wing tanks not being closed properly and did not result in the loss of a large amount of fuel, just a disconcerting view of it running off the wing. They would always caution you to not do any extreme maneuvers as the cap might fly off and the fuel in the wing would then "cavate", which could result in a real emergency. A good walk-around pre-flight would preclude a fuel cap problem. I was looking forward to stepping into the T-33.

GOING ON TO THE T-33

The dual activity would end with a flight with another instructor whose task was to see if you could fly the airplane. It didn't have the feel of a check ride, but it was intended only to affirm that your instructor covered all the necessary phases of flight in the T-28. I flew my ride with a good friend of Doug's, named Lieutenant Polly Ibatuan. He also was quiet and seemed preoccupied as we went through all of the basic maneuvers and returned to the field to shoot a couple of landing, including one touch and go, where you had to be aware of the torque when adding power. All had gone well I thought as he had been noncommittal on everything up to now, when all of a sudden he remembered something Doug had passed on about me. He was told I was a bit weak on engine-out landings and approach. He proceeded to fly to the base and when in sight of the runway. Polly said as he pulled the throttle to idle, "engine out". He told me to hit what was called a high key! I should have remembered! My airspeed was faster than I liked for where I was at but managed to find a spot above the runway to start this emergency procedure. From the high key you would spiral down to the runway in two full turns. The start point (high key) was at a higher altitude than the initial approach fix. With the engine in idle and the aircraft clean (gear and flaps up) you would start from a point basically over the approach end of the runway and initiate a gentle, maybe thirty-degree angle of bank turn. It was intended to be a two full 360 degree turns, but you could adjust depending on your altitude. You could gauge the angle of bank to coincide with your need to increase or decrease the rate of turn to insure you were not too high or too low when turning final as there was no "go-around" with a dead engine so that approach had to be on the button. A short approach is obviously not a good thing and a long approach can be salvaged if not too long by bleeding off airspeed, slipping the aircraft to lose altitude, but you may blow out a tire or two or end up with "hot brakes" which could end up destroying the aircraft. The "too long" approach would mean the aircraft would be destroyed at the other end of the runway and you may not survive the ending. After turning away from the approach end of the runway, I waited until I could see the runway again and decided I was a bit "hot" so I would extend out a bit before continuing the turn. I was also too close to the runway, so I adjusted my bird from the runway and then continued into another turn. I rolled out closely aligned with the runway and started my last 360 degree turn, which was going to have to be good. After the first half I peeked to my left and saw the runway. I was still a bit "hot", but I liked my position and I could bleed the airspeed using the gear and flaps when I hit the limit speed for both. Hitting the gear limits, I dropped the gear and continued my turn and came over a "low key" as my flaps were coming down. I rolled out about 300 feet, flaps and gear in the green. It would have been a successful landing, but Polly added power and told me to go around. I would have touched down in the first five hundred to a thousand feet and Polly knew it. We didn't have to do another and instead reentered the pattern and shot an overhead with the touch and go, followed by a full stop landing. The debriefing was quick, but I gathered I did OK. He would probably have more to say to Doug over a beer in Nuevo Laredo, where I understand they went quite often.

ACADEMICS

Classes were very much a part of our daily regimen and they provided an array of things which we had to have knowledge of in order to fly an aircraft in the world we live in. We had many tedious classes, but the one I least enjoyed was learning "Morse Code". Trying to learn the alphabet in dit's and da's took great concentration and it was necessary as it was more than just knowing the difference between an "A" and an "N", which were needed to distinguish the "aural null" of a radio station in the "Adcock" range, during instrument flight, but also every station has an identifier that you had to know one from the other as you navigate the skies. They are three characters so to know a San Antonio from a Dallas, you had to be able to tell a SAN from a DAL which would be broadcast in "morse" code as you fine-tuned your VHF (very high frequency) radio for a station. After a while listening to various tapes with headphones on in class, you became good at picking up the letters as they were being broadcast. Practice made it somewhat easy, but it took a while to get the hang of what you need to know. Another interesting class, one taught by Captain Simler, was celestial navigation. We had star identification classes and used pointer systems to find identifiable stars. Before these classes I think I was aware of the north star as a constant, but little else. It was late in September and we were going out before dawn and picking up the planet Venus as it rose in the east. At night we were introduced to the "belt of Orion" And its major stars Rigel and Betelgeuse and best of all and easy to find was the brightest star Sirius, which was the anchor of the arc of Capella. There was a set up outside of the academic building where we could insert a sextant and given information to locate certain stars and come up with a three-star fix of our position. It was very interesting and even though the nights were cool it was our first foray into the mysteries of the sky. We also had more classes on weather delivered by Captain Litzenberger, who was able to keep our attention with his great photos of massive thunderheads, the "anvils", very obvious and foreboding. His words of advice stuck with us as "you may fly into a thunderstorm, but you won't fly out" and we all agreed we had come to a point where we now had a feel for weather conditions that effected flight and could cause serious consequences if not heeded. Frontal recognition and certain warning signs were addressed that we now felt we could recognize and take appropriate action. Lieutenant Stewart taught flight operations, where we learned how to file a flight plan and the use of various flight manuals, that is if we ever graduate and get our wings. Most classes were very educational, and the instructors were interesting and knowledgeable, but classes every day sort of wore on us. There was no end to them!

THE LAST T-28 SOLO

I t was the day after the loss of a T-33 that lost its left tip tank on a pitchout turn to downwind. The skidding, turning and then spiraling aircraft will long have a place in my memory bank. The slow revolving spin, followed by the black smoke rising in the air signaling a funeral pyre of sorts after it smashed into the ground, taking an instructor and soon-to-graduate student to their deaths has left me and my fellow students about to start our jet training in the same type of training bird, stunned and our confidence in going forward shattered. A second lieutenant's pay is not what you would call a great amount, but $341 a month is a lot more than I made while going to college, despite working almost full time at my brother-in-law's gas station, but $100 of that was flight pay and despite free lodging and meals, that additional money found ways to disappear from my wallet. I would push myself to be a pilot, despite the memory of that spiral into the ground.

Today was a day just like yesterday, a very hot September day with a swirling dry desert breeze that shifted the wind-sock thirty degrees left and right of the runway. Doug had walked to the edge of the ramp and this time he was talking, more of a pep talk than a flight talk. Very unusual for him! He said he did not know the instructor that "bought the farm". (Air Force parlance) He was not concerned with my psyche as much as he was about the need to keep my head out of my ass and you guessed it "stay ahead of the aircraft". We both looked at the 781, the maintenance history of the aircraft and saw it was in flight shape, no red crosses. I noticed it had been written up on the last flight for an oil leak. I asked the crew chief about it and he confidently told me that he found the problem and fixed it. The follow-on test had been multiple engine run-ups to full power for extended periods of time and there was not a repeat of the problem. Of course, it had been signed off by the maintenance supervisor. I gave the loose-leaf back to the crew chief and he stowed it in the cockpit. I checked the back seat to be sure everything was stowed, and the harness and lap belt were fastened together so they would not flop around during flight. I completed the walk around and found the aircraft very clean. Doug stood by as I started the two bladed prop engine (the Navy has a three bladed prop) and as the large puff of smoke filtered away, disappearing almost immediately. I saw Doug slowly backing away, looking a bit concerned and allowing me to turn out of the parking spot. I closed the canopy and hoped the air conditioning would kick in soon even though the power was such to merely sustain taxi speed not induce cool air. There were a string of T-33s going out for takeoff, many, I had been told to complete their final check before getting their wings this Saturday. This graduating class had lost three students due to T-33 crashes. Two of those this last week, the other one was at the beginning of their transition into the "Jet" phase of training. I wondered what was going through their minds. The entire class had been made up of 1955 West Point graduates. I watched as one after the other took the active and started down the runway, spewing the swirling vapor trail of the jet engine as they took to the sky. All gently turned right out of traffic and disappeared in the haze of the desert day. I taxied into the number one position on the hammerhead and called out the aircraft identification and "solo student". "Roger that" was the reply. "You are cleared to take the active and hold". I turned to get on the centerline, brought the power to idle and stood on the brakes. "Shotgun Solo you are cleared for takeoff" came over my headset. I started adding power and pressing on the left rudder pedal, while watching the center line and releasing brakes. At full power I felt the surge of adrenalin when accelerating the aircraft down the runway. It's a great feeling, one of elation, but it was filled with caution. I glanced momentarily at my flight instruments, passing the "no-go" speed and then feeling the need to apply back pressure to the stick I was hitting take-off speed. The shallow climb was enhanced by the raising of the gear and the starting of the flaps to the full up position. Raising the flaps always causes a slight sinking feeling, but once having a clean aircraft, the rate of climb indicator becomes a matter of attention and then the climbing attitude becomes very obvious. Everything was in the green as I started my turn to exit the pattern and looking at the empty and brown ground below me. I was very aware that the air was full of individuals doing what I was doing, flying solo and looking for space to spend time safely. The climb was uneventful and suddenly I felt very alone. There was only the sound of the engine and of wind flowing over the canopy. The radio was silent.

Sometimes this feeling is one of elation at accomplishing a goal, but today it was more of an attitude of maybe I don't belong as a pilot. A semblance of that knawing, insidious fear arose, and I didn't like it. I have felt it before and promptly remembered getting back safely was my sole responsibility. No one was going to help me. I remembered Dick Coyle in primary, listening to his hyperventilated voice. I held my breath to make sure I wasn't doing the same. I was in the acrobatic area right now and leveled off, stopping the climb at about five thousand feet. I pulled back the throttle and maintained a speed of two hundred and fifty knots. I realized I had my head in the cockpit and should be checking outside for the traffic of other trainers in the area. The T-33s would be much higher, but most acrobatics was done at the four to eight-thousand-foot level for the T-28. I was beginning to collect myself, but still had a strange feeling about what I was doing. I had to take my mind off the negative sensation of not really being there. Was I having a physical problem?

Too much thinking I needed to do something. I decide to climb to a higher altitude and so started a chandelle to the right. Why did I always go to the right? I thought, who cares? But continued in my climbing turn in that direction. It was a good maneuver as I leveled off at seven thousand feet. Feeling better I started a basic roll to the left, fighting the nose to keep it on a point of a cloud I spied as I started the roll. After rolling out well off the point I did one to the right. It was better, but not good. By now I was hearing some radio transmissions, most were of the normal level, but one was from an instructor in a T-33 asking for clearance to land straight ahead as he had a tip tank that was not feeding and didn't want an overhead pitch pattern. The memory of that spinning aircraft yesterday more than likely influenced his request. I was still trying to do an adequate roll when my windscreen showed black spots accumulating. I leveled the wings and then pulled back the throttle to see if that would stop the oil spitting from the cowl in front of me. As I added power to maintain altitude there was more oil coming back and now my windscreen looked like a surrealist painting. I could see ahead, but it was disconcerting! I called mobile control and told them of my problem and requested a return to the base to land. They asked a couple of mundane questions, the last convincing them I didn't have a steady stream of oil, but "merely" a minor leak and they told me to continue the flight. I never knew there was anything leaking that was considered minor. Perplexed by their answer I asked them if there were any activities I should not attempt. The response was nothing was prohibited on a solo flight so proceed as planned. I realized I didn't have a plan, but I would work on controlled climbs and dives and set as a limit a thousand feet up and down. In every climb the spray of oil was apparent and in the dive the airflow would spread the oil across the windscreen in a different prosaic giving me a sort of strange entertainment. I continued this process until I couldn't make out anything forward and the oil was now spilling off to the right and left of the cockpit. I had the designated flying time for the period finally, so entered the overhead calling out my solo status, but didn't mention I could not see out of the windscreen. As I pitched and looking at the ground below I decide I would do better just flying altitude and airspeed for the pattern and not looking forward except to peek out on final to see what I had to see. The wind was not down the runway and was about thirty degrees off the nose so I could crab on final and look out from the left of the cockpit and see the runway. As I rolled out on final, I could make out the runway and as I started to drift to the left, using my rudder pedal I put a slight crab in and could see fairly well out of the corner of the cockpit all the way down final approach. I rounded out and landed without a problem. I did employ a series of S turns to the parking slot and when parking I could see the troubled face of the crew chief as he signaled me to cut the engine. I spent a bit of time filling out the 781, making sure to give them time in the air before the leak occurred and describing the severity of the problem. He asked me one question before I left and that was why I hadn't landed when it first occurred, and I told him I was refused clearance to come back and land. He was wiping off the windscreen as I left. I was happy to have seen the last of not just that one, but the T-28 as a training aircraft. Doug was not in the flight shack when I walked in. One of the other instructors said he would be back shortly. He showed up about ten minutes later, walked right over to me and asked why I hadn't done a straight in approach, which would have forced me to ask permission to do that from the mobile tower. I told him the story about being denied clearance to return early. The crew chief had seen him when he was walking back to the shack and told him about the windscreen. He shook his head and swallowed whatever he was going to say, then told me that in the future to declare an emergency, call a "Mayday". That would leave them with no decision as that is a statement that has to be acknowledged. As a student pilot there was one thing I didn't want to happen and that was to call attention to myself, an emergency declaration would have certainly done that. If a simple oil leak was found to be the cause I would be guilty of a "cry-wolf" syndrome.

THE JET EXPERIENCE

Watching the T-33 as a student flying the T-28 you can think flying a jet aircraft is not a big deal, but it is! The transition is dramatic, however mental as well as they are very different! Everything happens quicker and mistakes can be fatal. You will see there are many changes that you need to gather in very quickly. The engine is simpler as you are not concerned about mixture and your prop functions. The primary engine instrument is the EGT (Exhaust Gas Temperature) gage. It's a simple instrument but has many functions. You combine that with the RPM (Revolutions Per Minute) gage to start your engine. Lack of EGT is a flameout which equals no power. That equates to that stationary prop I experienced in Primary. A bad thing! Also, there in an EGT reading outside the normal range (green). Anything above green is serious. Red says there is a fire in the engine, also bad! You must shut the engine down, very bad! In pre-flighting a T-28 you can readily see a potential problem on the engine as you will see signs of oil or other obvious indications that the engine is of dubious condition. You see nothing in a jet engine, however there is one check that will immediately cancel your flight. This critical item in the aircraft is called the plenum chamber. It was located right aft of the cockpit and was viewed by pressing open a small access panel. It was a must check item on the walk around during preflight. It was a simple check as all you had to do was to make sure there was no sign of fuel in the area. It was the top of the engine and it had a sort of a circle segment on the top of the engine that was about a half inch raised off the engine itself. There were a series of small bolt heads around it and it had to be perfectly dry. Fuel flowed through that area to the engine and there could be zero leakage. Unlike the T-28 and its fine taxi characteristics the T-33 had a small problem when you started to taxi as the nose wheel was prone to cock if you didn't start your taxi straight ahead. Don't anticipate the first turn until you were rolling! It was more of an embarrassment than anything else as you needed ground assistance to unlock the wheel. But a more important item about the T-33 was that you had to get used to the absence of torque from the engine. No prop, no torque! These were some small items that the Engineering classes for the T-33, taught by Lieutenant Turpin did not cover, but they were among the first items Anson talked about before we even saw up close the aircraft. I loved the smell of the fumes of JP-4, the kerosene jet fuel used in all training T-33s. As I said before it was an aroma that every pilot is attracted to and felt its close association to flying. It is the standard fuel for almost all jet engines.

There were different reactions to flight situations in the Jet-T-33, from prop driven aircraft. You were more sensitive to a stall in the T-33, the warning was quicker to establish itself and had to be controlled immediately. There was no spin demonstration in the T-33 and in fact there was almost no recovery from a spin in the T-33, as almost any input while in a spin could possibly invert the aircraft and make it uncontrollable. An inverted spin was supposedly unrecoverable. The emergency reaction to an inverted spin was to eject! The T-33 also had a speed limitation that if exceeded would result in a high-speed buffet and could, given the right circumstances place you in a "coffin-corner" situation where there is a small airspeed difference between a stall and a high-speed buffet and recovery depends on where you are in that limited speed difference. Recovery must be swift, or you will lose an aircraft. I forgot to mention two things that signaled the large step you were taking as the pilots were sitting in explosive ejection seats that were used to exit the aircraft in the event of a necessary with-drawl from an uncontrolled event. It was now standard procedure to use a helmet throughout the duration of the flight in the T-33. In the T-28, there were times on low altitude work we could fly with our ball caps and a head-set microphone. There was a pin inserted into the seat with a red flag attached to it that "Safed" the seat while on the ground. The removal of the "pin" from the seat before flight signaled you were sitting on a "hot" seat. You showed the pin to the crew chief before taxiing. If a situation arose in flight where you had to leave the comfort of the aircraft, you could exit by pulling up on the handle of the seat and you would be on a vertical flight away from the aircraft. You would kick away the seat at the top of the exit arc and pull the cord to get a life-saving chute at lower altitudes. If you were above 14,000 feet, you would free fall and the chute would open automatically at the 14,000 level. The parachute was only good above a thousand feet as below that the chute would not open enough to salvage the attempt to survive. (In a matter of five years new technology had seen the advanced "Zero-Zero" chutes, which would blossom on the ramp at zero airspeed—That technology would have saved the pilots in the T-33 that lost the tip-tank on the overhead break.)

THE ALTITUDE CHAMBER RIDE

One requirement that was necessary before the start of the T-33 flights was an altitude chamber ride. It would be our first experience at flight above an altitude where we would suffer from "hypoxia" or lack of oxygen as most of our flights up to now had been eight thousand feet or below. It was with some anticipation we approached yet another obstacle to completing our training. The Physiological Training instructors, Captain Deneau and Lieutenant Kaiser had spent the greater part of a week preparing us for this adventure. The chamber would take us to an altitude that would require oxygen to fly un-impaired. They would tell us to take off our oxygen masks and have us perform simple tasks, like counting cards, identifying simple objects or merely asking us simple questions, like when was your birthday. There was a time element involved to make sure we could recognize our individual symptoms of hypoxia and to test our personal tolerance to a lack of oxygen. You could put your mask back on yourself if you felt impaired or if they recognized you were in some type of difficulty, they would reattach your mask for you. After everyone was back on oxygen, they would spend some time taking us to a higher altitude, usually around 25,000 feet pressure altitude and spend a certain amount of time there and then tell us they were going to decompress the chamber. They told us there would be a cloud like atmosphere that would occur. The decompression would come while we had our masks unattached. Our procedure was to reattach our masks quickly and wait for the fog in the chamber to disappear. They would then take the chamber down to a safe altitude. All this was to take place in the days before we started our flying in the T-Bird.

The Chamber itself was in a separate building. There was to be three sessions, with each group consisting of 12-14 students. I was in the first group alphabetically and so was to report to that building at 0800 hours. Dugan, of course was in the same group as was another good friend I had made at Laredo, Bobby Dantzler. He was a southerner through and through from Hickory, North Carolina and had a twang that resonated, especially when he would talk about one of his flights. He was slight in build and indicated to us he was not athletic. He walked with an assurance of who he was and was fun to be around. As we gathered inside the door of the chamber building, all in our flight suits, carrying our helmets in the bag we were given, we were ushered directly into this long circular chamber with bench-type seating along both sides. It looked like you could comfortably fit eight people on each side. We were told to take a seat and take out our helmets and attach the oxygen hose at each of the sitting positions to the outlet at the position you were sitting in. Once attached we were given a simple briefing on what was to occur, covering basically all that we had learned in our initial briefings and how to react to each situation. We then put on our helmets and attached a microphone cord as all transmissions would now be through that method. There was a consul outside the chamber where Captain Deneau along with two others I had never seen before were sitting and observing the inside through a very thick window. There were two enlisted technicians inside, plus Lieutenant Kaiser. Once "plugged" in the voice I heard was that of Captain Deneau. The chamber outer door was then slammed shut and we were talked through the altitude the chamber was going through, until we "leveled off" at 18,000 feet. They were constantly checking our masks to see if they were fitted properly and the captain would ask if everyone was feeling OK. We had numbered positions, so the voice would come over and ask if number so and so was having a problem. They had advised us to not answer directly, but to merely nod our head, yes or no when asked a question. Satisfied we were all tolerating the altitude they started increasing the altitude, stopping at 21,000 feet. After going through more inquiries about how we felt, they seemed satisfied and starting a clock they told us to un-attach our masks. Doing so I looked around and was peering into Dantzler's face. It was vacuum like and still. They told us to try and talk to someone and at the same time I was given a set of cards numbered 1-7 and told to shuffle them and put them in order. Similar tasks were being given to others. I shuffled my cards and then placed them in order. The sergeant looked at Dantzler and then checked back with me and asked me to make another try at shuffling and placing them in order. Dantzler was shuffling his cards as I completed the task again, one to seven without a problem. I noticed a couple of students were reattaching their masks, among them was Dugan. Dantzler was looking blankly at me as I was shuffling my card for the third time, his eyes were blinking a bit and then our observer reached in to fasten his mask. I looked at the clock at it looked like three minutes had passed, but I couldn't be sure. I looked down at my cards and found I had misplaced the numbers, so put them in the right position and smiling at the masked individual looking at me. I heard someone ask to check on my number and I shook my head back and forth indicating I knew they were talking about me. I was all right! When I started to giggle the sergeant reached to attach my mask, but I beat him to it. The first intake of the flow of a hundred percent oxygen seemed to clear my head. I looked around and everyone had their masks on and I was hearing that all did well. We were informed that the chamber would be pressurized to approximately 8,000 feet, which coincidently was the pressurized cabin altitude of most jet aircraft. They were going to bring the simulated flight altitude up to 25,000 feet and level off. When we did level off, we were once again briefed on "explosive decompression" and the effects. Our inside the chamber would instantly go from that pressurized altitude of 8,000 to the chamber's 25,000 feet. They told us to make sure there were no loose articles around us. They had collected all the cards they had handed out. Our helmet bags were secured and after a brief pause, Captain Deneau told us to unfasten our masks, but to have a hand on them to make sure it didn't leave our helmet or hit us in the face. Doing so, there was a pause, then suddenly the world turned into a fog bank and the air left my lungs. Nothing was flying around and the three individuals observing us were coming into view, helping students to get their mask on. I quickly secured mine and I checked Bobby who nodded his head showing me he was good. When everything settled down, we were told they would slowly take the chamber down to the starting altitude, but not too fast. There was a possibility of oxygen being trapped in our bodies and we could experience what to deep sea "divers" is known as the "bends". It took us awhile as they were careful to keep the descent very gradual, but finally they announced we were back at our starting altitude. The chamber door was opened, and we were all told to go back to our operation center. As we exited, the next group was waiting for their ride. I was glad it was over, just another hill to climb in this never-ending quest to reach a goal. I had no ill effects from the experience. The last thing I heard was we would be given a "chamber card", certifying we had completed the ride. We would be good for three years before we would have to do it again!

THE T-33

Doug initiated everything about this new aircraft, much like he did the T-28 by bringing the three students to the link trainers and the cockpit mockup to familiarize us with the cockpit and the instrument panel. It seemed tighter than the T-28, but the instruments were easy to pick up in a cross check, but like every aircraft the "needle and ball" were prominent in the sight pattern. The gear lever was to the right front and the flap handle was very easy to reach. The throttle was forward left, so your right hand was on the stick for all phases of flight. The trim button was on the stick and by this time all student pilots have discovered the mystery of trim. Any force experienced needed to be alleviated by using trim, a heavy nose needed nose up trim and the opposite if the nose was forcing you to push forward on the stick. You were looking for zero pressure on the stick, easy to do and it made for a smooth and coordinated flight. We could even compensate for a heavy wing to keep pressure off the control stick. It had become second nature to push against any force that appeared on the stick. It's hard to believe how difficult it was to understand trim in the early stages of primary. How I struggled over the concept of trimming an aircraft, now I am constantly working to keep everything on a constant level keel, even while flying formation I realize I struggle to keep the stick from grabbing in my hands. Each student was told to get "cockpit time" to familiarize themselves with the inside of the aircraft. Why do they have critical instruments, like hydraulics on a very small round indicator and place it where you can't see it? Oh well now that I know where it is, I'll look at it, even if in order to see it I have to turn my head and look to the side. Doug would tell us to find an airplane and sit in the cockpit with our checklist in order to identify location and placement of the essential items for flight, touching the spot or the handle to familiarize yourself with each item. Of course, don't play with the red flag attached to the pin that safes the seat from launching you into the blue as it would end up in a fatal fall. With the graduation of the West Point class, aircraft availability was wide open, so we had plenty of empty aircraft on the ramp.

After a couple of days of talk and simulated activity it was time to fly. Doug chose me to be the first at his table to fly the T-33. We strode out parachutes around our shoulders and accompanied by Clark and Fong. We took the toe hold and crawled up on the wing and placed our parachutes in the cockpit and before leaving to do the walk-around we opened the "push-open panel" behind the instructor position cockpit and checked the Plenum Chamber as Doug wiped his finger around the circular and raised top of the engine. He showed me his dry finger. We did the walk around and he pointed to the nose wheel and how it was supposed to look when sitting before taxi-out. He wanted to make sure I avoided cocking it on my initial taxi out. The rest of the check was intended to look for abnormalities in the structure of the aircraft and obvious leaks from areas of the aircraft that housed oil and hydraulic fluid. Both tip tanks had red flags to safety them on the ground. The tips were jettison capable from a switch in the cockpit, having a red cover that had to be lifted to reach the switch. Doug pulled out both and gave them to the crew-chief. When finished we were about get to into our student-instructor cockpits. As I was about to crawl in, I had a surreal moment. What exactly was I doing here and how did I get here? I had built model airplanes as a kid, balsa models, gluing together wing spars, spreading thin tissue paper on the wings, using a thin spray of water to tighten them up, all were rubber band models, where you wound the prop until tight and then launched them, hoping they would fly. Most did, but the landings weren't always the best. I crawled over the edge of the cockpit with that thought, knowing I was about to fly in a jet aircraft, Wow! Now, firmly in the aircraft I adjusted the seat and rudder pedals to accommodate my height. With my models still on my mind I fasted the chest and leg straps to my parachute. Many of my later self-built models were of aircraft that had flown in World War Two. My bedroom was one made by my Dad, in the garage as we lived in a two-bedroom house and I had three sisters. My Dad had constructed it by himself. He could do anything. He was a painter by trade but was also good at carpentry and electrical work. It was cozy with a set of bunk beds and an electric heater if needed. On the ceiling my dad had set wires in a rectangular crossing pattern, about a foot from the top of the ceiling and I would hang my completed models across the wires, hanging down by stout string. The collection grew and I often thought what it would be like to fly. I think I always thought I would someday be a pilot, flying aircraft like the ones hanging in the garage, fighters, many I had seen locally as there were factories all around where I lived, Douglas and Northrup were close and here I was about to launch in an aircraft that would prepare me for that dream. I had a half red and a half white silk scarf that my mother had made and it was around my neck, showing above the neck of my flight-suit. I looked out to see my table mates watching and now saw the crew chief off to the side with a set of ear-phone-type headset to combat the sound of the engine. After I put on my new, I think fire proof flight gloves, which I picked up yesterday afternoon I placed my helmet on my head and plugged in the microphone cord to the box on my left and checked with Doug on our connection. He "roger-ed" my call and asked what was taking me so long. I sort of smiled to myself as I secured my "knee-pad" on my right thigh, fastened my checklist under the clasp, inserted my sun, glasses under my helmet and started the reading of the start engine checklist. Before starting the engine, the interior checklist called for checking the position of switches and to pull the red-flagged pin from my ejection seat. After showing the pin to the crew chief I announced to Doug I had the pin out and stowed. ENGINE START was the next item and as I pushed the engine start button I had to wait until it reached the nine percent point and then I opened the throttle to the stop or idle position. The engine lit up immediately and I looked to insure the EGT gage was in the green. Unlike the T-28 I could leave the canopy open for taxi. We completed the before taxi checklist and I looked up to see the crew chief with the three, wheel chocks and the tip-tank pins in front of me, waving his taxi wands to come forward. I added power and with the first movement I touched the brakes, maybe too hard, for that check and I ground to a very temporary stop and released them to continue forward. I was relieved to not cock the nose gear as I went straight forward. After about ten feet I gently pushed on the right rudder pedal and turned toward the taxiway, then turned right again to parallel the runway and continued to the end of the runway. There were three T-33s waiting for takeoff on the hammerhead and because it was early in the period and no aircraft in the pattern they took the runway and departed with a minimum sequence between them and I was now the lone aircraft waiting to take the active. I closed the canopy and then completed the before takeoff checklist. Doug called the tower requesting clearance to take the active and hold. It was a very good day to fly, no clouds, no wind and a moderate temperature on an early October day. Cleared to take the active I applied power and nosed to the center of the runway. As I pulled to a stop on the runway, I was aligned with the centerline stripe. When I heard "Shotgun you are cleared for takeoff" I added power and firmly held the brakes down. Once power was stabilized and all instruments were in the green, I released brakes, pushed the throttle forward and was thrust back in my seat as the aircraft gained speed. No rudder pressure needed, but I had my feet firmly planted on them, out of habit, I guess. Pinky would approve. There was a speed check at sixty knots, all instruments were still in the "green" and at a hundred and twenty knots I pulled gently on the stick. Just like that I was airborne, I reached out and raised the gear with my right hand, waited and put the flap lever in the up position and felt the sudden sinking from the loss of lift and trimmed nose up to alleviate the change. The airspeed had snuck up above the designated climb speed and I felt Doug pull the nose up to compensate. He remarked that you had to pay attention on initial climb as one of two things can happen when you are raising the gear and flaps. You can pull the nose up and over-trim, losing climb speed or you can let the nose down, under-trimming and allow the airspeed to exceed climb speed limits. I muttered something in response as I watched the "rate of climb" needle pushing well beyond anything I had ever experienced before.

It was a great feeling and I felt secure as Doug was with me and was explaining various aircraft characteristics as we were climbing to the training area for the T-33. We leveled off temporarily at eight thousand feet and throttled back to maintain a cruising airspeed of 280 knots indicated airspeed. Doug proceeded to start simple maneuvers to demonstrate the feel of the aircraft. "The lazy eight" was first. He carved the horizon in a pretty wide and flat eight, and the variance in altitude was over fifteen hundred feet. He was very smooth, and proceeded to cut another, this time the maneuver was a nice round zero on both sides of the eight. A snap roll as he completed the maneuver was a surprise and three in a row was fun as I watched the stick being pumped forward and aft to keep the nose above the horizon. I was given the aircraft and did a reasonable lazy eight, followed by a series of snap rolls and finally I was asked to do an Immelmann maneuver. Let loose by Doug I did a very good one but lost too much airspeed so at the top after a 180 turn and climb, Doug said "I got it"! What followed was a surprise, but also a lesson. He pulled the throttle back and continued the climb, until the stall occurred. It was dramatic as the nose sliced down into a dive. He immediately added power and gently pulled the nose back to level flight. That was a demo, but it came as we were doing ordinary stuff. He advised me to apply nose down pressure to the dive after a stall to keep from going into a spin. He reminded me that few have ever recovered from a spin. We did a quick climb to altitude as he demonstrated the rate of climb, then dive capability of the T-33. I was now very happy to be out of the T-28, but I had one additional engine instrument I needed to keep in my crosscheck, the EGT (Exhaust Gas Temperature), a green line around the circular gage was all I needed to see when looking at it. There were also two less engine instruments, so the trade-off was a good one. Doug told me to descend to 6,000 feet and head back to the base. I complied and started my descent and as we came close to the overhead approach to the runway, he pulled the throttle to idle and announced he would demonstrate a flame out pattern. I suddenly was aware that it had become very quiet except for the sound of air passing over the fuselage. As he turned toward the runway, we were slowly losing altitude, but maintaining an airspeed above what the glide speed of the T-33 actually was according to the Dash-1. He announced he would trade off that airspeed when he needed to trade speed for altitude. He leveled off over the end of the runway at about 5000 feet and started a wide turn to the left and was now on the engine out speed and losing altitude in the turn. He was talking to me the entire time, telling me how to gauge the turn, making it wider or tighter, depending on altitude. It was necessary to complete another 360 degree turn as our altitude was too high to make an approach to the runway. He talked about the need to extending the downwind leg if necessary, but most of all keep the runway in sight. Not accustomed to the T-33 and its characteristics, I was more of a spectator, but I could see how he milked the aircraft to a final approach, lined up perfectly down the runway. About a hundred feet above the runway he added power, called a go-around and sucked up the gear and flaps, turned tightly, leveling off at 2500 feet. We took a position to enter the "pitchout" path to land. I remembered that a few days earlier I had witnessed a T-33 pitchout that ended in disaster. I tightened my shoulder straps as we approached the turn. Suddenly we were at 40-50, degree bank angle. My eyes seemed dull for a few seconds but cleared up as we rolled out on downwind. The gear went down, and flaps started down. Doug was talking at every move he made in a very nonchalant voice and did so until we touched down. After a short rollout down the runway he added power and said, "Your airplane". I grabbed at the stick, hit rotation speed and was instantly airborne and, reached for the gear lever and placed it in the "up" position, then started the flaps climbing straight ahead at full power I heard the gear doors shut and peeked at the "up" indicators and proceeded to climb when he said, "OK, reenter the pattern", so I initiated the turn back to repeat in some fashion what he just did. Unlike the T-28 I felt comfortable with the way it handled. The thought of the pitchout turn did not occur to me this time as I cranked out to a 45-degree angle of bank and held it till I was on the downwind leg. I was a bit awkward and rolled out like I had not seen a downwind leg before, but there was no sound from the back seat. Doug instructed me to do a touch-and-go. Finally settled in the pattern I was having no trouble at all maintaining downwind altitude or airspeed. This was a smooth aircraft, no prop in front of me, the clear vision seemed strange, but very comfortable. Turning base with the gear now down I started the flaps and continued my turn right through the base leg to lineup down the runway. On final Doug reaffirmed we would do a touch and go on this approach. My landing was good and elicited no comment from the back seat. I did the second closed pattern and I found the right altitude on downwind leg and was close to the proper airspeed to drop the gear and did so. I was a bit better during the turn to base, rolled my wings to level for a brief second and was in good position to complete the turn to final. As I rolled out I was at three hundred feet and right down the runway. The round-out was a bit premature, but the fall to the runway was not too painful. The words I heard as we rolled down the runway were "we'll work on landings". I was able to turn off the second taxiway, clearing the runway and after completing a "After Landing" checklist I managed the short distance to our parking slot. Doug made a comment going in that I needed to watch my taxi speed, must be the lack of clearing turns I thought. I felt a bit light-headed, knowing I had just had my first flight in a jet aircraft, and I knew I could fly this bird. I let his comment go and felt relieved to have finished my first ride in the T-33 without and major events, at least I thought so. Parking the aircraft was easy as I felt we floated to a stop, without cocking the nose wheel. I brought the throttle past the idle position to cutoff and the engine wound down to a stop. As we exited the aircraft Doug nodded to me and we walked together back to discard our chutes. George and Dick had been to the "Link" trainer and hadn't returned. Doug gave me a quick and dirty rehash of the first jet flight and mostly he talked about what not to do in the T-33, not what I had done and ended the conversation with some words on of all things "stay ahead of the airplane". Now that was something I had heard before and I'm sure would hear again.

T-33 SOLO

My second and third rides in the T-33 were a carbon copy of the first, with the exception that I spent a lot of time in the traffic pattern with emphasis on the precise flying of the pattern and landings. Attention was constantly on airspeed, altitude and head on a swivel. When on downwind you had to be aware that there were aircraft entering the overhead as well as being established somewhere in the pattern. It was nothing to have to extend the downwind due to conflicting traffic. The pattern work was to my way of thinking easy and putting the T-33 on the runway was a piece of cake. It just seemed smooth as you placed the throttle in idle and floated down to a soft touch. I would shoot four touch and goes on those two flights and although it was sweat producing, I thought the pattern work was a lot of fun. Adding power to go around was a real kick in the backside and each time it was like waking up to a new adventure. Though feeling the effects of the constant action in this type of flying I was disappointed to hear we would make a full stop on the next landing. It wasn't until we exited the runway after the full stop that I realized I was really wet. My flight suit suddenly seemed to be clinging to my body. My flight gloves were wet around the wrist and I was running fluid from somewhere into my mask. On the first flight I told Doug I was opening the canopy and he affirmed the idea. I didn't ask the second flight I just called out "canopy clear" and started it up. It was October and the air outside was fresh and cool as we would taxi to the parking spot. I would unfasten my mask and it was a feeling of total relief as when we were back on the ground I would begin to feel the effects of those flights. Interesting, as when in the air I was energized to do the next task, no matter what it was. After parking and exiting the aircraft Doug and I walked with our chutes unfastened at the chest and legs but kept them on our shoulders, helmet and knee board were in the helmet bag and the checklist was stuffed in my lower left ankle pocket of my flight suit. After each flight I was totally whacked out and I had an afternoon of academics ahead of me! At the end of the period we marched back to the barracks. I knew if I lay down, I would fall asleep and miss academics as well as a bite to eat and decided to not even go back to my room and just head to the mess hall instead. It was cool enough to have soup, so I would fill up a bowl of hot tomato soup and crush some saltines in it. I also grabbed a newly made taco and a glass of milk and sat down. Slowly those who had gone to their rooms after the morning periods waltzed in. Most of my friends, including Bob and Joe had their first flight, but not the second. I told them how exhausted I was after spending a great amount of time in the pattern during my second flight. Joe volunteered that Doug was probably going to solo me if he spent that much time in the landing mode. I laughed and said something to the effect that I had barely enough time to solo as I only had two hours and forty minutes of dual time in the

T-33. To top that off I was not at all ready to do any maneuvers in the aircraft, having practiced really none of them, except snap rolls and a couple of lazy eights and a one-time Immelmann. The conversation died down and the soup had done its job. Maybe it was the threat of soloing, but I felt energized and now ready to go to the academic building for the two afternoon classes, more T-33 engineering and our first class in Celestial Navigation. Don't know what we can do during the day with that class.

THE EVENING BREAK

Despite my doubts the Celestial-Nav class was very good. Captain Semeler spent most of the time telling how to identify stars from very obvious pointer systems. The end of the work day came soon enough and there were four of us who had decided to leave the base and go to a newly discovered steak house about two miles outside of the base. It was Polly Ibatuan, the instructor from the other side of 56-H and Doug's close friend who led us to this place. WE had been talking among ourselves one day in the Link Trainer building that we were looking for a good restaurant on this side of the border. Polly told us to ask Doug about the steak house. We did and he told us it was the best place around for a good steak. After being given nothing but high marks from Doug we were anxious to try it out. We departed early enough in the only car that had four doors, mine and found the steak house outside of the normal travel (actually, we had to travel on a dirt road) area to the border. It was an all-white building with a black front door. Inside it was cool and busy. It was a good size place with many tables of varying sizes and just a few small booths. Parading around inside was a platoon of waiters, with white aprons and white caps on their heads and all wore black trousers. Bob Higbee was our fourth member and he pointed out an empty booth to the mater-de and we were seated, looking back at the clientele. Most of the customers were men and most were very well dressed, obviously a business man hangout. It was the middle of the week and almost every table had four men involved in conversation. There were a couple of tables with women seated toward the back, but they were most definitely in the minority. We did note a few individuals we recognized from the flight line, but there was no one else from our class. Mexican beer in a filled frosty mug appeared, seems that Kelly had signaled to the waiter as we sat down to provide the beer. The menus were very simple, different cuts and sizes of steak and a couple choices of chicken and thick pork chops. There was one item on the menu, only Dugan was tempted for, it was a sixteen ounse stake, that if you ate it all, it would be free. We all opted for steaks of a normal size. All items came with a baked potato and a salad. The salads were all the same, very fresh and colorful and arrived in huge bowls. Different containers of dressings were placed on the table to choose from. Dugan tore into his salad and muttered something to the effect that why hadn't we heard of this place before. I was about half way through the salad when four sizzling steaks arrived. A bowl of green beans was placed in the middle of the table with a huge spoon in it. We were four happy want-to-be pilots. As we ate our steaks and emptied the bowl of beans and we ordered a second mug of beer. Soon the table was clean, and we deferred on a third beer as morning came quickly. I was not scheduled to fly tomorrow, but all the others were going for their second or third flight in the T-33. The bill was ridiculously low, and we paid it with a handsome tip for our great waiter, Eugenio. We waddled to my 54 Ford Victoria, climbed in and made our way back to the base. It was a very mild evening with the sun setting in front of us as we entered the gate. The two-stripe guard checked the decal on the windshield, saluted and waved us through. It had been a glorious evening and we all were ready to hit the sack, as the alarm would go off at six in the morning. Would it be another normal flight day?

INITIAL SOLO

The next day dawned and it was bit cool and a slight wind out of the east, but crystal clear or as they say CAVU (clear and visibility unlimited) in the daily weather briefing. After a great breakfast of coffee and SOS we arrived at the flight line. We were immediately waved in and received our morning flight briefing. Dick Clark was scheduled to go dual with Doug and Fong was scheduled to get yet another session in the Link Trainer. Doug muttered something that sounded like be loose or something to that effect. The flight shack thinned out and I was left with a couple of guys who came from Malden and a married lieutenant that was grounded for a cold. They had a name for it, DNIF (duty not to include flying). We chatted for awhile and then settled in to read the Dash-1 for the T-33 for the umptinth time. I knew Doug would be giving Dick a long ride so just occupied my time by writing a letter to my folks, something I was not too good at, but did keep them advised of how I was doing from time to time. I managed three pages when Dick walked in. He didn't say much other than it was a good ride and he shot a lot of landings. I asked where Doug was, and he said he had gone to the maintenance shack on the flight line. I assumed there had been some sort of problem with the aircraft and started to finish the letter, when Doug came in, he nonchalantly told me to get my chute as I was going solo. Stunned for a second, I paused, letting what he had said sink in and raised myself from my seat. He emphasized to hurry up as the period was going to be a bit short anyway. I grabbed my parachute off the rack in the next room and followed Doug outside. He motioned me to an aircraft a couple of rows down and on the inside position and told me to do the walk around and he would check the flight forms. Finished with my portion, I crawled up on the wing and pushed open the Plenum Chamber access panel. The round ring was very visible, and it had a very wet surface on the inside of the ring. I was instantly relieved as it was an automatic abort. I told Doug and he climbed up to see. He shook his head and we both came off the wing, while informing the crew chief it was a no-go, due to fuel seepage on the plenum. We started walking back to the shack, my gait ever more strident, when Doug turned and spied a maintenance truck. He stopped it while I continued to the shack. He suddenly yelled to me that he had found another aircraft. It was further down the ramp, but the truck would take us there. My heart started the wild pumping that raised my pulse out of sight. I hopped into the truck dragging my helmet bag and chute. We stopped about a hundred yards down the ramp, jumped out and found the aircraft number given to him by the maintenance supervisor. It was only two aircraft in from the roadway. Doug told me to get in the aircraft and do the before start engine checklist and he would do the exterior check. I got to start engine checklist while he stood on the wing telling me everything on the exterior was good. He started whirling his index finger, informing the crew chief we were ready to start engines. As he left the wing he yelled to me to declare "initial solo" before I took the active. I shook my helmeted head, called ground control that I was starting engines. After a successful start I motioned to the crew chief to pull the chocks. I sat there waiting for him to appear in front and spied Doug to the side with his thumb in the air. I knew I was hyperventilating, so held my breath as I saw the crew chief signaling me to taxi. I applied power and moved straight forward. The thought crossed my mind that I could cock the nose wheel and that would be the end to the solo as the period time would not allow any further delays. After going straight ahead and leaving the parking slot I pushed in the right rudder pedal and the aircraft followed my direction in a right turn to the taxiway. Again, I turned right, paralleling the active runway on my way to the hammerhead. I passed right in front of the tower and just knew everyone was watching me going out with less than three hours in the T-33 and waiting for me to splash. I even imagined Doug had gone to the tower to watch. Maybe I was taxiing too fast, hardly, I wasn't in any hurry to get into the air. I closed the canopy and immediately felt locked in. I pulled by Mobil Control which was almost adjacent to the hammerhead, but safely tucked back from the runway. Stopping on the hammerhead, I completed the prior to takeoff checklist and checked final to check for landing traffic. Unfortunately, there were no aircraft in sight, so I hit the "mic" button and in a halting voice called out my aircraft number and tacked on "initial solo". The reply was "roger, aircraft initial solo, you are cleared onto the active and hold. It was now hot in the cockpit, despite the foggy stream of cold air coming at me as I pulled into position straight down the runway. I was holding the brakes when I heard "initial solo you are cleared for takeoff". I hesitated as I looked for some reason not to add power. My process was interrupted with "solo aircraft, repeat, you are cleared for takeoff". I nodded my head for some insane reason as I added power, releasing brakes I was caught by the silence of everything. I couldn't hear the engine, nor was anyone talking. Suddenly I was at takeoff speed. I had missed the seventy-knot check. I gently pulled my silver bullet into the air, sucked up the gear and then the flaps, with a very slight loss of lift with the flaps coming up and was climbing straight ahead. At 800 feet I started a turn to the south away from the flight pattern and the base, continuing to climb. What was I going to do? I had barely gone through simple flight maneuvers with Doug, but I was in the air and I couldn't enter the traffic pattern yet as I had a full fuel load. I would have to wait until the tips were empty before I could shoot my landings. I flew further south toward Corpus Christi, sort of thinking I could do something like a lazy eight as that was simple and I would keep it shallow to preclude a dumb move. I set up myself sighting the horizon. I noticed a set of fluffy clouds to my right and so used that as a target for my nose. I proceeded to turn 30 degrees off heading to the left and descended, then pulled my nose up and around on a right- climbing turn, topping out and then descending through the horizon, completing the flat eight when I came around facing my fluffy clouds. I decided to do another and do it a bit better. So, I started the maneuver again to the left. When getting to the climb and turn to the right I applied a bit more pressure to make sure I got a true eight. I was very pleased with myself as I could feel the positive "G" force. After rolling out I felt it was not too bad (Pinky might disagree) and decided I would forgo any other activity and do a bit of sight-seeing. There was really nothing in the immediate area, but desert, so chose to continue south, toward the gulf, but obviously I wasn't about to get too far away from the base as that was my refuge. I had calmed down and was sort of enjoying the feel of accomplishment, although I hadn't done anything but takeoff. I eased my flight location to a point east of the field and actually did some gentle climbs and dives and waited for the tanks to feed out. Finally, both lights came on and I was on an internal fuel burn. I did not hesitate, and I entered initial about five miles away from the base on an early entry to the pattern and called "First Solo Flight on initial." The response was comical! "No visual solo flight, are you sure you are at the right field?" I responded with the fact that I was on a long initial. They acknowledged my position only as I hit the end of the runway with a surly acknowledgement that I was indeed in sight. My breakaway turn was passable and certainly not extreme. My wide downwind was noticed by mobile control as they gently hinted, I may not be able to see the runway from where I was with a call asking, "initial solo can you see the runway from your present position". I replied that I had the runway in sight. Needless, to say, my turn to base was a very gentle turn and I did get my gear and flaps down at the proper time. I lined up straight down the runway and made a smooth landing, turning off at the second taxiway. After I cleared the runway, I had this amazing feeling of relief and satisfaction. That was one full stop landing and I had to make two more so completed the after landing checklist and taxied back to the hammerhead. This time I had to wait for an aircraft on final but was then cleared on the runway for my take off to get my second landing. I applied power and went screaming down the runway as my reduced fuel load made for a rapid acceleration and launched into the blue half way down the runway. As soon as I got to the end of the runway, I started my turn to downwind, rolling out right at 1200 feet and was almost in position to turn base. It was a good pattern and with the turn still ninety degrees from completion, I rolled out momentarily and then completed the turn to the runway and I split it down the middle. There had been no comments from mobile and as I touched down and rolled to an early taxiway, I was happy and now confident in what I was doing. I hurried to get back on the taxiway and after a very short distance was at the hammerhead and before I could set the brakes I had a call notifying me to get moving, "initial solo, you are cleared on the active for immediate takeoff". I felt I had arrived and proceeded to continue down the runway, adding power as I got on the centerline and leapt into the air and patiently waited till I got to the end of the runway and once again turned to downwind, adjusted power and once again dropped the gear and started the flaps. When I reached my turn point, dipped a bit low as I turned base, so leveled out with power, then finished the turn, leveled at 300 feet and put it down in the first portion of the runway. I cleared the runway in what was a blur, taxied back and saw my table mates and Doug waiting as I parked. I thought I was the ace of the base and know I had a big grin on my face as I took off my helmet and crawled out over the wing. They all congratulated me, and as I was walking away asked me if I was going to leave my chute in the airplane for another trip around the pattern. Embarrassed I returned to get my chute as they all laughed at my gaff. We proceeded to the squadron center and from the ensuing conversation it was apparent that Doug was in mobile to observe my landings as he mentioned my wide pattern, however he never mentioned my landings, which were, in my estimation very good.

After a fast lunch and a period of euphoria I was basking in the fact that I was the first to solo in "Alpha" flight. It was reminiscent of my solo in the T-6, because neither of my instructors told me ahead of time that I was going to make that jump on that day. Dugan was still waiting for an indication he was going to solo from his German instructor and was grumbling about it. I knew that Clark would surely go tomorrow as he had his third ride today so being first didn't mean anything other than I've done it. I won't have to announce "initial solo" the next time I come to the hammerhead.

The first hour afternoon class was physiological training, taught by Captain E. W. Deneau. It was interesting because it brought back the incident at Malden when the student hyperventilated and lost the use of his hands. The Captain had heard of the incident and told us that an instant cure is to hold your breath for an instant or longer if you can and exhale gently before the next breath. It is a matter of controlling your breathing. You can also turn your oxygen to 100 % and gulp it to control your breathing. Now that our flights are all performed with a helmet and oxygen mask it makes sense to take advantage of the oxygen that is available to you. It also is good for hangovers they tell us. It was an interesting class

After an afternoon of classes I was too tired to think about doing anything but eating in the mess hall and going to bed. After a shower and a quick trip to wash my sweaty flight suit, I sank into my bed, only to be awakened by Dugan charging through our shared bathroom, who wanted to talk about the threat that he was possibly in line to solo on his next flight, but Herr Meinig had said nothing. I told him among other things, it was a "piece of cake" and he seemed satisfied and allowed me to turn over and go to sleep. The next morning was a bright October day. Knowing I had already soloed I was a bit loose as I walked to breakfast with Dugan, who was nervous, thinking this was his solo day. Herr Meinig had given him a "wring-out" ride yesterday, concentrating on landings and after the flight gave Bob an uncharacteristic, "good flight" nod. Dugan felt this was a sure sign he would go today. We sat down at a table in the mess hall with Roland Ford and Gerry Gable. Roland had been at my table with Pinky. He was one of the married students and he related he had soloed yesterday in the early part of the flight period with "B" flight. We shared our thoughts and experience as Gerry, like Bob felt he was going today, and he was bemoaning that possibility. He had a knack of worrying about things, but I've heard he was a good pilot. We both made the comment it was better to get it over with than to keep worrying about it. That line didn't seem to calm either one of them, so we changed the subject, finished breakfast and got in line for our route step march to the flight line. I felt very at ease, knowing that Clark would be going on a solo and Fong would get another dual ride. Fong had seemed to be improving and it didn't appear he was any longer in jeopardy of washing out. I settled down with the two table mates waiting for Doug after entering the operation center. He sauntered in with his gloves stuck in his thigh pocket of his flight suit, a small smirk on his face and before he sat down, he said he had three aircraft given to him for the morning first session. Being there was only one of him and three of us it meant we were all going to fly, and Fong would be his student and Clark and I would go solo. He casually told me where my aircraft was parked and that I should get some good "air time" and pattern work, and that I didn't need to include landings, as low approaches would work fine. I was still numb and didn't respond too quickly, but as I was about to get up from my seat, he told me my aircraft was being refueled and wouldn't be ready for fifteen or twenty minutes. He took Clark with him as he was telling him the rules of first solo flight and told Fong to wait for him to return. I settled back in my chair and noticed Gable was walking out with his instructor, Lieutenant McNew, a Texas native that Gerry said was a very good pilot. Dugan's table was empty, so I figured out that one of them was soloing and the other two at Meinig's table went out to watch the process. Fong was not a great communicator and so I thought I would get my helmet bag and chute and walk out to the aircraft. I didn't see Doug and Clark anywhere as I walked about a hundred yards to the line my aircraft was in. I didn't feel like an old hand, but at least this time I didn't have to call out it was my first solo flight. I spied a fuel truck next to an aircraft and assumed it was mine. I checked the tail number and noticed that the fueling was complete and the truck was ready to depart. I saw the crew chief working on his forms and approached him, asking if it was ready to go. He nodded his head as he closed the notebook and gave it to me to check. A couple of red dashes, no deferred work needing to be completed before flight and a full fuel load, which meant I would be up for at least an hour and change. Faced with reality I put my chute in the front cockpit, checked the plenum chamber which was perfectly dry and started my walk-around. As I finished and was about to step over the rail when I saw Doug standing at the end of the line of aircraft with his right thumb raised. I responded in kind and attached my chute and cinched the shoulder harness to the seat belt, took out my checklist and as I looked back up, noticed Fong and Doug were getting into an aircraft in the next line in the parking area. I vowed not to sound nervous when talking to mobile control or the tower as Doug would notice. I started the engine, saw the crew chief with the pins in his hand monitoring me to taxi. As I moved forward and started my turn, I heard Clark's call of initial solo. I didn't feel any more relaxed today than I did yesterday, but today I was just another solo student. When I arrived at the hammerhead, I was third in line to take the active. Both aircraft had two pilots, probably the last dual rides before solo. I knew the pattern will be full when I return and touch and goes would add to the melee in the pattern. By turn came suddenly and I pushed my aircraft into the air with no real plan. After launching I decided to go straight ahead and climbed to 8000 feet, well above and to the east of the T-28 practice area. Turning south I climbed and decided I would just stay level until I felt the need to do the easy and non-dangerous acrobatics, but as I reached a level off I had a sudden urge to do a snap roll and did so and as I came out of it I had to pull up the nose as I hadn't pushed the stick up hard enough when inverted. I critiqued myself and did another, much better and realized I was not looking around enough, so glanced in both directions and saw no aircraft. Where was everybody? It made you think all those morning aircraft were somewhere. I had an urge to call Clark on the inflight discrete channel, but felt he had enough to think about, so didn't. Another snap roll and then another. Very good! I decide to turn to the west and was now on the edge of the student flight area. The horizon was well defined so a lazy eight was a logical option. I picked out a central point on the horizon and proceeded to start my turn and descent to the left. (Why did I always go left first?) Started pulling the nose up and banking to the right, back through the horizon and completed the "eight". Pretty good, but knew it was a tad flat. I could do better and did another. I was satisfied with that one. My tips were still feeding, and I hadn't tried a chandelle. It was an easy maneuver and was just a max climb and turn of a 180-degrees, which I had done many of when solo and perfected under Pinky. I opted to go right and started my turn to the right and pulling forcefully back on the stick. I could feel the positive "G's" and glanced in the cockpit for no reason. Suddenly, I was in a stall and the nose angled right and fell through the horizon toward the ground. I suddenly realized I had stalled the T-33. I pulled the throttle to idle. All I remembered was "don't spin the T-33 as it will likely invert and there is no recovery! I began to pull back on the stick as my nose was pointed to the ground, but when doing so that action was met with severe buffeting. The altimeter was unwinding, what altitude did I start the maneuver? I relaxed the stick and realized I was in a high-speed buffet, not a stall. What had I done? Once again, I pulled back on the stick, trying to pull the nose up. I was again met with buffeting, so relaxed my hold again. I pulled back again, and the nose did seem to come up a bit so despite the shuttering I kept pressure to pull out of this dive. Were my tips still on the aircraft? I would relax the pressure a very small bit to stop the buffet, then pull back again. The shuttering abated and I brought the nose to level flight and added power to sustain flight. I have no idea how much altitude I lost or how long it took to get back to level flight, but it seemed like forever and I did feel that I was going in a near vertical attitude at one time. I was in a "coffin corner" in flight parlance as I had stalled the aircraft, but I was within a couple of knots of a high-speed buffet, due to the angle of attack in my dive to the ground. There was only about four knots difference between the stall speed and the high-speed buffet. I was shaken and decided level flight was all I was going to do until my tips went dry. I followed Doug's instructions and after my initial I stayed in the pattern and shot three low approaches, before my full stop. The pattern had been busy, but not to the point where my downwind legs stretched too far. The landing had been a good one, but I was engrossed in the experience I had while in flight. After clearing the runway my thoughts were about what could have been and vowed that I would never put myself in a position to endanger my aircraft with inattention. I taxied to the parking location and parked the aircraft. As I left the cockpit I wondered if there had been any obvious indications of stressing the aircraft. I exited and did a quick walk around under the suspicious eye of a crew chief, wondering why I looked the way I did. I signed the forms and gave no indication I might have stressed the aircraft as everything looked OK. I really wanted to talk to Doug! Clark was already sitting down at the table. I think I heard him call initial solo when he entered the pattern and told him so. He was very casual about his ride and shook hands as I congratulated him. Unfortunately, I never had the opportunity to get to Doug as just as he was walking in the door with Fong he was followed by Dugan with a big grin on his face. He had soloed and it was the first time I saw him really laughing about flying. I had to shake Dugan's hand and Doug slipped away as he often did, disappearing into the outer room.

Back to class that afternoon and more discussions on lack of oxygen symptoms. As we took our break, I noticed the T-33 Engineering officer Lieutenant Turpin and Captain Garret Smith, the flight operations instructor, were standing near the class break area. I sauntered up to them and told them about my incident today. They were good listeners and Captain Smith explained how the "coffin corner" of flight works. He thought I did a good job in the recovery and said patience was the byword. You can't panic and try to force the aircraft through either of the two extremes. I joked with him that time and lack-of-altitude do not mix very well. He agreed and laughed as he told me that's why we had ejection seats. Hopefully you are above 1000 feet, the limit for safe ejection and you still must pay the price for losing an aircraft. It is best not to put yourself into that position and they both agreed. The next day will be a busy one for the rest of the students in 56-H as many will be getting their first solo. I was tempted to talk to others about it as I knew some others would take the plunge tomorrow, but I would not have to tell my tale as in the next class the instructor in flight operations, Captain Smith discussed the problem of finding yourself in the "coffin corner" and the recovery technique to follow during the late day class without mentioning my name or my experience. Everyone listened!

LITTLE THINGS

The next day brought with it some fierce winds and lots of dust and other stuff flying around. They cancelled the morning flights and sent us to the trainer building for some initial instrument work in the T-33 simulator. It was mostly to accustom us to the instrument panel in the aircraft, but we were given tracking problems to solve as we shared time in the "box". It passed quickly and with time to kill I took the opportunity to talk to Doug about yesterday's incident. He also listened! He said he had never experienced the problem, accidently or otherwise, but had been in the neighborhood while doing stall recovery demonstrations. He gave me further insight on the amount of stress the T-33 can withstand and to not be afraid to let it shake a bit. I told him I would feel better if I had some more dual time and he agreed. He had already informed Fong he would solo the next flying day, so that would clear him to go dual with us. Since I had almost as much solo time and dual, I could use more time with him to refine other parts of flying the T bird. In a later conversation Doug volunteered to tell me that that Fong was "dating" a girl across the border. No wonder he had trouble concentrating on flying. Why he told me I don't know, but maybe to be more cordial to Fong as I didn't attempt to be overly friendly.

The severe winds disappeared as quickly as they appeared so while Clark and Fong were soloing the next two days I was riding with Doug. He would do a maneuver and I would follow trying my best to duplicate his effort. I told Doug that I entered the day before yesterday's problem while doing a chandelle and he had me do one to try to discover what happened. During the maneuver I knew I had pulled the nose up too severely in the turning bank as I remembered the "G" force I felt on that occasion. The combination of the bank angle and the force I placed during that climbing turn was the problem. We played around and I told him I enjoyed doing a loop and an Immelmann (starting a loop and at the top, roll out, keep from dishing the roll-out and heading 180 degrees from your starting heading. We compared attempts, mine were not as good as his, but about the third try I had it mastered. You gain a ton of altitude and the art is keeping the heading on the roll-out. After two days with Doug it dawned on me that I had gained a new confidence in flying the T-33. I had been doing maneuvers that I had not wanted to try, but the competitive spirit of outdoing my instructor kept me from thinking about my bad experience and my enjoyment of flying soared. I even got to the point that I was comfortable in doing a power-off stall and doing a recovery in a steep dive, without feeling the need to accelerate the recovery technique. Then entering the overhead pattern, I think I outdid him on the pitchout, my thirty plus degrees bank was tighter than his. The little things!

BACK TO SOLO FLIGHT

Doug, of course had other obligations and Fong was a concern. He had soloed and seemed to be doing well, but on a subsequent dual ride Doug was not pleased. I was back on my own and despite the sense of doubt that I sometimes felt, I had to be a bit confident in my flying ability. I think everyone of us had a moment where we had to feel our way into gaining confidence in their personal ability. I was now someone who found my own avenue of performance. Little things also applied to solo flight. My biggest concerns were above the traffic pattern. I knew I could land. It took me some time to break out of being a "thirty- degree bank pilot" at altitude. The really, safe maneuvers did not require any great skill. In talking to most of the others we shared experiences. The break had to be something you try only with your IP (instructor pilot). It came down to doing a stall series. My experience of inadvertently getting into the coffin corner had immunized me from doing a power-on stall alone. On a cool, crisp day after being airborne for thirty minutes and while my tip tanks were still feeding, I decided I would do a power on stall. I started a steep climb with a cruise power setting and saw my airspeed rapidly decreasing and suddenly the shudder. I applied left rudder as the aircraft fell off toward the right wing, I applied full power and as I slipped into a shallow dive; I slowly leveled the aircraft off. I probably lost a thousand feet, but I had full control. I climbed back to a safe altitude, a plenty safe altitude and pulled the power off and held my nose above the horizon. The abrupt shudder hit and again the aircraft plummeted to the right, left rudder to get level wings and a nose down attitude completed the recovery. I then applied full power and was in level flight. It was a textbook recovery. Having overcome my reluctance to stall the T-33, I was satisfied that was enough. I knew I could recover from an inadvertent stall and would recognize one if it occurred, and I don't think I ever practiced another stall in the T-33.

I did other things to amuse me and pass the time until the tips went dry. Sometimes going low over the desert in southwest Texas and going northwest to a giant lake where there were many sailboats coursing the various wind patterns, not aware of the joy a pilot could feel buzzing them and spilling their sails. I wasn't the only one as the word gets around and I think it started when a hint was given to a student by an instructor as to how much fun and invigorating it is. As in all good things it had to come to an end as it ultimately led to violent phone calls to the base. The response to these calls was always "did you get the number of the plane"? At three hundred plus knots that wasn't likely, but the warning put out to student pilots was enough to stop the practice for me as the threat was if caught you would be washed out. I would find other areas to quell my desire to experience the thrill of speed.

As time elapsed and the time flying solo was being compromised by new areas that were part of the curriculum, like navigation and formation flying I worked to hone my ability to fly the airplane. I would practice steep turns, maintaining altitude. I even made turns, banking rapidly, pulling back on the stick, testing my ability not to "grey" out, forcing the blood into my head so I would see through narrowed vision points on the horizon. Another new adventure was navigation using a map. It seemed easy at first, but when you see one small town in the Texas plains from the air you see them all, however there are discerning items that distinguish each town therefore if you denote such items on your map. Use the shape of the town, the road structure going into it and distinguishing features that can be seen from the air, a runway, or a railroad yard, a lake or other such item and mark them on your map. When you are unable to rely on radio stations for navigation you revert to following visual aids. A poorly prepared map can lead to lost aircraft with student pilots cranking their aircraft off predetermined headings ever so slightly until the next town is actually not the town you are looking for, you make a turn at what you think is the right spot and soon you see the town that is supposed to have a railroad yard and there is no such animal on the ground, thus you are lost. It's not too difficult if you are following the shoreline of the gulf and you come across Corpus Christi, a town you can recognize as you know it has a Navy training base and you see the runway off the gulf. It is recognizable and you can recover, but now your arrival back at Laredo is maybe ten minutes past your due time. So much for "dead reckoning"! Fortunately, only you and your instructor know you flunk navigation using this method. However, there was the previously mentioned, alternative of using radio stations and set navigational points that send out beams for aircraft to follow. We saw a bit of this in primary, but we were now traveling at a much higher speed so reading maps and using dead reckoning, were matched to the "A" and "N" beams closing rapidly as you intercept and close and hurtle rapidly to a fix. Flying under "the hood" became a standard and difficult adventure, but it was something I did well. The classes in "Morse Code" were good and I became accustomed to identifying the code identifiers from various towns in Texas, but more important I seemed to pick up the "A" and "N" beams from navigation stations and follow them to the fix. I never quite conquered the complete alphabet in Morse Code, but I could pick up most of the letters and I did not have a problem distinguishing a "dit-da" from a "da-dit". The real key was to recognize station passage and take the proper measure, usually to enter a holding pattern over the fix, until you received final instructions for a penetration and approach to a landing field. When received there was a standard penetration to the field in question, where you either flew a Ground Controlled Approach (GCA) or you intercepted the Instrument Landing System (ILS) and flew that to the runway for landing. The ILS system was one where you had to keep the vertical and horizontal crosshairs down the centerline of the runway you were going to land on. At the minimum altitude, you would execute a go-around, unless you were in a position, visually to land. The instructor in these cases would either take the aircraft for landing or he would have you follow the instructions from the controller on the ground after you initiated a go-around.

THE BROOKLYN DODGERS

On one memorable solo ride which was flown on a beautiful October afternoon I was upset about a pivotable baseball game. I was bummed as the Brooklyn Dodgers were playing in the World Series and I was scheduled to fly. I have been a Dodger fan since I was young enough to hear games on the radio. Pee Wee Reese, the Dodger shortstop was by boyhood hero. I knew the entire roster of the Dodger players and followed them as a real fan should. As I prepared my gear to go to the flight line Doug passed me by and I told him I would miss listening to the Dodger game. He said I could tune it in on the AM radio band in the aircraft and listen while still monitoring the common aircraft frequencies. Feeling better I as I got into the cockpit before start engines, I familiarized myself with being able to touch the radio without having to stare down as it was on a lower side panel. I counted the knobs to make sure I would be using the correct one in the air as I didn't want to lock out my traffic communications. Once sure I could find the knob I wanted, I knew I would still have to tune to find the right station. Once in the air and climbing to altitude I fumbled around and finally found the right station and heard the voice of Red Barber and his sidekick, Vin Scully discussing the present status of the game. Johnny Podres was the Dodger pitcher and was pitching a shutout in the fifth inning and the Dodgers were leading 2-0. I leveled off at 8000 feet and proceeded to go to the solo area southwest of the field. It was a clear day and the only thing I wanted to do was to listen to the game. For the next hour and ten minutes I was just punching holes in the sky and dodging low cirrus clouds. Finally, my tips had gone dry and it was time to return to the field to land. It was the bottom of the eighth inning as I entered the traffic pattern with the score remaining the same. The left-handed Podres had limited the Yankees to three hits and only had to retire the side in the ninth to give the Dodgers their first World Series victory ever and it would be over their nemesis of years passed, the Yankees. Unfortunately, I had to enter the pattern for landing and did so, and turned off the radio, not knowing what was going on in the top of the ninth inning. After landing and taxiing back I shut down the engine and exited the aircraft, frantically trying to find out who won the game. A "bread truck" carrying my crew chief stopped and got out and told me the Dodgers won. 1955 World Series Champions! My day was complete. I don't remember anything else about the flight, but I was a happy camper!

GROUND SCHOOL

The daily trek to the classroom was almost as adventurous as going to the flight line as the instructors were very good fully qualified pilots for the most part and they were entertaining. The weather instructor Captain Litzenberger was not a pilot, but he made weather seem like dancing with a beautiful woman. Cumulus formations were three types of woman, buxomly and tall, furious and deadly and calm and serene. Fronts, both cold and warm became friends on the flight line as you remembered his words on ninety-degree wind switches with frontal passage. This was a most informative series of classes, and one I played close attention to. One of my favorite platform instructors was Captain Semler, who taught celestial navigation. He made the heavens come alive and it led to many interesting night flights trying to find various stars in the clear Texas skies. One night we were on a night navigation and dual formation flight. The instructor pilot in the lead was Lieutenant McNew, a Texas native. My good friend Gerry Gable was his student and in the front seat of the aircraft. Roland Ford, my table buddy with Pinky at Malden was also at his table, but obviously not on that night navigation flight. I was number four in the flight with Doug in the back seat. Lieutenant

Mc New was on the aircraft radio frequency constantly talking about the beauty of Texas and as we approached a major city, whose lights, unlike the smaller cities, lit up the horizon, he called out that we are navigating using a three star fix, Deneb, Dube and Dallas. It was a clear night and I had no idea at the time which star was which, as I didn't know one from the other, but I could see Dallas from afar. The inability to identify stars would change as our class moved outdoors to eliminate our deficiencies regarding the heavenly bodies. We started our night classes where all students would have a sextant, fixed in an overhead frame and were given the information to find various stars. It was always a search that ended in a great discovery, mostly finding a star you have never heard of and sometimes leading to the discovery of a constellation. All was retained to the extent that when I flew, I was now looking for various celestial fixes to orient myself. When the Celestial classes were over after eight hours, four of which were outside, I was sad, and star identification became an obsession with me. I could identify any number of stars and would find dark places at night out of the reach of intrusive lights, where I could look in any direction in an attempt to locate my favorites. Physiological training and celestial navigation were my highest grades in ground school and my favorite subjects. Captain Deneau was the instructor for Physiological training and was surprised when I maxed out the chamber ride, being able to stay off oxygen the longest at a barometric pressure of twenty-five thousand feet. He verbally made me put my mask back on so they could do a depressurization procedure, which was required to qualify for flight in the T-33. This course was the longest in duration for the classes we had, other than the aircraft engineering courses in the T-28 and the T-33. In the flight operating instructions course for the T-33, our instructor, Lieutenant Turpin emphasized once again the fact that you did not want to spin the aircraft as it would go flat and maybe invert, making it very difficult to get out. I didn't have to dwell on that as I had no intention of trying to spin the aircraft. The T-6 was easy to get into a spin and get out. I never hesitated to practice them. The T-28 was easy to get in but hard to recover as the stick wanted to bruise your knees. When solo I avoided the pain and it was practiced only on dual rides. Recovery was something else as it just took a hard rudder depression in the opposite direction of the spin and holding pressure on the stick to save your knees when it resisted you. Don't give up! Ground school classes were always given at a time where it fit our flying regime as celestial classes were given as we started our night flying and navigation, when we were immersed in finding our way through the sky. The Engineering courses were placed in a timely manner and were meant to familiarize us with the functioning of the aircraft, not the mechanics of them. The instructors were very knowledgeable and easy to listen to and always seemed to be cognizant of our need for information.

FORMATION FLYING

Four instructors with four students, was the makeup for the first foray into flying formation. We took off individually with Doug and I as number two to launch from the east –west runway. After wheels up Doug talked about the lead ship going into a slight turn to the left and from the back seat talked me into closing on the lead ship who would be in that shallow turn to the left. With him on the controls we snuggled into a position on the left wing of the lead aircraft. I glanced out to see the third aircraft closing to my left. The briefing before takeoff from the lead aircraft instructor, Lieutenant Halverson was that we would form as an echelon left and fly loose until level off at fifteen thousand feet. At which time number one and two would be a separate, but close group from three and four. We would keep in sight and ultimately change leads to afford each student time to fly on the wing of an aircraft. As each student received time on the wing of a lead aircraft we would form as a four ship and return to base in echelon to land. Lieutenant Halvorson and his student pilot Lt. Dezil Boyd would again be the lead. After we broke into two flights of two, Doug maneuvered our T-33 into a position on the left wing of Lieutenant Halverson. I could see Denzil, in the front seat watching as we closed on the wing. We were very close! Doug started talking about reference points and the fact that you don't watch the whole airplane but pick out a reference to keep up tight on the other aircraft. He said he used an exhaust vent on the side of the aircraft and flew in its relation to the trailing edge of the wing from that point. As he snuggled even closer, I began to see what he was talking about. He told me to get on the stick with him and put my hand on the throttle. I grabbed the throttle and the stick and after nestling into a spot, suddenly I didn't feel pressure on the stick, and I felt I was flying the aircraft. Doug said, "It's your aircraft, I'm hands off". I couldn't believe how easy it seemed. I was totally fixed on that vent and was holding it firmly in position. Suddenly we hit an air pocket and the position was gone. I had let a smitten of turbulence shake me from my spot. Doug said, "no sweat, just move right back in". The term no sweat did not apply as I was feeling moisture creeping inside my helmet. I sashayed around and about and then finally settled a couple of aircraft lengths away, but I was stable and slowly worked back to the slot I had been in. Sweat was rolling into my mask and I could feel moisture now coming out of my helmet, but finally got settled. It is something to be fixed on a spot, where the slightest tug or slice of air can disrupt your concentration. I was intent on holding that spot and Doug was saying nothing. Finally, I heard Lt. Halverson sound out. "O K you have been in position for over five minutes, let's let my student have a shot". I couldn't believe I had spent that amount of time, but more than that I was delighted to move into the lead and let someone else do the work. Doug interrupted Halverson and said, "Let me show him something first". He told me to pull off the throttle and fall back to the left and below the lead, which I did. When clear of the lead aircraft and a bit behind, he told me to move back and turn under the tail of lead, being careful to not get in his jet wash. It was a gentle turn, just "wishing" the aircraft to the other side. I was to then climb up and close on the right wing and pull into position as I had on the left wing. I found a similar vent on the right side and slowly inched my way to see that vent as I had viewed the other one. It was not easy as we hit some turbulence and I fell away, now drinking my own fluids accumulating in my mask and dripping out of my helmet in rivulets around my ears. Finally, moving in I came to a halt, and was where I wanted to be and Doug said to pull out and clear lead. I found it harder for some reason from the right side. Once far enough to the right he took the aircraft and pulled ahead of Halverson and Boyd. It was now Denzil who had to find the spot and get his time in position. I watched as the now number two pulled smoothly into the crease and stopped. After a moment or two of gyrations in and out, up and down began and the aircraft fell away and then suddenly stopped. Once again it ventured into position and stabilized, only to fall back. I could only imagine what Denzil was going through as each time the position was gained it was lost. Finally, there seemed to be a stable pause in position by the other T-33 and it held for minutes, with only minor fall backs, and some vacillating up and downs. This ordeal was interrupted by the voice of Lt. Halverson saying, "Snowball Flight, lets regroup and assemble and echelon right". I glanced out to see the other two aircraft slowly closing from the rear and lead was now pulling in front of me and the group. Back to the number two position, this time on the right side. Doug urged me to keep the number two position loose with wing tip clearance and slightly aft of the trailing edge of the lead. Of course, that didn't bother me a bit as it was now actually fun! However, being number two in a four-ship cell was like being in the middle of a traffic jam. You held your position and didn't think about the guy on your wing. You just fly on the aircraft you are tucked into. Whatever he does you are doing and it's not a matter of what he does, you are on his wing and if he goes into a loop so do you. When he turns, you are turning, adding power as necessary and increasing your angle of bank when he does. The only way you really know is the increase in the "G" force from a turn or a climb as you feel the pressure on the bottom of your pants and the possibility of the need to trim the aircraft or add power.

We were returning to the base to land. I had often watched the four ship formations coming into the pattern as they pitched out one second apart and then landed virtually together, touching down and then rolling out to a turn off the runway. This would be my first time, so I was fraught with anticipation. Don't screw up the pitch. It had to be tight enough to match the lead aircraft as you turned to the brief downwind leg and then the constant turn through a base leg and rollout on the heading to the runway. If it's too tight you will be inside of the lead and if it's too loose, you're a wimp or worse yet, a Navy pilot. The pitch controls the entire pattern. It must be right, but I'm a student so I have some leeway, once! As we entered the approach to initial, Doug said "count one" and initiate a quick bank of 45 degrees and hold it for an 180 turn, then roll out, drop your gear and check the runway, start your decent and turn to final, while milking your flaps. Lead should be very visible and already in his turn to final when you roll out on downwind. Follow and prepare for some minor jet wash. Flaps should be full down, check gear in the green, check your final approach airspeed and complete your landing. Sounded simple! I forgot all about the four ship and became fixed on the lead. The lead started his pitch to the left, I counted to one, one hundred and turned and rolled right through the desired angle of bank, but quickly adjusted my pressure on the stick and found the right level and held my altitude to the reciprocal heading, rolled out, dropped the gear, looked for lead, found him and started the turn to final. My airspeed was a bit hot and I needed to lose some altitude as I held my heading and altitude too long. Doug gave the stick a push forward to remind me there was a plane on my tail and to get down. I started the flaps and surprisingly rolled out on the runway heading, while watching lead touch-down. I was finally on airspeed, gear and flaps were set and I coasted over the approach-end overrun of the runway and set it down. Doug reminded me to stay off the brakes and let it roll out to allow the number three room to roll. Lead had taken the right side of the runway, so I went to the left of the center line. I was feeling good as we rolled in a sort of formation down the active. I finally relaxed my hold on the stick and pushed the right rudder pedal full in to exit the runway behind lead. I thought my first day of formation flying had gone well, but I would wait until the debriefing to make sure. Lt. Halverson's debriefing was very short and only spoke of the join-up and how some lagged to get in position. He thought number two was above average in the join up for the first attempt.

I liked that but knew Doug had really made the move to cut him off. Doug's debriefing was succinct and to the point and took less than two minutes. He said I did Ok and was pleased that I held position for a good period, nothing about the pitch or rest of the pattern. Doug was intent on his students being at ease when flying formation, if there is such a condition during that type of flying.

After two dual rides in formation flying Doug said I was ready to go up as a solo student. Clark received the same clearance, but Fong became the odd man out and continued with instructors for an additional flight or two. The regime became the three of us and an additional student flying a four-ship, with the solos changing from lead to another slot in the four-ship. When Fong was cleared it was up for grab who you might fly with as a solo student. Instrument flying was starting so the tradeoff was a solo flight with another instructor or a dual ride under the hood. Sometimes all three of us were flying on the same day, two flying in a formation flight with another instructor. I found it was strange flying with another instructor as a lead, with his student and you stuck as a "tail-end-Charlie", the number four slot of the formation. The first of these was with 2nd Lieutenant H.P.M. Meinig, Bob Dugan's instructor, who was reverently called "Herr Meinig", due to his background as a pilot with the German Luftwaffe, as an eighteen-year old, towards the end of World War II. He obviously had proved himself as a pilot and hopefully was not holding a grudge over the outcome of the war. Dugan said he had a great ego and was always showing his prowess as a pilot. Here we were ten years later subjected to whatever hostility he might still have.

HERR MEINIG

Dugan was constantly talking about the threats of his instructor, Lieutenant Meinig, who didn't think anyone could fly formation to his liking and made it known to his students that he could shake anyone from his tail. Of course, everyone listened as he had flown with the Luftwaffe when he was eighteen. Bob was impressed with his instructor but didn't feel very happy to be his student. Bob had gone through his initial solo ride later than most of the class and felt Meinig was holding him back. He was blunt and outspoken and when he was critiquing a student, he could be heard throughout the briefing area in his guttural German accent. When Doug informed me, I was flying a solo formation as number two with the infamous German I was thunderstruck. Doug noticed I was apprehensive and said, "just suck into him when he goes in-trail, and don't let him bother you with any aerial hi-jincks, just back off and watch." He softly said, "at least you are not number four". I slowly walked to Dugan's table and when Bob saw me coming, he had a big smile on his face. I found he was not going to be Meinig's student in the front seat of the dual T-33, it would be Mark Blizzard, someone I didn't know too well, but knew he was one of the married students. He was a serious fellow, always had a stern look on his face, but at Herr Meinig's briefing he seemed to be relaxed and ready to fly. Why not, he would be in the lead and not subjected to the instructor's attempt to shake a flight of student greenhorns. Number three would be 2/Lt Cecil Greene, an Alabama native, who had a sweet southern drawl and number four would be a good buddy of mine, Bobby Dantzler from Hickory, North Carolina, whose drawl was even more pronounced than Cecil's was. It would at least be good listening as three and four acknowledged the lead's instructions in flight by a resounding, "Ragaah that"! It was interesting how the term "roger" became the compliance call, but even more interesting was to hear "rodney" or royer" used instead as you flew with others. Anything to break the monotony.

The briefing was fairly, normal as the leader briefed the normal sequence of launch and join-up. Once in our echelon we would climb to eighteen thousand and proceed to the formation area. We would practice various states of formation to include changing position and going from echelon right to left, then practicing position changes with Blizzard getting some time as number two or three, but he would be the leader at the end of the flight. We would finish in trail position, before heading to the fix for initial and landing. The forecast had called for some building and scattered cumulus clouds, but after an hour they would be closing in a bit, but never forming a ceiling and to add to the sweaty palms, we would encounter some mild turbulence thrown in to distract us. As we left the table, Bob pulled close to me and repeated what he had told be before that Meinig liked to start a loop when in trail and milk his flaps to widen the loop, without telling his students and watching them fall off before the top of the loop. This was usually at the end of the flight. He liked coming back to the initial fix without students, just to emphasize his prowess as a pilot. I was forewarned and pre-armed for his antics!

The four aircraft were parked in close proximity on the ramp, so as we reached our individual aircraft, I could keep tabs on Meinig during pre-flight and his walk around the aircraft. I would make sure I would get out of the chocks and follow him closely when taxiing to the hammerhead. I didn't need a critique on the taxi out. I finished my walk around, looked in the plenum chamber access panel and paused to check the back seat and locked the shoulder harness and seatbelt together, then climbed into the front cockpit and strapped on my chute and fastened my seat belt and shoulder harness, went into the checklist and looked up to see lead starting engine. I hurried through the checklist and circled my finger to the crew chief and started the engine. I did remember to not start my turn too quickly to freeze the nose wheel and pushed the throttle forward to start my taxi, then made the turn to the parallel and followed the fumes of the lead. I closed the canopy to keep from inhaling too much of the JP-4 smell and fastened my mask and adjusted the oxygen input. I saw Cecil and Bobby waiting as I passed their row of aircraft and knew they would be right behind me. We were all on the hammerhead going through the before takeoff checklist and I heard, more than saw, lead taking the active as he called out to the tower for clearance. "Deadeye Flight of four cleared for takeoff," Came through my helmet. Lead rolled into position and continued his roll, as I came to the centerline, adding power and proceeded to launch fifteen seconds after him. I could easily see his trail on this clear, bright day and turned to the left in a thirty- degree bank, watching his shallow, climbing turn. I quickly overtook him and slid loosely into his left, sighting my position on the fuselage vent. I know Cecil and Bobby would be to my left but did not look to see them. I called, two in position and waited. The call came "Three in position" and still waited. Finally, the last call came, "Four in position". With that last call lead announced he was adding climb power and leveled his wings. The four-ship was intact and climbing to altitude. During the climb, lead called for the flight to go echelon right. I waited for four to call in, then three, before I went to a loose position, cut back power and slid down, aft and under lead. It was interesting looking up to see the underside of an aircraft as you float in close to his tailpipe. I didn't dwell on it too long though as I had to stop the right turn to get in position on the right side of the lead. I knew where two and three were supposed to be, so once aft and under I slowly pulled up to my reference point and once again held position, this time a bit tighter as I knew Herr Meinig would be checking me out and called to let lead know I was where I was supposed to be. I took a quick glance to my right and saw Cecil loose on my wing then just tried to keep my eyes on lead. It was becoming a bit turbulent and was distracting as I was bouncing up and down trying to lock on my vent. When all were in position again Meinig started a slow turn to the left. This, of course means we were all stacked above him in the turn, which became more pronounced. It wasn't bad for me, but I could imagine Bobby, as four was sweating in his mask. Mine wasn't too dry! We finally leveled out and were now on top of a few clouds, sort of brushing against the tips and staying in position now was more difficult as the washboard effect of these clouds caused me to lose my fix and I became a loose two. Herr Meinig called to tell us we were going to take another turn, this time right. Fortunately, we had cleared the clouds for the moment, and I was able to get back where I belonged, hoping he hadn't noticed my "momentary deviation". A term used often in evaluations to give some hope to a beleaguered student. The turn was fairly, steep but didn't present a problem. The turns and then climbs and dives followed. It was brutal and I was feeling the effects. My knees were shaking, mostly as a result of trying to remain stable and I was very uncomfortably wet from sweat. Finally, he called to send us to a loose formation. I waited to pull away from his wing, until I was sure three and four had moved out. A loose position was about two wing widths away, still close, but much more comfortable. I got a break as lead was going to pull back and assume the two slot and I would be the lead aircraft to allow Blizzard to get some wing time. We would be in a fingertip formation for this exercise. I was told to exercise gentle turns left, then right. We flew this way for a few minutes and then Herr Meinig came on and said we would change position again with number four assuming lead. Dantzler was to move away and accelerate ahead and I would form on him, continuing in Echelon as number two on his right-wing. I had to wait until I saw "four" pass our three aircraft and go ahead of us. I then started a turn to get on his tail and catch up to complete the process. I finally pulled into my spot on the lead aircraft, confident I hadn't lost anyone. Once steady the good German announced we would go back to his aircraft in the lead. Poor

Dantzler would now drop back to the "four" spot and Blizzard would accelerate and take the lead. I would be two again. Once back in echelon it was Blizzard's voice calling out to go entrail. I knew the German was going to try and shake us, but would he try the loop maneuver or something else? We all fell back and stacked down on his tail. Once all were established, he started turns, first right and then left, not too bad, but they intensified. Being two was not too bad as I had a chance to be on his wing, maybe a little loose, but think of poor Dantzler. He was on the end of the whip and slow but sure he would fall away. It was like being in a dogfight! Then after about five minutes it came! He leveled out and you could see his power increase and he went into a wings level climb. He announced we were going to do a loop. As it steepened, I was tucked in close and tight, at least I thought so, looking right at his tailpipe and decided to fall back a bit so I could see the trailing edge of his wings. As we hit vertical, I could see the flaps extending, not much, maybe 10 to 20 degrees, so I reached up and started mine, while still holding a decent position. I didn't extend mine for long as his was steady and I was holding on to him. As we reached the top of the loop, I couldn't hold position any longer and fell back. I had no idea where the two aircraft behind me were, but I could still see and follow lead at a distance. He did not finish the loop but chose to roll out into level flight. As he leveled out, I was a good stretch behind and above him as I had waffled out of the inverted position. We hit a couple of clouds and I momentarily lost him but climbed to keep clear of the clouds and when on top I could see him darting below me towards the base. I followed at a fairly, close distance, still above him, but now close enough to make sure I didn't lose him. He hit the high key and called out "Dead-Eye Flight of one initial". I hesitated, dove down and looked at the end of the runway below me and called out, "number two initial", and turned into a forty-five degree bank to the left, rolled out on downwind, dropped my gear and spotted Herr Meinig dead in front of me turning base to final and it was then I realized I still had partial flaps. I finished placing the flap lever in the full down position. I'm sure I exceeded the flap limit speed and saw I had stopped at 10 degrees. I would write it up, but I wasn't going to tell the Luftwaffe ace at debriefing. I hesitated to turn and lengthened my downwind, then turned to follow at a safe landing distance, and touching down as lead exited the runway at the second taxiway. I followed suit and as I turned, I saw a T-33 pitchout, followed closely by another. It could be Cecil and Bobby and silently hoped it was. I hadn't heard either calling their initial, but I had switched to ground control after touching down. I was directed to the same parking location I had before and saw a pair of parking wands pointed my way. As I shut my engine down, I looked to see Mark Blizzard and Meinig exiting their bird and pulling their seat packs out of the cockpit. As I jumped onto the wing, I saw two T-33s taxiing toward the parking area, saw the tail number of Bobby's aircraft. I would have waited for him but didn't want to keep my flight leader waiting and so hurried in for the debriefing. I entered and hung my chute on the appropriate rack and saw Dugan scurrying away from Meinig's table. Blizzard was sitting down and was looking at the blue flight suit of Herr Meinig. I waited a second and then pulled out a chair and sat next to Mark. The quiet was deafening. It seemed endless, but then the door opened and in walked Cecil and Bobby, the marks of a tight face mask was prominent on Bobby's face as he turned to enter the parachute storage room. Finally, all of us were seated waiting for the flight lead to speak. He addressed the other two and asked why they fell out of the formation and berated them for their lack of airmanship, then turned to me and asked why I wasn't on his wing at initial. I told him I fell back at some part of the loop and could not catch him. He nodded and said, "It was an overall good flight, but we need to pick up our reaction to flight conditions". He talked a bit about changing from the right to the left but said our communications while doing so was very good. It really was a compliment! I saw Doug peeking at me from our table but saw no emotion or a seeking gesture. We were excused and I walked by Dugan, with a grin as wide as the Rio Grande River and sat down next to Fong, who just had an elimination ride from Doug. He too had a nice smile on his usually somber, serious face and I knew he must have done well. Doug asked how it went and I muttered something like great or fine, I'm not sure and he too smiled. It had been a wonderful day for flying and I felt I had been fortunate to be the one who could say I flew formation with Herr Meinig and was still with him through the landing. The only drawback was I had to write up the fact that I had exceeded the airspeed for partial flaps. The crew chief didn't seem very concerned but did acknowledged the write-up.

NIGHT FLYING

A new segment of the process to achieve our silver wings was to experience flying at night, solo in the T-33. After flights on a dual basis at night, including night dual rides, employing our navigation skills, the entire class was to do their first solo night flight this week. There would be two to three days where all of us would break our maiden and fly a solo night flight. There would only be one flight period for the night solo missions. Mine would be Tuesday, Clark on Monday and Fong, now seemingly safe to graduate, on Wednesday. I didn't feel any anxiety over flying at night, but I admitted some rumblings in my gut as it was another new experience.

It would be followed by our solo night navigation flight as an item in the table of requirements to achieve our pilot wings. We assembled outside the housing area student apartments after dark in early November and marched to the flight line. It was a perfect Fall night, clear, no moon at all, windless and visibility in flight terms, CAVU "ceiling and visibility unlimited"! When arriving outside the flight shack, we came to a halt and waited for the door to open to admit us, which was standard. When Lieutenant McNew opened the door, we walked in and were greeted with an all red interior. All lighting had been changed to red bulbs to adjust our eyes for night as red lights do not affect night vision. We entered in this red hue and went to our appropriate tables. Those who were flying the Monday schedule were asked to sit at a table up front and they proceeded to that table to be briefed for their indoctrination flight. It wasn't long before Clark came back to the table, picked up his flight jacket and went to get his chute. The rest of us spent the next two hours in the flight center doing basically nothing. Slowly the students came back from their flights, Dick Clark was among the first. He indicated it was a no-brainer, but very dark.

The next day I was taking a break from my first class and asked Jack Cheketts, who was at the same table as Bobby Dantzler, while they were engaged in conversation, how the flight was last night and he said it was very calm, no turbulence and very clear. He also commented on that without a moon how dark it was. That night as we entered the red lit room I barely sat down and was told to go to the table for a group briefing on weather and other items pertaining to the night flights. It was a short briefing and as we walked away Doug told me to be aware of the total darkness of the environment around the base. I nodded and uttered some comment of knowing what he was talking about. That was three people who mentioned the darkness, so I tucked into my head that it would be dark. I picked up my chute, got my aircraft parking slot and left the flight shack for my aircraft. When I left the flight shack, I was amazed at the coolness outside, compared to the stuffy and warm interior of the room I had just left. There was no perceptible wind and the sky was alive with twinkling stars. I made no effort to give more than a furtive glance to make them out. The crew chief saluted me. That was interesting as most of the time they give you the aircraft records and wait for you to ask questions. I took out my very bright pen-light with a red lens and looked for discernable indicators and found no latent discrepancies that would preclude flight. I thanked him and started around the aircraft amidst the sound of multiple power units starting up. Having completed the walk-around I picked up my chute off the wing root and crawled up next to my cockpit and looked into the rear seat to see the seatbelt and shoulder harness har already been fastened together, pushed the panel over the plenum chamber and viewed a very dry ring and tossed my chute into the front seat. Finally situated and ready I cranked up the engine, whiffing the JP-4 fumes as I sat thinking about the very dark environs about the ramp as other than the discernable tail glow of other about to taxi aircraft, there was nothing that was emanating light. I got my clearance to taxi and added an "inch" of power and moved forward and started out from the parking area and fell into a line of aircraft ahead of me. I watched as one after another went down the runway spitting a fiery tale, breaking ground and disappearing into the night. I sat on the hammerhead and watched as the aircraft in front of me departed. I was told to take the active and hold. I lined up right down the centerline of the runway and waited for clearance and finally I got the call. I applied power and rolled down the runway, hitting takeoff speed I pulled the nose up and reached for the gear handle. As I looked forward there was nothing, I mean nothing. It was clear, yes, but there was no discernable horizon. I saw nothing, but total blackness mingled with tiny dotted lights. There was no definition of ground or sky. There was a moment of panic and then I came instantly into my instrument panel to insure I was wings level and climbing as my sensation was of anything but. My artificial horizon had wings level and a constant airspeed climb. I waited until I had passed 1200 feet before I ventured to look out of the cockpit, stealthily, peeking back to my left to see the city of Laredo and the base which brought back my sense of balance. Vertigo can be a fleeting thing and reliance on and seeing instruments you believe in can instantly restore your feeling of normalcy. Looking around after that brief panic moment, I could now break out the stars in the heavens from the single lights on the desert floor. Wow! I said out loud, that was hairy. I didn't have vertigo, but I would have if I had kept my head up. I spent the rest of the flight keeping my eye out for other aircraft and checking stars. The night sky, moonless, is a plethora of interesting pointer systems that seem to lead nowhere. I could run out of fuel trying to find specific stars that standout on the ground, however they are masked due to the large number of visual stars you can see without the evening haze or the moisture in the air.

We were told to not do any maneuvers in flight during the night and that was fine with me. There was to be one landing, no low approaches or go-arounds and after that takeoff I wouldn't welcome another launch into the dark, moonless night. When returning for my approach I was super cautious and executed a loose pitchout, rolled out on a wide downwind, some would call it a "Navy Pattern" and had a wing rollout on base that would have embarrassed Doug, but It was a nice approach and landing no problem at all. I could like flying at night if they could provide a moon to give me some idea of where the horizon was, as it was a nice, reflective and serene experience. Unfortunately, there was no second local night solo, but we did get to test the night sky again, doing the required navigation flight.

NIGHT NAVIGATION

Coming in from my solo ride on Friday all the students were briefed that we would be flying nights again next week in lieu of our afternoon schedule. Once again it would be a single period, starting as dark fell so you could count on an 1800 start time. One good note was that we would have a new moon in the eastern sky, which meant if the primary runway stays the same, we should see it on takeoff. We would have a weekend to think about it.

The programmed night navigation flight started out in the same manner as the initial solo missions, red lights dominated the room, and everyone was playing with an individual map that we all had to draw, outlining our flight routing. Our instructors were all there and ready for us to sit down for the briefing. Colonel Samways, our training Group Commander was there to observe. Major Allison, the 3640th Squadron Commander opened the briefing on words about air discipline, reminding us to keep our eyes out for other aircraft as the entire flight would be in the air and ultimately back in the pattern. We would be flying a Navigation leg and takeoffs would be one-minute separation. There were thirty-seven student pilots in "A" Flight, so the final aircraft would not takeoff until almost an hour after the first. There would be a five-minute break after the first twelve launched, then the next twelve would take off, and a final group of thirteen would follow. Many of the instructors would launch before the students. They would be in the air to monitor the groups and even guide them if necessary. The initial leg would be north to Dallas, turning southeast to Houston and then back to Laredo. We all had prepared those maps the previous day and annotated them with time and distance, with headings noted on each leg. Captain McDade, the "A" Flight Commander said a few words about recall procedures in the event of problems in the air and call sign use for check-in at the turn points. He also covered procedures for return in the event of an air abort. We were then briefed on emergency bases or airports to use in the event of an emergency. We were told to use strict radio discipline and to keep our oxygen masks firmly attached throughout the mission. Our enroute altitude for the navigation legs was twenty-two thousand feet and we were told our indicated airspeed for each leg would be 270 knots. Lt. Scwartz and Lt. Baron, senior instructors, would be in the air to assist stragglers and monitor the turn points. Doug informed me he also would be one of the instructors in the air, along with naming three other instructors to check on deviants from the route. Each of our turn points could be monitored on the navigation frequency of each location. A weather briefing followed with our academic weather instructor, Captain Litzenberger telling us it would be clear for the entire night and winds aloft would be from the northwest. Turbulence would be light, with a possibility of some moderate bumps close to our second turn point. Wind velocity on landing would be light and variable. As he said to close the briefing, "it is a perfect night to fly". At the end of his briefing he mentioned that there would be a nice sliver of the moon to help anyone who has a vertigo problem.

THE NIGHT LAUNCH

I was to be in the first twelve to launch. Each of the three groups was given a color and each pilot a number to identify them in the sequence of launch. I was going to be "Red Three". Following flights were green and orange. The first group left the red light "district", grabbing our chutes and went to our parking slot. I put my chute in the cockpit and then started a comprehensive walk around, using a small red and white flight suit-fitting flashlight that I had almost forgotten to bring. I had washed my flight suit this morning and when putting items back in the suit the little cigarette box looking flashlight was left out until I put my pencils in the left forearm holder. I noted that the zipped pocket under the pencil sleeve didn't seem the same as usual, so luckily turned to retrieve it and zipped it up in the pocket. I checked the 781 aircraft maintenance log and saw no red cross (can't fly) items, a couple of red diagonals (meaning could fly without endangering the aircraft and those in it) and otherwise it was ready to go. Was I? This was a very nervous time as thoughts of others not coming back from night solo missions plagued me. The three stripped, crew chief was very alert to my walk-around and kept a large flashlight, pointed as I walked around the aircraft.

I then had a thought about my night vision, thinking it was all for naught, being in a red room for forty minutes and then walking out into the dark and using a flashlight with no red lens to read the 781 and be ushered about with a flashlight marking the way. Maybe I should stop thinking! I noticed others were completing their walk-around and beams of light, signaling there were other flashlights, to be in use. Then I heard, then saw the first of the instructor launches, flames coming from the tailpipe as it rose into the black night. There was a very thin moon, casting little light, making the night sky seem full of stars. I crawled into the seat and pulled my parachute strap around my chest, fastened it and pulled the shoulder harness down, fastening my leg straps and then inserting the shoulder harness into the seat belt and pulling the latch over the top and locking it in place. I looked down and pulled the red flag from the side of the seat and pulled the ejection seat pin it was attached to. As I looked forward the crew chief, anticipating my engine start was stationed to my left. I showed him my seat pin and he acknowledged it was pulled. I heard the call to start engines from a lead instructor for the "red" group and immediately pushed the starter switch. At seven percent I brought the throttle out of the stop to the idle position as the rumble of the engine fire took hold. The crew chief had moved directly in front of my aircraft with two lighted wands held directly above his head, then moving them backwards and forwards to indicate I was cleared to taxi. There was another T-33 moving from a slot to my right and I would follow him to the taxiway. I heard his call "red two" taxiing and I followed with "red three, on the move". I had the canopy still open and could smell his jet fumes through my mask, so promptly reached for the closure switch. Red one was on the taxiway and as I pulled on to the parallel taxiway, I could see others waiting for us to pass to keep the number line correct and in the proper order for takeoff. It was interesting to see the night activity on the ramp, the wing lights of each aircraft, blending and fading into the floating exhaust of the aircraft, giving them a haunting look. The lead instructor aircraft was on the hammerhead and without delay pushed into position and barely slowed down as the flame from his engine lit the area and he rapidly thundered down the runway. The lead student took the runway, took his position and was cleared by mobile control to takeoff. As he rolled down the runway red two took the active runway. He too, was cleared after the one-minute pause, so I pushed the throttle forward and lined up on the centerline of the runway waiting for my clearance to go. I was breathing rapidly, but I felt calm and despite some perspiration I was comfortable in my ejection seat. Remember I thought, you need a thousand feet to safely eject from this bird. Why did I think that? I don't know! "Red three cleared to launch" cleared my mind and I brought the throttle to the full-open position and then released brakes. I loved doing that as I was thrust back in the seat, the runway lights were passing as I hit a "No-Go" speed. Everything was good for launch. Takeoff speed and a gentle pull on the stick as the last of the runway lights I could see passed under me. With my previous experience on takeoff into the night sky I prepared myself for the utter void in front of me so as I sucked up the gear, my attention was inside the cockpit showing the wings level as I climbed to a safe altitude, again assuring myself that my wings were level by checking the

Laredo brightness back behind me. I turned and picked up my initial heading to Dallas and continued my climb. The night was brilliant, stars everywhere, sprinkled lights on the ground and virtually no visible horizon made for an odd feeling that you were in a bubble. Leveling at twenty-two thousand I reached over and switched my oxygen lever from normal to a hundred percent and adjusted my cabin heat upward. I could make out the wing lights and a faint glow from the tailpipe of the aircraft in front of me. He was slightly to my left and now I could see the lights of a small Texas town straight ahead, giving some definition to the ground and the sky. I would glance at the twin red and green lights on the wing tips of the aircraft in front of me, steady in the distance and then go back to my heading indicator and artificial horizon and then bumping up or back the throttle to keep my airspeed constant. The small town passed under my nose, but now there were others as we cranked our way north, leaving the very uninhabited southern part of the state. Small groups and shapes of light were now making a pattern on the ground seemingly saying look at your map. I turned on the red cockpit light on the right side of the canopy ledge and glanced at the map. My drawn line on the map was bisecting some of the nameless towns below and the pattern was right on. I turned off the light and looked for red two but couldn't see his lights. Suddenly I was aware of an aircraft close by on my left. Could that be him, I wondered? No, that aircraft was much too close. The aircraft waggled its wings at me and turned away. It must have been one of the monitoring instructors as no one else would venture that close on a night navigation I thought. Straining my eyes to the left I still could not see another aircraft.

I scanned to the right and saw the lights of red two. Either he or I had wandered off heading and I had been fixated on the left side of the track to Dallas. Look around dummy, I thought! The stream of students would continue for a long time and although Air Traffic Control was well-aware of the long line of aircraft and would be monitoring our route, there were still other aircraft in the sky and we had to be cognicent of that. I had not seen any other aircraft, but I knew they were there. It was a strange feeling to be alone, yet not alone. There was little chatter among aircraft, not even from instructors in the air, eerie to say the least. The sky was so bright with stars now, made even more vivid because there was this thin moon. I started to try to find some of the more familiar and dominate stars, so looking to the east and just rising was the "Belt of Orion". I could never remember which one was, Rigel and which one was Bellatrix. I did remember "Aldeberon was on top of it as it rose, and Capella would be the bright star to its right. I had read that Betelgeuse, Procyon and Sirius, which was not up yet, made up the winter triangle, if only I could remember which one is Betelgeuse? Straight ahead I could make out the "Big Dipper" or "Ursa Major" as it is known, as it pointed to the North Star, Polaris. Its long tail goes to Arcturus, which I could not find, must be too low. The stars kept my mind active as I searched to identify them. Under all of this I could now see the bright lights of Dallas looming up ahead. Our turn point was actually short of Dallas, about ten miles. I was looking and listening for station passage, but really didn't need it due to the obvious illumination dead ahead. I could see the instructor aircraft's turn to his right and that was followed by red-one in his turn. I believe Roland Ford was one, but I didn't pay attention to who it was during the briefing. My ETE (estimated time en-route) was coming up so I wanted to see number two in his turn. I would time down when I saw him. I then picked him up in his turn as his red, left wing light went above his green, right wing light in an obvious change of direction. I was getting station passage and my time was winding down. I started a gentle thirty-degree bank to the programmed heading, leveled out, now heading to Houston, or at least to a small city, twelve miles to the west of that town. I started my instrument clock for the twenty-one- minute leg and settled back in my parachute. I had been leaning into my shoulder harness and my helmet, all of a sudden, felt heavy. I put my head back to the top of the ejection seat for a moment to relax the pressure and noticed my airspeed had bled down three or four knots and pushed the throttle forward to get back on the indicated airspeed. My right hand was a little numb from holding the stick, so flexed it a bit and added nose-up trim, just a hair to take the pressure off. I unfastened my mask to wipe some water out of the flaps on the side of the mask and hurriedly put it back on, although the cockpit pressure altitude was steady at seven thousand feet in the pressurized cockpit. I felt comfortable with the mask on as it didn't seem to feel like it was a cramping my face and I didn't have to reach up and press it closed if I was communicating with anyone. The class chamber ride has tuned me to believing I could survive without oxygen, for some time, but I wouldn't press my luck, plus I like the idea of turning on 100% oxygen during flight. It was cool and seems refreshing and I think it sharpens my night vision.

, although the lights on the Mexico side were not very bright in comparison. The time passed quickly on this leg and the Gulf loomed ahead. The stillness and calm was suddenly interrupted by some conversation going on from one of the student pilots who had a panel light of some kind that came on. It was resolved by one of the in-flight instructors and it was again silent. Once again, I could distinguish aircraft turning in front of me and the time was running down for me to be at the turning point. Houston loomed large and the darkness of the Gulf of Mexico was distinguished by the abrupt demarcation from the land. You could make out moving lights on the dark surface, showing boats moving in the water which made me pause, until I realized what it was. My time expired and I initiated the turn back to our launching point, Laredo. The radio lit up as someone was asking for some assistance in getting his tip tank to feed. There was talk of a circuit breaker that he needed to check. That did the trick and he muttered some sort of thanks to whoever helped him. To my left as I rolled out, I could make out what I thought was Corpus Christi as the Navy Base beacon was rather apparent in the clear sky. This leg called for a check in as we got closer to the base and before we started our approach to the runway. We were going to do an enroute descent to initial for our approach and landing. The cockpit was getting a little close and my butt was aching from the long time in the seat. I felt hot and tired as it had been a long day and I didn't get any sleep this afternoon and chose instead to get in a game of handball at the outdoor, three wall court across the street from the Base Chapel. I was learning the game and some of the instructors played there often. The gym was not air conditioned and was very hot and I wasn't into the indoor sports so took the advice of Lt. Planamento, one of the other handball players and took up the game. I liked it, but I was now thinking today wasn't the best time to play. We had the afternoon off because we were flying tonight, and I wouldn't have slept anyway. At any rate the base and the town could be seen, and it occurred to me that the area seemed well lit now, but when I took off it was very dark. The Rio Grande river was like a large snake and the demarcation between Laredo and Nuevo Laredo was very apparent. My mind had wandered off what I needed to be doing.

The lead instructor came on the headset and indicated he was starting his descent to the base and reminded everyone to stay alert for this visual approach to the runway as our initial breakaway was away from the lights of the town into the dark desert. Red one called his decent, followed by two and I started down, cutting the throttle to idle and picked up my programmed descent speed. Killing off the airspeed was a problem so I held altitude for a time to get on speed, then went into a gentle glide to the base. When I got antsy and the speed built up I would momentarily stop going down until I got back on speed. I was too fast for starting the flaps, but as it turned out I leveled out and was at 1200 feet and still a distance from the runway. I had lost sight of the lights of one and two and had heard the lead instructor say he was breaking away from the runway to check on incoming aircraft. I droned forward until I heard red one call initial. I was lined up with the runway, still looking for two and heard his initial call, then saw him in the turn. I came over the end of the runway and called "red three initial", broke to the left and went on instruments. It was so black outside I didn't trust my sensations and locked on to the attitude indicator and stopped my turn at forty-five degrees. Halfway through I looked out and could see the runway and started my decent to downwind, now sure of my position I dropped my gear and turned base pushed the flap handle to the down position and insured they were full down, glanced up to see the gear was in the green and rolling out straight down the runway. I was right on 120 knots. The runway rushed up as I rounded out and felt a slight drop and then touchdown. Not a "squeeker" to be sure, but adequate. I had finished the night solo navigation requirement of pilot training and it felt good. I left the runway at the first taxiway and hit the parallel and opened the canopy to the very cool evening air, turned right to the parking slot. The crew chief picked me up and waved his parking wands, turning me into the same place I left almost two hours ago. I shut the engine down as he chocked the wheels. I found my seat pin to safe the ejection seat, pushed it in the small hole and crawled out of the night bird, 781 in hand. I told him I didn't have any write-ups, which pleased him greatly. I pulled my chute from the hard metal seat, crawled down the ladder and headed for the flight shack.

Opening the door, the lights were now normal and there were two pilots sitting down, one was Roland, so he had indeed been red-one. We smiled as I secured my chute in the adjacent room and the experience sharing began. Slowly others joined us and when Gabe walked in with Dugan I laughed, wondering if Bob had any difficulty finding initial. I asked him and he gave me some obscene gesture as he walked into the parachute storage room. Soon the room was full of happy "pilots" and the noise was deafening until an instructor poked his head in and asked if we heard anything from red twenty-one. Who was that I wondered? I looked to Lt. Curry's table and didn't see Jesse Hocker. His table mates, Jim Hudson and Roy Hoffman were there, but no Jess. It became very quiet. They called out two of the pilots, one in front and one in back to inquire if they heard anything. In the midst of all that, Lt. Curry walked in and said they located Jesse. He had somehow ended up over the Naval Air Station in Corpus Christi, thinking it was Laredo. He called over "Guard Frequency" and asked why the runway lights were out. They flashed them on and off and when he responded to that they told him where he was and gave him a heading to fly to Laredo. Curry said he should be landing any minute. There was a discernable sigh of relief and the conversations once again started up. When he walked in the door a red-faced, Hocker laughed off the taunts in his deep, Kentucky drawl and sat down. The debriefing was short and sweet. Captain Mc Dade was obviously very pleased and thanked us for our professionalism and air discipline. When dismissed Doug came over to me and told me it was he, who had been on my wing the first leg. He said he wanted to make sure I was awake. Fat chance of that!

THE CHRISTMAS BREAK

E ven United States Air Force Pilot Training takes a break at Christmas. We would have two weeks and for all reasons I decided I would drive home for the break. One of my friends in the barracks, Abe Tanaka told me one of the students at his table in the other flight of 56-H was going home to California and was looking for someone to go with him and share driving. His name was John Williamson and he was going to Pacific Palisades, which was not too far from my home. I told Abe to tell Williamson I was interested. Because Abe and his friend were in "F" Flight and on the opposite schedule from me I found them at lunch after they had flown in the morning and we agreed on the trip. He wanted to take his car and I happily agreed. I would leave my fifty- four Ford safely on the base for the break. Friday was an afternoon "Fly Day" for me, so Saturday morning would be our departure time. I packed my bags after flying and settled in for a night's sleep. Saturday dawned and it was a beautiful day to get out of town. We left early in the morning and drove straight through the night, stopping to change drivers every few hours and arrived at my home on late Sunday afternoon. We traded segments of driving and sleeping so our fatigue factor was rather light. Our only stops had been for gas and food and the traffic throughout the trip had been good to us. We traveled light with only two bags apiece. When we arrived at my house it was barely a stop for John as he waited only long enough for me to get my bags out of the trunk and waved goodbye to me as he wanted to get home before it got too dark. My Mom and I waved as he sped down our street. It would only take him thirty to forty minutes to get to his home. We had agreed that he would pick me up after Christmas and just before New Year's day, which fell on a Saturday, early in the morning, as we had to be back on Sunday night.

It was a very relaxing break and Christmas was always a time for family. My older sisters were both married and would come to my parents home to be with Mom and Dad and sister, Judy and I. Most of my friends were also available to get together, but for some reason it was not the same. Most of them were involved with their girl friends and my closest, growing up friend, John Richey, a Navy Veteran, was married so it was mostly hanging out at home as I did not leave anyone when I left that I had to see or date. I did try to get ahold of a girl I had dated before, but she was not impressed that I was an almost Air Force pilot, nor for that matter, that I was even home. When John showed up to pick me up, I was happy to be going back to Laredo. It would only be five weeks before graduation and I knew the flying would be intense, but it was the downhill time. I still had some requirements to fill, but they should be "no-brainers". John, who I hadn't heard from for almost two weeks, showed up right on time early Saturday morning and as I was about to get into the car, he pointed out to me one of his Christmas presents, seat belts! His mother had had them installed on his Chrysler at Sears and expected him to use them. I was used to wearing a seat belt in all the aircraft I had flown, so this made sense to me, even though I had never worn one in a car before. It sounded good to me, so I said goodbye to my mom and dad, threw my two suitcases in the trunk of John's car, jumped in the right front seat and fastened up. We had two days to get back to Laredo and planned once again on driving straight through, trading driving time every two to three hundred miles. We took off through the Riverside area, through the Cajon Pass to the California desert, crossed into Arizona as the sun was sinking in the West. I took over the driving in Phoenix and we traded once more before I drove the rest of the night. We stopped in El Paso for some breakfast. John had slept much of the night and was ready to take over, but I said I could drive a bit farther. I did make it down the almost deserted road another 40-50 miles, but fatigue took over and I said enough. We were going through Marfa, a small town at the northern end of "Great Bend National Park" it was time to let John take over, so we stopped, got a cup of coffee at a small café just off the highway and John took over as the driver. I had faithfully used the seat belt since we left, so as I settled into the passenger side of the front seat. I fastened the belt around my waist, but very loose so I could turn on my side to sleep. The sun was coming up in what was now a south heading direction to our destination.

I slipped into a deep sleep almost immediately, only to be awaked by a sudden lurching and felt myself flying to the extent of the fastened belt. My head touched the windshield ever so slightly as I fell back in the seat. Dust was rising outside my window and

I was suddenly very awake. The car came to a sudden stop and again I flew forward, once again, touching the windshield and then silence. I looked over at John and he was holding on to the steering wheel, a look of complete wonderment on his face, but obviously not hurt. We opened our individual doors and crawled out into a depression that had stopped the car in its downhill slide. The top of the car had buckled behind the driver's seat and most of the car was wedged in this depression. As the dust settled, I began to see what had transpired. We had run off the four-lane highway and plummeted down this desert hill. Looking up toward the road I could see a group of people standing at the top of the incline, maybe thirty yards away. The trunk had popped open and our bags were exposed, but undamaged. It was a miracle that neither of us had even a scrape. I felt my head but felt only a slight sign of where I hit the windshield. By now it was apparent we wouldn't be driving John's car any further and that the new seat belts had saved us from serious injury. I was very aware that I had been stopped by my belt as I "touched" the windshield. Without it I'm not sure what would have happened. We both paused and looked at one another, still uncertain what happened. I grabbed my small bag and John grabbed one of his, as we knew we couldn't manage both on any attempt to get to Laredo. It was rather cool, but sunny outside and the sweater I was wearing seemed enough, so I didn't remove anything else from my other bag. We were able to close and lock the trunk. We walked to the top of the grade as one of the people on top was walking down to meet us. It turned out he had seen us go off the road and stopped with his family to see if they could help. He was a Mexican farmer traveling to El Paso in a small sedan that seemed to be packed with belongings. He had with him his wife and four young children. We asked if we could get a ride into Alpine, a town about seven miles away. He agreed instantly, stacking his children, two up front on his wife and the other two scrunched together in the back seat with John and I. In his conversation with us, he kept asking if we were OK. Despite the plunge down the hill and the sudden stop we were both amazingly unscathed. I could now feel a slight bump on my head, but surely would have had greater problems if the belt hadn't stopped me from hitting the windshield full force. It was also apparent that John had fallen asleep as the benevolent farmer said we just went straight ahead as the road turned and John didn't remember anything until the first lurch of the car going off the road. The chatter of the driver was the only talking going on as we retraced our way back towards his destination, El Paso. He dropped us off in Alpine, only when he was sure we could manage. We found an AAA office in Alpine and they promised to send a wrecker out to pull John's car out of the side of the hill and bring it into Alpine. The agent said they would retrieve our other bags and keep them in the office until we could come back and get them. I hated leaving mine there but had no choice as it was too cumbersome to carry as we had decided to hitch-hike the remainder of the way to Laredo. It was Sunday and there were no buses scheduled until late that night. It was already almost nine in the morning and we had to sign in by midnight tonight. We would immediately be back in the mix and my flight was flying tomorrow in the morning.

At this point we had no way to know what an adventure it would be! Getting out of Alpine was not a problem as a salesman, going to San Antonio picked us up on the outskirts of town. He would take us to the turnoff of highway U.S. 90, leaving us about 90 miles short of Laredo. It was now early-afternoon and it was a mild, sunny day. We were on standing on the westside a "roundabout", going in four different directions. To our left, going east was the road to San Antonio and to the right the highway led to Mexico. Straight ahead we saw the sign pointing to Laredo. There was little traffic heading south, or for that matter any direction. At least two hours passed and most of the traffic that did appear was going east to San Antonio. When we saw a car approaching the circle we would stand up, hoping they were going south. Finally, as the sun was getting low to the west, a few cars and some small trucks passed us by heading in a southerly direction, but no one even slowed down. Finally, a Pontiac Firebird coupe came whistling from the west on the road to Mexico. As it turned, I could see two men in the front seat. It sped by us and suddenly hit the brakes and backed up, stopping a few feet away. It was a two door, soft-top convertible, red and as the door opened it had white leather seats. The passenger asked where we were going, and we yelled together "Laredo". He said, "climb in". By that time the driver had emerged and was opening the trunk. We threw in our bags and thanked them for stopping. I detected the smell of liquor as we met the driver at the trunk of the car. Climbing in the back seat as it was held forward by the passenger, it was obvious that these two had a few drinks under their belts. We screeched away from the side of the road and headed south. They asked what we did and we told them we were stationed at the airbase outside of town. They told us they would take us right to the gate and that they knew the area very well. It turns out they were both Pontiac dealers, one had the dealership on this side of the river and the other in Mexico. They offered us a drink from and open bottle they had up front and we declined. We were streaking down the road that fortunately had very little traffic. We couldn't see the speedometer, but we were well over the speed limit. The conversation never stopped between the two, laughing and telling us stories as they would turn around to talk to us. John was very nervous, and I wasn't feeling too confident either. After about forty-five minutes they spied a place on the side of the road and pulled in to "have one for the road". They invited us in, but we said we would wait in the car. After they disappeared into the bar, we discussed whether we should get out and see if we could get another ride. We had at most two hours before we had to sign in and the lack of cars and the total darkness outside on the road and our inaccessible bags convinced us we should wait for them, despite their condition. In our minds it was our only chance to make it on time. After what seemed a really, long time, but maybe only a half hour they immerged. The two literally stumbled to the car, still laughing about something. They crawled in and tore back onto the highway, without uttering a word to us. It took us almost another hour before we got to the crossroad to the base. We told them before they got to it, we would walk the half mile to the gate as it would be out of their way to turn off the main highway to go to the base. They protested, but finally said OK. They pulled to the side of the road and the driver got out and opened the trunk and said something I didn't understand. We both thanked them and took our bags and greatly relieved, gladly walked to the gate.

We showed our ID cards to the guard and made our way to the headquarters building, where the OD (officer of the day) showed us where to sign in. It was twenty minutes to midnight. A bed had never felt this good.

THE LAST NORMAL WEEKS

The flight schedule for this first week back was very skimpy for me on the return to flying, one instrument ride and one solo ride, all in the morning on a blustery week, lots of wind, mostly down the runway. It didn't affect flying too much, but it was cold. It was time to wear our thermals again or experience the discomfort while walking to and from certain areas of the daily routine. On some afternoons while in academics the rise of a few cumulus clouds in the east became the subject of "day-dreaming" of times at Malden and flying with Pinky. He was always talking about the beauty of the growing cumulus cloud and quick to tell you how dangerous it was to fly into one in any stage, but early in the "growth" you could be subject to rapid changes in altitude and heavy turbulence. Of course, we heard similar things during our weather classes, but Pinky was the one who impressed on me to avoid even getting close to one. In the T-6 I never had the opportunity to fly high enough to see the top of one as it grew, but the boiling sight of one growing as I looked up always impressed me. Once in the T-33 seeing the rapid growth of one as it materialized in the distance always reminded me of the danger within this act of nature. Even getting close was dangerous as spouting from those clouds was hail the size of baseballs that could break the strongest of windscreens on any aircraft dumb enough to test the proximity of one.

One of my last solo rides stood out as memorable as I had been doing my usual light and non-violent aerobatics and noticed as I was half way through a lazy eight my tip tank light was on. Staring at the light I checked to make sure I had selected the feed pattern for my fuel and saw the tips should be feeding. The fuel panel was set properly. But they weren't feeding! I remembered in previous conversations that there was a circuit breaker that controlled that, but I couldn't remember which one. I had leveled out and stared at the panel trying to remember which one it was, but no luck. There also didn't seem to be any that were extended or popped up. I had to call mobile control. They answered promptly and I told them my tips were not feeding and they gave me the one to pull and reset, which I did. The light remained on; still no feed from the tips. They told me to rock the wings abruptly and I did, still no feed. I became the object of a great deal of attention now. There was a conversation going on down below and intermittently there would be a question and after my response there was silence and then another question until a long pause dominated the radio. I thought maybe a snap roll might do it, but didn't want to, without asking. I hesitated and while thinking about it, mobile control started talking to me about a jettison area for the tips, which really got my attention. I was listening to the instructions for getting rid of the tip tanks, when the urge to roll the airplane took over. I did two consecutive rolls and as I rolled out the light went out and my tips started to feed. I thought something other than the pilots in mobile control compelled me to do that maneuver. I paused and made sure the tips were indeed feeding and then radioed that the tanks were feeding. Another pause and then they asked what I did. When I told them how I did it there was a silent moment and then someone said something like finish your flight. Roger that I replied; Nuff said!

INSTRUMENT FLIGHT

nstrument Flying in the T-bird always provided a stable platform, after takeoff and then putting up the "hood" in the back seat had a mysterious effect as you would go from sunshine to darkness and then be told to take control of the aircraft. Most of the handoff were very normal and after a few seconds you were acclimatized, and your eyes were riveted on the instrument panel. The "attitude indicator" was always the first in your cross check of the instruments in front of you, however it didn't take much to divert your attention to other sources needed to sustain flight, such as the airspeed indicator and the heading indicator. Your inner sanctum didn't necessarily close in on you, but it definitely gave you a feeling of being alone. Tuning in to a given range identifier would be an immediate task given to you by your instructor and then a "radial to intersect and home into the station. Once you effect station passage, the choices were many. You could be told to hold in a racetrack pattern and use two minutes for each leg and doing that on a certain radial, or you could just track outbound on a radial for a certain time. The instrument ride would end with a penetration to the desired runway, most were "teardrop", and pick up a radar controlled,

Ground Controlled Approach (GCA) with you being vectored on radio to your landing by individuals tracking you on the ground. You could also use the Instrument Landing System (ILS) where you follow the instrumentation in your cockpit to fly the approach to landing. All in all, the flights were usually a draining effort as you are locked on and in for a long period of time. When the instructor in the front seat finally takes over for the landing you are physically and emotionally spent. Those were the normal instrument rides, however in the ride this week the turbulence from takeoff through the entire flight was hard on my ability to maintain altitude and heading. It was much more pronounced close to the ground, flying an ILS (Instrument Landing System) to minimum altitude, 200 feet with a go around, picking up another instrument approach. I flew a GCA (Ground Controlled Approach), and thought I was on a washboard, bouncing all over the sky. Trying to follow the voice directions on final was insane. I would bounce through low and high on glide slope. Doug kept telling me this was light turbulence, but I knew better as I had read the "Airman's Guide", which outlines the degree of turbulence, but said nothing. Fortunately, Doug took the aircraft at minimums and made a full stop landing. I was drenched from the effort and welcomed his offer to open the canopy as we taxied back to the parking spot. The rush of cold air was way more than I bargained for, so ducked down behind the seat in the front station. Exiting, Doug looked at me and said, "good ride", a surprise as he usually didn't comment until we debriefed. Today there was no debriefing.

THE CROSS-COUNTRY NAVIGATION LEG

Time was fast approaching to the 56-H graduation just a month away, when Doug approached me and said I had a requirement to complete a cross-country navigation flight. He also added that I needed an instrument check and that could be done on the return flight. It got a lot better when he then told me I could go anywhere I wanted within limits and it would be an out and back to some destination preferably over a weekend, returning to Laredo after an overnight. It would be limited to a one stop out to the destination and one stop back to the base. That left out a flight home as that would require at best two stops. I had thought about it for a couple of days and finally said, "how about Denver?" That had been my early childhood home and I had a lot of close family members my age in that city and it would afford an opportunity to see them. Doug was agreeable to the destination and set about trying to come up with a plan to get there. There was an Air Force base in Denver, called Lowery AFB and in checking, it was open to transient flights in and out and would provide us with all the support we needed. We could go into Lowery AFB on Saturday and return Sunday night. Looking further for possible bases enroute to Lowery, a good refueling stop would be Biggs

AFB in El Paso Texas, however that might be stretching it a bit. In checking, Doug said we could make it, as long as we didn't run into unfavorable winds aloft. From there Denver would be a sprint. Leaving early on Saturday we could be in El Paso by 1100 hours and no more than an hour later we can be in the air for the short hour, plus to Denver. That would be the first day and staying overnight in Denver, taking off the next day to come back. Doug had used Love Field, a commercial airport in Dallas previously. with a refueling stop at Love Field, in Dallas, an Air Force reserve unit was based there, and it would provide us with the fuel and support as they were used to T-33 aircraft and we would then fly back Sunday night to Laredo. I would call my cousin, Tom Young and have him pick me up for a night of visiting the Young-Phelan (all my mother's side of the family) cousins.

I called Tom and asked if he would be able to accommodate the trip and he was happy to do so. It was all arranged; it should be a great trip. Tom Young was an all-state running back football player in high school and my cousin by marriage to Charlene (called Chuck) Phelan. Although he was a bit older, we had always gotten along very well and I had always admired him, not only for his athletic ability, but he had come back from a terrible auto accident to lead a great life. He was fun to be with and a totally dedicated family man. He would pick me up about 1700 in the Officers club at the base. I set about doing the necessary flight planning, cutting and pasting maps for both the going out and coming back flights. Doug had indicated he would be happy to spend a night in Denver, a place he said he had never been.

Early Saturday morning Doug and I met in an almost empty

flight ops building. Bob Bilbro, one of the married students was in there with his instructor, Lieutenant Nestel. They were also going on a cross-country, but I didn't catch to where. One of the academic instructors was going on a weekend solo flight to March AFB, his home was close by in Riverside. All in all, I was excited to go to Denver. My cousins and I had been close for many years despite the fact, that we lived 1200 miles apart. I had spent many summers in Denver visiting my Mother's family, staying with one of my mother's brothers, who my father had as good friends before my mom and dad were married. I felt my uncles were like second fathers and their sons, who I had shared many experiences together, were closer than cousins. We were the same age and it would be great to see them again. Knowing Tom would spread the word, I looked forward to the return and hoped to see some of my many relatives.

We picked up our already prepared maps and flight plan I had meticulously prepared on Friday and proceeded to base operations to submit our flight plan and get our enroute weather. As it turned out it was going to be a beautiful day all the way to El Paso and then to Denver. This, of course, was all new to me, as I had never filed a flight plan before, and weather had always been part of our daily briefing before our student's flights started. The weather officer was very specific about what the great day it was and told us the winds aloft should not have an effect on our flight to Biggs. Once the flight plan was filed, we walked out to our T-33, parked a short distance down the ramp, carrying our chutes on our backs and carrying a light overnight bag in our arms. Reaching the aircraft, the crew chief had already opened a panel on the side of the aircraft for our thin bags. We stored them as the crew chief fastened the dzus fasteners, insuring, the panel was flush and tight. The pre-flight was uneventful and I went up the ladder into the front cockpit and Doug hopped in the back. This would be our arrangement until the return flight Sunday out of Love Field, where I would switch to the back seat and start my instrument check on the flight back to Laredo. After strapping in I saw the crew-chief was standing fire guard and was ready for me to start the engine. I rotated my index finger and initiated the turbine, followed by bringing the throttle around the horn and immediately getting ignition. Placing the throttle in neutral, I waited for the chocks to appear at the side of the aircraft and saw the crew chief, chocks at his feet, motioning for me to taxi out of the parking slot. I pushed the throttle forward and moved slowly out on another first adventure of my training program. Doug would not give me any help in the instrument departure from Laredo and as far as the en-route navigation, I would not get any help from the back seat. I needed to find a radial outbound to pick up any of the various air routes and legs to Denver. The first task, and obstacle, was to get my route clearance for this endeavor. There was no mobile control to talk to, so the tower gave us clearance to launch and pick up our first enroute leg to Biggs AFB in El Paso. Once that was accomplished it would be just another dual ride, but the destination would be a new one, not Laredo. Once in the air I intercepted the outbound leg from the Laredo radio range and picked up my heading to the first "fix" on my route map, which I had laboriously worked on Friday. I had folded it carefully so that I could attach it to my "Knee Pad" to show the first legs of the flight and made sure it was readable, with call signs and identifiers for each turning point. The weatherman had hit it right on the nose as it was nothing but blue sky for as far as you could see, no turbulence and looking ahead, much the same. I leveled out at twenty-seven thousand and settled into the routine of selecting beacon legs for each of the position points and identifiers I needed to intercept. At the same time, I was conscious of my fuel state and the last vestiges of my tip tanks as they were being exhausted. Both tip tank lights illuminated, and I switched to my internal wing tanks. The body tank, the final ninety gallons of fuel would be the last used tank. When on that tank there was a tiny clicker in the cockpit that would count down from ninety in double digits in such a way that you could not ignore the roll downward to a dry tank and flameout of the engine. On student normal training missions this tank was seldom used, however sometimes it would come into play as you were entering the pattern for landing. I was intent on being attentive to being on heading for my navigation legs and anticipating my destination fix was a prime need. I would tune that in as soon as I got in range of that beacon. Using the outbound leg radial was an ideal way to stay on course. Doug was busy listening to some radio program and I'm sure keeping notes on my progress, despite seemingly disinterested in what I was doing. I had trimmed the aircraft to the point that I had little pressure on my right hand on the stick, but occasionally I would use my left hand to shake the stiffness that came about. Time passed quickly as I picked out significant items, I had marked on my map to hone my dead-reckoning skills. As I approached the El Paso area, I was given permission for an enroute penetration to Biggs. The wing tanks were almost exhausted. I pulled back the throttle and started a controlled descent to the field when the first sound of the "clicker" began to roll down. Eighty-eight appeared in the tiny window. I adjusted my heading and started a turn inbound to the outer marker and ILS start descent point to the runway. Seventy-eight gallons of fuel remained, and the clicker sound signaled the fuel level was going down that two gallons at a crack. Click, Click, Click started to interrupt my thinking as I dropped my gear I started to milk the flaps, Click, Click, Click. I could see the runway visually and declared for a visual approach, terminating my looking at the instrument panel and glancing toward that infernal sound, Click, Click. Doug had not said a word as I called out gear and flaps and going visual. I was over the end of the runway and still about twenty feet in the air, but right on airspeed. I rounded out to a squeaky landing and rolled to the second turnoff. I cleared the runway and switched to ground control and was told to pick up the "Follow-Me" vehicle. I spied it coming toward me so paused to let it turn in front of me. I was cleared to a parking spot right in front of Base Operations. I asked Doug if the canopy was clear and received an affirmative, so brought it up. The somewhat cool, not cold air seemed very refreshing and I opened the mask clasp, letting it fall from my mouth and turned off my individual oxygen lever. It was a very nice day, sunny and no wind to speak of. It was announced by approach control that the temperature was 62 degrees, not bad for a Late January day. As I pulled into the parking slot, I took a final look at the clicker and saw fifty-four. I cut the engine and waited for the chocks to be set. We had been in the air for an hour and fifty minutes and Doug had been silent for most of that time. His comments were sporadic to say the least. He did indicate that it had been "smooth", but no mention of the final fuel state which I'm sure he followed closely as there was a duplicate display in the back seat. We went into Base Ops to get updated weather for Denver and renew our flight plan for the legs to Denver. Inside I asked Doug how far we could have gone with the fuel left in the body tank and he replied, "about ten to fifteen minutes". He then told me if I had made any mistakes in my calculations and route decisions he would have taken over and brought the airplane into Biggs. He said I had done fine. When arriving at the weather desk to get our updated information Doug asked about the winds aloft and seemed satisfied when he learned that we had hit a head wind that was not in our original forecast when we picked up our northwest heading, causing our ETE (estimated time en-route) to be off some fifteen minutes. After filing our new flight plan and grabbing a Pepsi out of a machine in the lobby, we walked back out into the sunny Texas day and crawled into our refueled aircraft. I felt a bit unsettled as I had blindly pressed on despite my fuel state and the fact that my times between fixes were off by a minute or two at each turning point. Doug, knowing the weather at the destination was clear, had allowed me to continue. It was a lesson learned!

The flight to Denver was uneventful, cruising at 28,000 feet in relatively clear skies. The time en-route was on the nose. One thing that got my attention was how difficult it was over that time period to hold heading and altitude, flying manually as the slightest movement of the stick would move you ever so little a degree off your heading or a hundred feet off your altitude. Winds aloft were as predicted and as we hit the high penetration fix, I could see the Denver skyline below. The snow-covered Rockies seemed to stretch far to the west, but there was no apparent snow around the city below.

My Uncle Grat was the vice president of the Denver National Bank and his son Don and I were the same age. We used to sunbathe and swim in Washington Park, which was close to his house on many summer days. I had spent lots of summers in the cellar bedroom of the Phelan home. Uncle Grat was a hero for me. He was a self-made man, who had risen from a teen-aged "runner" for the bank to his present state as the Vice President for oil development in the bank. He received his college degree well into his fifties and was a highly respected individual throughout the city. He was never too tired to play catch with me or play a round of golf and he was good at both.

I more than likely would not see the grown-up cousins I used to visit as they were not in the area, Don was in the Army and others had jobs outside of the city. There wouldn't be that much time to round up many of them for the one night. Tom had agreed to pick me up and take me to their home in South Denver and wanted me to spend the night. They had a group of children and wanted to put me up for the night so it might be crowded, but fun to see them again. He also said he had a few of my relatives coming by the house to see me. It would be an interesting night.

Enough thought for now as I had to get on the ground and land on this short runway at Lowery AFB, located over five thousand feet in altitude. Lowery was located almost in the middle of the suburbs of Denver, so the approach to landing would be over residences that had been allowed to rise after the base had already been there. Many of the WWII bases had been built in outlying areas, only to be overtaken by development. It was only later that the government placed restrictions on building around those fields. Even then the surrounding residents, who moved into these areas, knowing that a noisy airfield was there, were the constant complainers about aircraft making too much noise. It was an interesting conundrum that the base officials were faced with. I started the penetration to the field. It was a "teardrop" from twenty thousand and the outer fix for the ILS (Instrument Landing System) was a tad over seven thousand feet indicated, but only 1200 AGL (above ground level). I was on the "glide-slope" and visually was lined up with the runway. As I got to the base perimeter about two hundred feet AGL I noticed we were going over fencing that surrounded the runway and the base proper. I touched down about a thousand feet down the runway and rolled all the way to the end of this, 7500 feet long, very short runway, especially for jet aircraft, made shorter by the altitude, having to apply the brakes more than I was used to. Turning off and clearing the runway we were told to taxi to the front of Base Operations. Again a "Follow-Me" truck appeared to lead us to our parking location. We were steered into a slot just opposite to the front door. The only other aircraft close was a B-25 parked nose to me just across the parking taxiway. The "Follow-Me" truck disgorged a fatigue-clad individual, who carried a set of wheel chocks and signaled me to shut the engine down. I quickly noted that the body tank was still full and that we had been in the air one hour and thirty-five minutes. I placed the safety pin into the ejection seat and made sure the red flag was visible over the arm rest. The chocks were set and I unbuckled the seat belt and shoulder harness and leg straps on my chute. I remembered we were going to leave the chutes in the cockpit overnight, so unfastened the chest strap and stepped out onto the ladder placed next to the cockpit. I jumped to the ground and Doug and I took our helmets, placed them in their bags and tossed them into our seats, closed the canopy, opened up an access panel on the left side of the aircraft and took out our small bags with overnight clothes and toiletries, closed the panel and walked into base ops. It was a crisp early evening, about 4:00 PM local. We had closed out our flight plan and got an USAF moto pool transportation vehicle to take us to the BOQ (Bachelor Officers Quarters) located right next to the Officers club, got a couple of rooms and then I called Tom to tell him we had arrived. He said he would be there in a short time, time enough to take a shower and get into civilian clothes and out of the green bag. I told Doug I would see him tomorrow and headed to the room. After a brief time, I was ready to go and went to the O'Club to wait for my ride. Doug was sitting in the lounge outside the dining room, so sat with him, when Tom walked in. I introduced him to Tom and before I knew it Doug was going with us for whatever party there was to be. Tom convinced Doug he shouldn't be alone so the three of us piled into Tom's car and headed to Englewood, a suburb of Denver.

Doug had accepted the invitation and was in for a night he would never forget. The party with "cousins by the dozens", mostly on Tom's side of the family. It was a fun party that lasted most of the night and ended with Doug and me in a set of bunk beds, usually used by two of Tom and Charlene's boys. The boys awakened us early Sunday morning and led us to a breakfast prepared by Charlene. After eating we were driven back to the base where we made a quick stop at our unused rooms, changed into our flight suits and drove to base ops. It was a real treat for the boys to walk out to our aircraft and Tom said they would stay for our takeoff from Lowery AFB. We filed our flight plan and gathered our clearance to Love Field in Dallas and during our weather briefing we were happy to get favorable weather with favorable tail winds en-route. There was a note of caution as we reviewed our takeoff data as the temperature for takeoff was at a level that increased our distance for takeoff almost to the length of the runway. It was not to the point that we exceeded our critical field length, but very close. Doug felt we would be OK, so we pressed on to the aircraft. Once ready for start engines Doug asked the tower for the current temperature and it was as forecast so he told me to start the engine and press on. When ready to taxi I saw Tom, Charlene and boys standing in front of base operations watching as we prepared to leave. I waved as did Doug and went to the end of the runway. On the hammerhead, Doug once more asked for the current temperature. This time it was two degrees warmer than forecast. Doug instructed me to not do a rolling takeoff, instead to take the active as close to the end as possible and hold, set the brakes and bring up full power before releasing brakes. When settled, after a sharp, almost 90% turn to the runway I stood on the brake pedals, brought up power, stabilized at 100%. Everything was in the green and released the brakes. It was still all good at sixty knots and then again at our go-no-go speed of a hundred and twenty knots. At one hundred and fifty, I pulled the nose up and Doug beat me to the gear handle and pulled the gear up. I couldn't help but be watching the fence at the end of the overrun as it loomed large as we got to takeoff speed. We cleared the fence by a fraction, and I felt that Doug was on the controls with me to insure I kept the nose at a desired takeoff angle to maximize our climb over the fence. It was very close! (Later when talking to Tom on the phone, thanking him for the night, he said it was so close that he thought the gear, still coming up would hit the top of the fence.)

On the departure out of the base we were given a climb on course and were told we were clear of traffic. Leveling off at 29,000 feet I felt the need for a shot of 100% oxygen as my head was a bit fuzzy. Doug wasn't talking so I pulled out my map and folded it out to display our route to Dallas. The trip from level off to Dallas Love field was routine as I made all my airborne flight paths fix to fix on time and had a straight in penetration to Love. This is where the change would take place. We only need a top-off for our fuel but ran into a delay due to some mix up with our clearance back to Laredo. Once that was resolved we got to the airplane, took out our parachutes and made the switch to the back seat for my final instrument check. I remember taxiing out past people, watching prior to their departures on commercial aircraft. This tiny single engine jet trainer was moving among large, reciprocal engine planes. We seemed very small, but I felt buoyed by being in this situation, qualified to fly a jet aircraft in a period of reciprocal engines being the common mode of travel. People noticed too!

We had refueled on the military side of the airport, where a small detachment worked for transient military aircraft. I asked Doug if there were any permanent aircraft stationed there and he said no. We were well taken care of by their transient services on a Sunday in Texas. Now taxiing across to the commercial side was like an entrance into the big time.

The final instrument check I was to be given on the return to Laredo didn't seem like a big deal as I had been tracking routes between fixes for two days. We went to the end of the runway and had to wait for two airliners, one a TWA tri-tailed aircraft and the other was a United that looked a lot like a familiar military aircraft. I think we called it a C-54, not sure. We finally took the runway and with Doug now at the controls, took off. Once safely in the air I was told to raise the hood around the interior of the back cockpit, (the back seat had a hood which could be installed prior to flight for use to insure a student could not look out during an instrument ride) and fly the programmed departure out of the airport. It was just after sundown and there was a hint of a sunset, but it was fading fast. It didn't matter as once the hood was fully, engaged I was locked on my departure heading. The weather at Laredo was to be clear and we should be there before 2000 hours according to our flight plan with no traffic in the area on this Sunday night. We had gained an hour going into Denver and we were losing that hour on our return. Forecast en-route winds were not programmed to be a factor. It should be a "no-brainer" and by now Doug, despite the remnants of a slight hangover was in a good and joking mood, something I hadn't seen in him since I started flying with him in "Basic". I have the feeling he too took part in using 100% Oxygen going to Dallas.

This departure was a matter of following the standard route for going out of "Love" in a southerly direction. I had placed the copy of the map I picked up from operations on my knee pad and had memorized the outbound heading I would intercept to climb to altitude. This would take me to a departure fix to pick up the outbound heading as I reached altitude and level off. Once level it was a simple matter of going from fix to fix, staying on the heading while I flew straight and level. Tuning radio frequencies was another matter, then intercepting a radial inbound to a new fix, fortunately Dallas to San Antonio was easy, then going outbound from San Antonio to Laredo and finally picking up the Laredo radio range and going inbound to Laredo. It was now a moonless, dark night outside of the hood and It was very tiring holding altitude, however it was a smooth night with virtually no turbulence and according to Doug a beautiful clear sky. Finally, I had reached the inbound heading to the Adcock range that signaled Laredo AFB. According to Doug on our mission planning I would have to complete identifying station passage, enter a holding pattern, make the published penetration, and complete two instrument approaches. (The plan would be to identify station passage then I would enter a two turn holding pattern. It was a "racetrack figure". Legs would be two minutes long and then a 180 degree turn on each end. The second time I hit the fix I would start the standard penetration to the field. I would first do and ILS (Instrument Landing System)) approach, something I had practiced in the flight simulator and on other instrument flights. I would go around when I hit the missed approach altitude (two hundred feet AGL-above ground level). I would then ask for a radar approach using a GCA, (Ground Controlled Approach)) following the instructions of a controller who would pick me up and direct me to the runway and decent to a landing. This would complete my instrument check.) I had two minutes to my ETA (estimated time of arrival) and I had a steady pattern of Dit-Da, the Morse Code "A". Upon passage I would hear the Da-Dit for the "N". The range was divided into four quadrants, two of which you heard the "A" and two the "N". As my time was winding down, I wanted to hear that change and would then assume flying the holding pattern, by initiating the first 180 degree turn to the left. My ETA passed and no "N". Doug was silent and after two minutes he spoke out. "You missed station passage". It was like a knife to the heart. I told him I never got an "N". He said to complete a turn back to the fix, so I did an identification turn, a ninety followed by a 270 degree turn to go back to the station and this time had no problem going from the "A" to the "N", and picked up station passage. I completed the two racetrack patterns and called for a penetration to approach control. Given clearance, at station passage I pulled the throttle to idle and started the teardrop penetration to the outer marker for my ILS. It was flawless, even if I do say so myself. It was an excellent job. I was on the glide-slope; crosshairs were perfect and on airspeed. On the go around Doug took the airplane so I could take a break before flying the GCA. Outside of a momentary break at level-off it was my first time, hands off the stick in an hour. After we were established on downwind, I was given back control of the aircraft.

Following the directions of the ground controller I turned base, then final and started descent, gear and flaps were set for landing. I was virtually on heading and glide-slope for the entire final and at minimum altitude, rather than initiating a go-around, Doug took control and landed the aircraft. It had been a busy two days of flying and we logged almost eight hours of flying time and two hours of instrument time, however Doug informed me I flunked my check for missing station passage. I would have to have another instrument ride to demonstrate I can recognize station passage. It was a total fluke that I had gone from one quadrant to another and arrived in the same Morse Code designator, but I had and should have made some move at my ETA to resolve the problem. I did not! I was spent and tomorrow I would have to show up for the morning flying session, although I would not be programmed to fly. The aircraft had been good to us as we had no major write-ups, making the crew chief happy. Wwe dropped off our chutes and left the flight line. At least my cross-country requirement was finished. I would still have to do another instrument check to complete all the requirements to get my wings. The thought crossed my mind, does anyone flunk out this late in the program?

THE FINAL DAYS

Doug didn't make me wait too long to retake the check and went dual on an instrument ride two days later. We climbed to altitude and joined with two other aircraft for a little formation flying. With Doug in the front seat my reference point was a bit different, but I was able to establish my position. After a very few minutes Doug and the others decided they wanted to play so we had instructors in formation doing barrel rolls in echelon. It was very impressive. We were in the number two position and I was watching number three. He was tucked in so tight I could see the sweat coming down his face. I know they are experienced pilots, but I don't know if I can ever get to that level. They spent twenty minutes going through every imaginable maneuver and finally all had other things to complete with their students, so we broke off and went our own way. Doug immediately told me to put the hood up and track into the range fix, which was already in the display. In listening to the identifier for the range I immediately picked up an "N" and tracked into the station. We must have been close when we left the other two aircraft as I picked up the "A" after only a few minutes and immediately went into a right turn, standard holding pattern. Doug took the aircraft and split "S" to the field, called initial and completed the visual pattern, landing with a squeak of tires and taxied to the parking slot. After deplaning he indicated as we walked in that I had passed my instrument check and most of my remaining flying would be solo. I was relieved and very pleased and knew that the last couple of weeks I would be able to fly the programmed hours solo before graduation.

SOLO FLIGHTS

Most of the solo flights were basic flying out the proscribed, time type, being told to log a certain time as every student was programmed to have 262 total hours before graduating. There was one flight, however that was memorable. I was on a morning flight on a day with a forecast that should have prevented me as a student from flying. There was supposed to be a front passing through with some rain, but visibility in the area was to remain above student minimums. It was relatively clear on departure, but as I climbed out from the base to the east, I could see buildups to the north that looked ominous. I proceeded to an open area to keep my location to the east of the base, staying in the clear as much as possible and above all the clouds. Slowly I could see the field disappearing under the cloud cover to the west. I was contacted by the base and told the base was below student minimums and to proceed east and stay clear of the weather and look to land at Barksdale AFB for refueling and wait out the storm passage. I called Dallas Center and asked for clearance to proceed to my new destination and pulled out the flip chart for Barksdale and headed east. I was told by flight operations to call the squadron upon arrival for instructions. With clearance I flew directly to

Barksdale and got an en-route descent from approach control to this strange, new base (for me) and looked up on final to see this huge runway, seemingly as wide as it was long. After landing, I was directed to pick up the "Follow Me" vehicle and was asked my intentions. I told them I would need fuel but was not sure until I called my home base. I was led to a parking space in front of Base Operations. It was a SAC (Strategic Air Command) base and the security was suffocating. An Air Police truck met me as I left the aircraft and they too asked my intensions. I told them I didn't know as I had to call my home base for further instructions. In our discussion they actually asked to see my ID card to verify I was a friend (where did they think I got the airplane?) and then I was escorted into Base Ops. I asked for a phone and called back to Laredo and was told to refuel and head east to stay away from the weather as they wanted me to get flying time. They suggested I go to Pensacola Naval Air Station in Florida and RON (remain overnight) and check in tomorrow. I filed a flight plan for a direct flight to the Navy Air Station. Weather was to be good the entire way and arrival was to be clear. I should get there in daylight so it would be something I could easily handle. I was escorted from Base Ops by the same Air Police that led me into the building. Their vehicle still had its rotating beacon flashing red as I walked to my aircraft between two Air Policemen. I did my walk around and basic pre-flight, hoping I would find everything OK, under the watchful eye of this force around me. I checked to make sure I got a full fuel load, entered the cockpit and started my engine, signaled for the crew chief to pull the chocks and started my taxi back to that massive runway, and of course, followed by my friends in their vehicle. After being cleared onto the runway I pushed the power forward. I glanced over to see the AP vehicle, with lights out returning to somewhere, awaiting the next unsuspecting aircraft landing there. Taking flight into the clear Louisiana sky I was given an en-route departure to the east, cleared and climbing to FL 280 (twenty-eight thousand feet). I found myself enjoying the solitude, but now alone and flying away from my military home I was a bit unsettled, maybe even a little scared and was listening for any noise that was unfamiliar and for any light to come on. I fanaticized "flame out", bail out and other intriguing problems. I wondered what going to a single engine fighter, like the F-86 or even the new F-100 would be like. I admitted to myself I was a bit afraid, being solo and flying away from my familiar environs, landing could not come quick enough. This was the first time I was alone and away from my secure self and it was not satisfying! I was finally given clearance to start my descent to Pensacola. It was clear and I could make out the base from a distance, so honed in on maintaining the heading I was given and maintaining airspeed. The voice of a GCA Controller broke the silence and my locked-on spell, giving me a new heading to final approach to the runway. I could obviously see it but chose to not make a visual approach and follow his directions. As I was about to hit the final approach, it dawned on me I had not configured the aircraft for landing. I quickly dropped the gear and started the flaps, getting everything set for the descent. I completed the descent and make a good landing. The roll-out was short and I quickly exited at the second taxiway. A friendly "Follow-Me" truck appeared and led me to a parking slot close to Base Operations.

Exiting the aircraft, I was not met by security, but was met by a friendly, transient crew chief who asked me if I had any problems with the aircraft. I responded that there were no write-ups and all I needed was fuel. I also told him I was staying the night and would leave at some time tomorrow. He was fine with that and asked if I needed to open the side panel for my overnight bag. I told him I was not prepared to not return to Laredo, where I was in flight training. He laughed and said I could get a ride to the VOQ/BOQ (visiting officer quarters /bachelor officer quarters) in operations. It was a short walk to the building and when entering, walked to the desk and closed my flight plan and asked for transportation to the VOQ. I called back to Laredo and gave them my location and they told me to call back in the morning The all white clad seaman at the desk made the call and shortly thereafter a vehicle appeared and whisked me to the front of a columned white building, with a gold on black sign signifying it as the "Officer's Quarters". As I walked in, I was overcome with the white uniforms, with a smattering of khakis outfits and the impeccable surroundings. I could smell my flight suit and knew I was terribly out of place. The check-in was painless and the smartly dressed civilian behind the desk even gave me a towel, a toothbrush and a small tube of toothpaste with my key to a room at the top of the stairs on the second floor. I was pointed to a place to buy some fresh under-ware and a tee-shirt. He also told me that the dining room was around the corner and that it was ok to eat in a flight suit. After I bought the new clean underwear I chose to go to the room before eating and shower, put on the clean clothes and then pull on the smelly flight suit, even a new t-shirt could not close out the odor. It was an appropriate time to eat as the sun was sinking when I went down the stairs to the dining room. It was about half full, with navy uniformed individuals, some with dates or wives, but mostly two or three guys together. I was led to a small table in the corner, I'm sure to protect the fresh and clean clientele. Fortunately, I had a few bucks in my wallet and ordered a good meal and had a beer. I realized half-way through the meal I was very tired, and the beer didn't help. I finished my meal and went back to my overnight room and peeled the sweaty smelling suit off and crawled into bed. I, picked up the phone and asked for an early wakeup call and fell quickly to sleep. The next morning, I was forced to put on my stinky flight suit, however I had on clean and fresh under-ware and T-shirt. As I walked through the lobby, I peeked in to see if the dining room was open and of course it was. I ordered some coffee and scooped up some scrambled eggs from the tray and stuck in two pieces of bread in the toaster. Nobody engaged me in conversation, so ate my food and when finished I called and asked for transportation to Base Operations, checked out of the VOQ (Visiting Officer's Quarters) into a beautiful, crisp sunny day. My requested transportation was waiting between the white columns that spanned the front of the building. My driver was once again a cute,young, female, seaman wearing a starched white uniform. She knew my destination, even though I told her that I was going to Base Operations. I had had some coffee put into a container and carefully got into the front seat. She politely told me I had to sit in the back, so I obligingly moved, almost spilling the coffee as I got out. There were no words between us as we took the five-minute ride to the flight line. I walked into base ops, went to the desk and asked for the land line, to make a call to Laredo. The captain who answered the phone was aware of my "journey", and said the weather was good and that I should make the trip back to the base and gave me some options for each leg. I checked outside and my aircraft was right where I left it last night. I opened the canopy, took the ladder resting on the ground and reached in and picked up the "781" off the seat. The aircraft had a full fuel load. I went back in, to flight plan the trip, and used the first suggested stop from the captain at Laredo., Jackson, Mississippi and then I would go from there to Perrin AFB in Texas, which might be a stretch and then on to Laredo. I submitted the flight plan with the first destination and walked in to get weather and was met by a very attractive Navy Commander in a, you guessed it, starched white uniform. She had a nice smile and was very pleasant as she briefed me on the en-route and destination weather. She did seem to be trying to keep her distance as my flight suit, and its sweat patterns were obviously a distraction. There was a problem with the weather as I would be heading west into winter high altitude winds that are usually accompanied with turbulence and my ground speed would be much slower than I had anticipated. I may have to adjust my plans in the air, so I found a couple of bases short of Jackson that I could use if needed. I thanked her and walked back out into the crisp Florida morning. The T-33 sitting there looked very sleek and my thoughts went to my next aircraft after my hopeful graduation from pilot training. I had opted not to accept a three-year extension to my service commitment to get an aircraft of choice, more, so the likelihood of the next aircraft wouldn't be an F-86 or the new F-100. Instead an F-89 or F-94 would more than likely pop up.

I had grown up a very short distance from Northrop Aircraft in Hawthorne, California and often watched the newly finished aircraft, with their still green protective exterior, takeoff on the very short runway outside their factory at the Hawthorne Airport. They were stripped down aircraft, with only the fuel needed to go the short distance across the local mountains, on their way to another location, (Edwards AFB) to get the finishing touches on their development, loading other equipment, and bring out the silver finish on the exterior of the aircraft. It was a cumbersome, heavy looking, straight-wing aircraft with two outsized rocket-carrying tubes on the tips of each wing. It was an Air Defense Command aircraft as was the F-94. One day while heading to my college part time job at my brother-in-law's gas station there was an F-89 being towed into position to the far extent of the short runway. I was on a road that paralleled the runway. I slowed down to watch it take off for its final touches at the Northrop plant at Edwards Air Force Base. It was backed up to the ramp in front of the fence on Prairie Avenue. The ramp was an exhaust deflector as well as a noise-deflector device to protect the local area. When in place, as close to the fence as possible, the pilot brought the two jet engines up to full power and released brakes. I proceeded to bring my car speed up to follow him and as he passed me, he was still firmly planted on the runway. I hit 70 in my 1938 four door Chevrolet sedan at this point and I was maybe a third down the stretch of road that paralleled the runway. I watched and slowed down to view his takeoff. As he approached the 7-8 foot chain link fence, at the end of the runway on Century Boulevard. He was still firmly on the ground and he suddenly broke through it, going across the Boulevard, missing any traffic that was on this major road and plowing into a raised area where dirt had been piled up around a drainage ditch, launching into the air and crashing on the other side. There was no fire, no explosion only a large cloud of dust. I had stopped at the end of the road and could see the fence sprawled across the roadway. People were running to the place where the aircraft had hit the dirt embankment. Traffic had totally stopped in both directions. I was unable to get closer than where I was due to the debris on the road but knew no one could survive what I had witnessed. I was later to find out that the pilot did survive. He had been ejected or ejected himself as the aircraft launched into the air, but due to the downward point of leaving the aircraft he went parallel to the ground and because the field was a fully grown field of corn he was like a bowling ball going through the stalks. I never learned the extent of his injuries but was sure they were extensive. The fact that he had a very minimum fuel load for the short trip had kept the aircraft from exploding and catching on fire. I was not impressed with the 89 and hoped that it would not be my assigned aircraft.

I did my walk around and checked to make sure all the tanks were full. A Navy enlisted man jumped out of a "bread" truck came forward, having seen me as I opened the canopy to fetch the aircraft 781. He snapped me a salute and said, "good morning sir". I answered the salute and salutation as I checked to see if any comments had been made in the flight history. Satisfied, I proceeded to crawl on the wing, opened the plenum chamber

321

access panel, checked for any fuel. Seeing none, I entered the cockpit and was surprised that I was followed by my newly acquired crew chief, who was now assisting me in finding my shoulder harness. Satisfied I was strapped in he said, "have a good flight", jumped down, started the power unit, which was plugged into my bird and manned an adjacent fire extinguisher as I started the engine. Another individual had appeared from the truck and stood in front to direct my initial taxi from the parking stub. The chocks from my gear appeared to my left clear of the aircraft and seeing the motion of his raised arms, signaling I was clear to taxi, I brought the engine up and went forward and followed the signal to turn to my left toward the main taxiway, paralleling the runway. I got a snappy salute from my acquired crew chief which I promptly snapped back. I felt like a recognized real pilot! There was virtually an empty ramp, with only an orange painted tail T-33, a like patterned Navy T-28 and a couple of twin engine aircraft, which looked like C-45s, down toward the end of the runway. The tower cleared me for takeoff as I was turning onto the hammerhead, but I came to a complete stop to finish the before takeoff checklist. I took the runway and again pressed the brakes to the full down position and brought the power up to 100%. Everything was good and I released the brakes as I was pushed back in the seat and hurtled down the runway. It was a smooth launch into this cool, windless day and immediately picked up departure control and received clearance to climb on course to my next destination, Jackson, which was another Navy base. It was a CAVU day, (ceiling and visibility unlimited) and as I turned on course, I could see another "A" shaped runway to the south, with a number of aircraft on the ramp. As I continued the climb out, I was suddenly very aware of the quiet around me. I could hear my breathing and I once again became a bit apprehensive. I only hoped everything kept working! Pinky would say "get over it! I leveled out at 29,000 feet and I couldn't see even a small fleecy cloud. Cities passed under me at a rapid rate and as I checked my ground speed calculations I was doing fine and should not have any problem making Jackson. I was suddenly being cleared for another en-route descent to the Navy station. After landing a truck with the now normal "Follow Me" sign pulled up as I exited the runway. There was no mistaking it was a Navy base as the truck had a sign with large letters spelling out NAVY and the Base Operations building had a huge sign welcoming anyone to this Navy base in the middle of a landlocked area with no discernible body of water close by. After parking and informing the yellow jacketed transient crew chief that all I needed was fuel I went in to find a suitable base for my next stop and update my weather.

It became apparent I would have to make at least two stops before going back to Laredo due to winds aloft. They would not be too long, but it would save me having to stretch my leg on this next trip. The first would be about an hour and twenty minutes, but my final leg would be a short hour flight. My first stop was at a relatively new base in Arkansas, located just north of Little Rock and appropriately called Little Rock AFB. It took all of twenty minutes to top off my tanks, file a clearance and update the weather. Going in and out of the next two bases, the second, another visit to Love Field were without problems. There were always similar services for transients, fast and accommodating.

Coming into Laredo I was happy to get back to a familiar place and upon landing on a non-duty day I saw little activity and was directed to my parking slot, met by a bread truck, filled in my 781 with only minor writeups and walked back to the BOQ, only to find no one to talk to or tell my story. I was happy to have had the experience of a solo cross-country, even though my flight suit would not agree. The plus was I got in a lot of flying time; the negative was I would not get much in the air-time for the next week. I basked in the shower and put on fresh clothes which made for a new person, but where was everyone?

THE FINAL CHECK-RIDE

The last two weeks were a blur as it seemed every day there was something left to be done to complete various parts of the program. I must have signed my name a dozen times attesting to something and it came down to my last ride. As in any program everyone needed to pass a final check to put "the frosting on the cake", and insure each pilot was ready to leave training and be awarded the silver wings. The final proficiency check ride was with Lieutenant Charles Curry, a diminutive guy, who looked like he was about sixteen years old. I'm short, but it seemed he was at least two inches shorter than me. Two of my friends had him for their instructor, Jess Hocker and Jim Hudson. They seemed to like him, but never really said much about him. It was another nice early February day, no wind, mild temperature and clear skies. A great day for a flight, even if it was a check ride. Could they possibly wash out someone at this stage of the journey, I thought? Lt. Curry went over the scheme for the ride and we hustled out to the aircraft. Everything went well and our takeoff was to the east on a normal departure. On level off I was told to perform a "Lazy Eight", then a loop, a couple of barrel rolls and a series of snap rolls, right and left. I finished a power-on stall and on recovery the good lieutenant told me to go to the high fix. Upon entering a brief holding pattern, waiting for other traffic I did a "by the book" penetration, getting to a lower altitude, putting me in position to enter the pattern. I lined up on the runway and watched it come under my nose and broke to the left in a tight turn to downwind, rolling out a beam the end of the first segment of the active. Dropped my gear started the turn to base, milking flaps, finished the turn right down the runway and Lieutenant Curry pushed the power forward and said, "let's go visual", so I turned to enter the downwind leg, then hesitated. There were other aircraft going through the same drill, so the visual landing pattern had at least three others occupying the pattern. I extended the go-around and finally turned and fell behind two others. It extended the downwind a bit but I was familiar with the landmarks so I relied on picking up visually the aircraft immediately in front of me and held altitude a bit, delayed my gear and finally negotiating the turn to base and final, botched the turn to final and overshot the runway, made a nice landing though and Curry said to take it around and exit the pattern. We climbed to six thousand feet, away from the runway and he spit out as he pulled the throttle to idle, fly a "flameout pattern". There was a slight delay in my comprehension of this request as I mulled it over in my mind. This constituted two three hundred and sixty degree turns with the engine in idle, rolling out on final with enough altitude to complete a power-off landing. I must admit this was a definite weakness of mine. Doug had helped me through many attempts and I finally felt I was marginally proficient. Doug didn't feel the same way and told me so. He even indicated I should practice the flameout pattern on my solo flights, which I never did. The good lieutenant in the back seat I'm sure had been forewarned by Doug of my strengths and weaknesses, therefore he was talking to me as an instructor, rather than an evaluator as we came to the power-off time. I slowly bled altitude for airspeed and reached the high key, the designated entry level, so as I struggled to make sure I didn't overdo the first turn, stretching out the 360 on an attempt to bleed off altitude. You need to start that turn at the leading edge of the runway and make sure when you start the second three-sixty you have sufficient altitude to make the runway on rollout. By the time I started the second turn I was OK, but a bit hot. I tried to again extend the turn, but that's hard to do if you are on a turn to the base leg. Adjusting my bank angle, I was able to turn with the runway in front of me, but I was still hot on final. I would have made the landing, but I may have burned out all my tires, applying brakes to stop. It was definitely a marginal approach! Curry took the aircraft and said he would demonstrate one from the back seat, so we went back to a position above and south of the base. He pulled the power off and aimed for the end of the runway. I watched carefully for his turn and rollout points, after his first full turn and starting his second turn, he was in perfect position to start his final turn and on airspeed for final. Upon completing it perfectly he said I could do another, which I took as meaning I didn't pass the first one. We were getting low on fuel so I knew this would have to be good. We levelled off at about 5500 feet. Back at a lower altitude crossing at the end of the runway I knew I would have to tighten the turn and gain some altitude in the process before I entered the final turn. I entered my first 360 and made it very tight. When I started the last turn, I was positioned where Curry had been and felt this would work. It was another tight turn and when I rolled out, gear and flaps fully extended, I was right where I needed to be for landing. My airspeed was close to being where I needed it, maybe a little hot but there was no doubt I would make a successful landing. Curry called out that it was a good approach and told me to take it around and complete the pattern for a full stop. After a good landing and parking the aircraft we were walking back to flight operations and he said I did well and would use the second flameout pattern for the grade. I was stoked and felt Doug would be pleased. The next few days were clean up on time, with no real need as I had completed all of my requirements to graduate. I flew with Doug on my last flight, experimenting on acrobatics I had not tried before. It was a fun time knowing I would be getting my wings, no more pressure. Doug admitted to me on that last dual ride he also didn't pick up station passage on our return to Laredo on my instrument check, but felt obliged to make me do one that station passage was obvious. Thanks a bunch. I sweated that second ride.

THE ASSIGNMENT

The list of assignments came out with little fanfare as only those committed to an additional three years received name single engine fighters like the F-86D or F model. There was one assignment to the F-100, a new aircraft at the time and that went to a Hawaiian, named Mel Yen in "F" flight who was going to fly in the Hawaiian National Guard. Most of those not committing received Target-tow assignments to fighter units, a very unglamorous new entry assignment into the Air Force. They would be flying a T-33, not much fun in that. I received, as did a few others in my class, an assignment to the B-47, a new, six engine jet bomber that was programmed to take the place of the B-29s and the newer B-50s, both aging reciprocal engine aircraft. I was pleased with the assignment, but wasn't too sure about the location, Roswell New Mexico, but would make the best of it. The base was called Walker AFB and I heard they were just getting the aircraft and converting the wing from B-29s to the B-47. Reciprocal to Jet, sounds like an interesting switch for the older pilots. I would be joined at Roswell by a couple of students from my section of the class, Jess Hocker and Jerry Gable. Also, from the other section of 56-H, ("F" flight) I would be joined by

Tom Stanton, who, along with Gerry would be my house mates in Roswell. My pilot training roommate, Bob Dugan was going to Fairchild AFB in Spokane Washington and a good friend Bobby Dantzler was going to Altus, Oklahoma, all were Strategic Air Command bases. A couple of poor souls were going to the B-36, an amazing aircraft, but as third pilots. Advancement in the B-36 was slow and stick time was rare.

GRADUATION

On Saturday, February 6th, 1956 the class of 56-H were to receive their wings. We would be Air Force pilots, having completed over a year of training in the various aircraft that made up the training command. A similar group from this class would be getting their wings at Lubbock AFB, having completed their training as multi-engine pilots in the B-25. Also, about seven others completed their training at Luke AFB and Webb AFB. 56-H was a special class and as would be mentioned over and over in our ceremony, it was a class that had completed training without a fatality or even an accident of any kind. It was very significant as we were the first post war class to do so. The ceremony was not too long, a few speeches by the two squadron commanders after the invocation by Major Lewandowski, the Catholic chaplain and then a short congratulation type message from the wing commander, Colonel Milton Adams, with the awarding of wings that followed. We were all in our class "A" uniforms and as we exited the theater you could not help but notice that the chest of all those new pilots seemed to be a bit larger as the silver wings stood out in the bright sunlit day. Many of the new pilots had significant other to pin on their wings, but most of us were awarded the new status from the wing commander himself. As mine was pinned on by Colonel Adams I had to glance down to make sure this was real. It was! The congratulations continued for a long period as we stood basking in our accomplishment. All good things had to end and most of us were packed and ready to get to our next duty station or take some leave. I was going to go home for a short leave, before I reported into Walker AFB in Roswell New Mexico. Doug shook my hand and said goodbye. It was strange as we had spent a great deal of time together for the last six months, but I didn't know him very well. The instructor-student relationship was only close on the flight line. I had had a beer or two with him off the flight line once or twice and spent the night at my cousin's house in Denver on my cross-country, but nothing more. He would be getting new students next week and it would begin all over for him. I would be going to a new aircraft, a new beginning and a real learning opportunity. It will be a bigger airplane, six engines, and two pilots. I was looking forward to the next step as a pilot in the B-47. I said goodbye to Bob Dugan on the steps of the theater, knowing he had already packed his car and was not going back to the room; we had been roommates for the last year in two different bases. We had had many tough days and anxious moments together, but also many fun times and even hilarious moments and shared some secrets that were quickly forgotten. Despite that when he came back from Christmas leave, he announced he had married Martie, a great surprise and something I really had not anticipated. We too would separate, but I knew we would keep in touch. It was hard to say goodbye to him and I knew I had a tear coming out so just turned away and waved at him. There were so many friends that would leave to go to other bases, but we were bonded as successful members of 56-H, all wearing our silver wings and survivors of a year of checks by individuals looking for possible flaws in our ability to manage an Air Force aircraft. Many were looking forward to the next base, but one thing stood out in our conversations. We were all in need of a place to stay at our new bases, not wanting to have to live on base, so a number of deals were made about the next location. The bachelors were looking for roommates to share houses as most were hoping that they would find their bases stating their there would be no available quarters on base. Gerry Gable, Tom Stanton and I closed an agreement to find a place in Roswell. Most of the rest who were going to the same base were going through the same process. After a flurry of good-byes, the next move was out the gate with all your worldly possessions packed in the car for the next journey in this process of being an aviator. Laredo had many memories, but there were better places to have a duty assignment, hopefully Walker AFB would be one.

EPILOGUE

The second lieutenant started his flying career in the Air Force in the B-47, a six-engine jet bomber as a co-pilot in the 509th Bomb Wing and more specifically in the 715th Bomb Squadron. The 509th was deployed to England on his arrival at Walker Air Force Base in Roswell, New Mexico and he was sent to McConnel AFB, Wichita Kansas to go through a six-week ground school for the aircraft. There was no flying attached to the school but was intended to familiarize Lt. Dugard to the intricacies of this new bomber. Upon his return he was placed on a combat crew that was termed non-ready and spent time in simulator and flight training until termed "combat ready". He encountered two types of pilots during this initial phase as many of those placed in this aircraft had come from B-29 and B-50 reciprocal engine aircraft and had flown in Korea. Some of the younger pilots were very proficient, however many of the older pilots had difficulty crossing the jet line. As an individual from pilot training for jet aircraft Lt. Dugard was more proficient than many of those who were termed as "Aircraft Commanders". After over two years as a co-pilot at Walker AFB, logging many hours of flight under all flight conditions, he made a career decision to leave the service to pursue additional studies and a "Masters" degree in Education. He completed a semester and he realized his heart was in flying so the exit from the Air Force lasted ten months. He was approached by a former squadron commander who told him there was a limited recall of pilots and asked if he would like to return to the 509th BW. He quickly agreed and was summarily recalled to the wing. The 509th in the interim had left Roswell, New Mexico and was now at Pease AFB in Portsmouth, New Hampshire. It was a painless reintroduction to the aircraft and in a short period of time, now 1st Lieutenant Dugard upgraded to "Aircraft Commander", a position that accelerated him to becoming an Instructor Pilot (IP) in the aircraft and later to a position as a "select" crew in the Standardization Division within the wing. This position qualified now Captain Dugard to receive a temporary spot promotion to Major. He was subsequently dispatched to the prestigious "Instrument Pilots Instructor School" (IPIS), a six-week, forty flight hours school to qualify selected pilots as the leadership in Instrument flying, qualifying them to perform as platform instructors and give required yearly proficiency instrument flight checks to other pilots. Major Dugard finished first in a class of 42 pilots, including five skilled pilots from foreign countries.

During his tenure in the B-47 aircraft he accumulated over 3000 hours of flight time and participated at home as well as overseas on nuclear alert in Spain and England. With the phaseout of the B-47, Major Dugard was selected to fly the B-58 supersonic four engine bomber. The lead-in for the B-58 was in the single engine fighter, the F-102 where the similarity in the swept wing and high-performance shaped fuselage (called the "coke-bottle") provided a similar platform for entry to the supersonic B-58 bomber. He attended the lead-in training in the F-102 at Perrin AFB Texas. After sixteen plus hours in the single engine fighter aircraft and fifteen more in the T-33 he was assigned to Bunker Hill AFB (later named Grissom AFB) in Peru, Indiana. After four months of intensive training, he and his crew were declared combat ready. Major Dugard advanced to Instructor status in the aircraft and was selected to be a member of the Combat Crew Training Squadron (CCTS), training new pilots in the aircraft. After over 600 hours in the Mach-2+ aircraft and over twelve years as a combat crew member he was transferred to the Strategic Air Command headquarters at Offutt AFB, Nebraska as the head of the newly formed Officer Career Development Office (DPRD), with additional duty as an Instructor Pilot in the Headquarters T-39 twin jet aircraft, administering flight and instrument checks for current and incoming pilots to the command headquarters. While there he attained the rank of Lieutenant Colonel. Lieutenant Colonel Dugard was selected to become a B-52 Squadron Commander, with an entry into the Maintenance arena as a squadron commander of the 55th Strategic Reconnaissance Organization Maintenance Squadron (OMS) and served in that capacity for six months before attending a B-52 Checkout program for flying the aircraft. Once checked out in the B-52 he was assigned to Mather AFB in Sacramento California. Upon arriving he was informed that his squadron was deployed to Guam in a program called "Bullet Shot". He followed the squadron and was shortly flying combat missions to Vietnam, culminating in flights over Hanoi and Haiphong during the twelve day "Linebacker" raids. While in Guam he was promoted to Colonel and returned to Mather as the 320th Bomb Wing Director of Operations and due to his new role in the wing checked out in the KC-135 refueling aircraft. He was subsequently named as the 320th Bomb Wing Vice Commander. He served in that capacity for three months and was reassigned to U-Tapao Royal Thai Air Force Base (RTAFB) in Thailand as the 307th Strategic Bomb Wing Vice Commander, where after a short duration he assumed command, flying both the B-52 and the KC-135 on missions in southeast Asia. He participated in the evacuation of Saigon at the end of the Vietnam War and the recovery of the Mayagüez cargo ship from Cambodian forces. He was instrumental in the drawdown of forces from the theater and flew the final KC-135 aircraft from Asia after his one-year tour. He was reassigned to Barksdale AFB in Shreveport Louisiana as the 2nd Bomb Wing Vice-Commander. Seven months later he was named the Commander of the 2nd Bomb Wing. He was subsequently selected as the 410th Bomb Wing commander, at K.I. Sawyer AFB, Michigan, a B-52 H model super wing. He was later selected to become the 15th Air Force Director of Operations, managing all aircraft and missile forces west of the Mississippi, a position from which he retired from the Air Force after twenty-six years and more than 6700 hours of flight time.

Printed in the United States
By Bookmasters